Let's Get PERSONAL!

Second Edition

Creating Successful Relationships Through Effective Interpersonal Communication

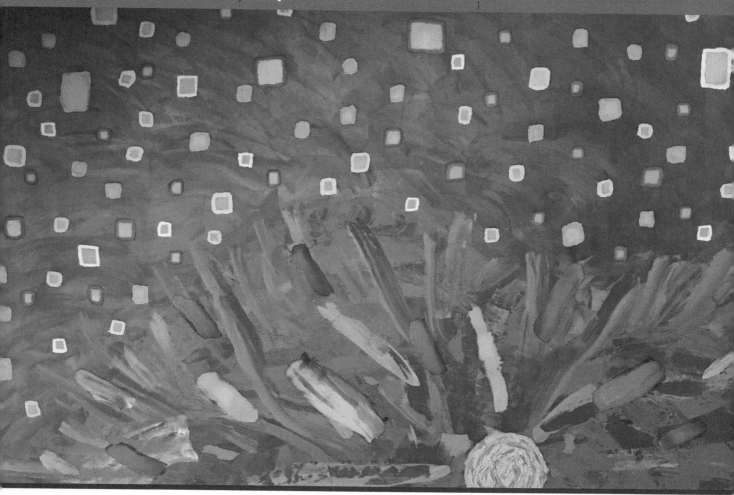

Dee Osorio | Michael Schulmeister | A. Todd Jones

Kendall Hunt
publishing company

Kendall Hunt
publishing company

www.kendallhunt.com
Send all inquiries to:
4050 Westmark Drive
Dubuque, IA 52004-1840

ISBN 978-1-5249-7081-9

Contents

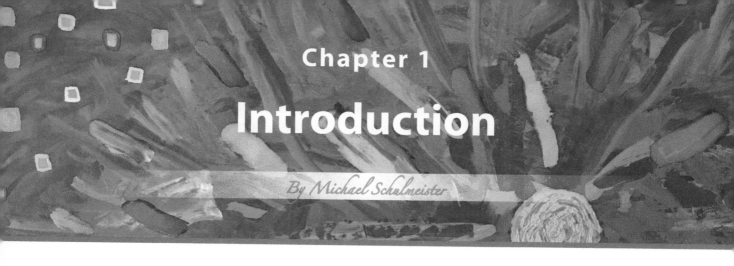

Chapter 1

Introduction

By Michael Schulmeister

Let's get personal...

Teaching interpersonal communication has transformed my life. Although I have a high IQ, after studying the concepts, theories, and skills that are taught in the field of inter-personal communication, I have come to realize that I am a "relational idiot." I have stud-ied and thought about many things, but for the first 40 years of my life, I put very little concentrated thought into my relationships with other people.

For example, I have been happily married to my wife Sarah for over 30 years, and I always thought we had a solid, satisfying relationship. However, after carrying out a very basic self-evaluation of my close relationships (provided in an interpersonal communication textbook), I realized that I could greatly deepen my relationship with Sarah through more intellectual and emotional intimacy. I am looking forward with great anticipa-tion to the next 30 years of my marriage knowing that there are very basic ways I can strengthen and enhance my marriage relationship.

To remind myself of the importance of interpersonal communication and relational development, I have posted this thought on my office wall—"Relationships matter most." I also ask to teach interpersonal communication regularly because I never want to forget the life-changing, relationship-transforming things I have learned in this course.

— *Michael Schulmeister*

Relationships matter most.

You need to read this chapter

- To understand both the quantitative and qualitative definitions of interpersonal communication.
- To learn how the academic study of interpersonal communication developed.
- To gain a basic understanding of the transactional model of human communication.
- To appreciate the importance and value of interpersonal communication.

Figure 1.1 Human relationships matter most.

Although you may have a satisfying relationship with your dog or cat, this relationship is not based upon or fostered by interpersonal communication because interpersonal communication is defined as communication between two human beings or persons. A **person** is usually defined as a *human* being regarded as an individual or as an entity that has the moral right of self-determination (Figure 1.1).

The German philosopher Emmanuel Kant defined human beings as "ends in themselves." Humans are rational beings that are called "persons" because their very nature marks them off as self-determining, autonomous creatures. Human persons are usually distinguished from pets or property.

Although pets can bring us great satisfaction, they are property, not persons. Dogs and cats are bought and sold. We often also lock them up in our houses when we must leave our homes. If we locked up or bought and sold human persons, we could be charged with criminal behavior. Nonhuman animals, on the other hand, are not usually charged with crimes because (unlike persons) they have no legal or moral responsibilities.

This textbook will not focus on your interspecies communication with your pets or other nonhuman animals because interpersonal communication is a subfield of **human** communication. Although owning a pet can improve your mental health, this owner/pet relationship is not the same as (and cannot replace) an interpersonal relationship with another human being.

We begin this introductory chapter by giving a brief account of the development of the academic study of interpersonal communication. You will learn that with the exception of public speaking, the academic study of face-to-face human communication is a fairly recent (20th century) development, and that the academic study of interpersonal communication proliferated in the 1960s (making this field of knowledge a little over 50 years old).

We will present and explain a basic transactional model of human communication that will help you to understand some of the basic concepts and realities involved in a human communication interaction. You will learn that human language allows human persons to interact in a way that allows "a meeting of minds."

We will also compare interpersonal communication to other subfields of human communication studies, and we will mark off two important subfields within the field of interpersonal communication itself: intrapersonal communication (the study of how persons communicate with themselves) and family communication (the study of interpersonal communication between family members or significant others).

After distinguishing the qualitative definition of interpersonal communication from the quantitative definition, we will discuss the ethics of interpersonal communication, and we will argue for the importance of recognizing human beings as persons. We will then end this introductory chapter with a list of reasons why interpersonal communication (and the study of interpersonal communication) is important and valuable.

The Study of Interpersonal Communication

In the Western cultural tradition, the form of oral discourse that has been studied the longest is public speaking. The ancient Greeks and Romans developed and systematized the study and practice of oratory, so public speaking has a 2,500 year history. Rhetoric (the art of public speaking) was originally one of the seven liberal arts in the classical world, so instruction in public speaking has been an essential element of Western education for over two millennia. Human beings have put a lot of thought into how a speaker can present a monological (one-way) discourse to a large, live audience.

Sometimes the study of public speaking in the Western world has been greatly stressed and promoted (as in the classical Greek and Roman periods), and sometimes it has been de-emphasized or relegated to a subsidiary role. For example, at the beginning of the twentieth century, public speaking was usually taught as a subfield in college English departments. In the early 1900s, college English instructors taught both writing and public speaking.

However, in 1914 the National Association of Academic Teachers of Public Speaking (NAATPS) was founded in America because high school and college instructors felt that public speaking deserved to be recognized as an independent academic field. Over the years, the name of the organization changed several times: in 1923, the NAATPS became the National Association of Teachers of Speech (NATS). In 1946, the NATS became the Speech Association of America (SAA). In 1970, the SAA became the Speech Communication Association (SCA). Finally, in 1997, the SCA became the National Communication Association (NCA).

One reason for the name changes in the organization was the increasing influence of the social sciences. An organization that once narrowly focused on public speaking over time took a broader interest in all forms of human communication. This new interest was accompanied by new research methods and programs that focused on the systematic development of scientific terms and theories that could help us better understand all forms of human communication, including face-to-face interpersonal communication.

Although public speaking as an academic discipline focuses on the monological (one-way) verbal communication of a public speaker with a large audience, interpersonal communication as an academic discipline focuses on the **dyadic** communication between two persons. Although speech is a *monologue*, an interpersonal conversation is a *dialogue*. **Interpersonal communication** is the study of how two people share messages and meaning in a communication transaction or dialogue (Figure 1.2).

The study of interpersonal communication overlaps with two other social science fields—psychology and sociology. Interpersonal communication involves **you** interacting with **others**. Human psyches and personalities are formed and developed as baby humans interact and communicate with other human beings which we call "significant others." The significant others that communicated with you when you were a child helped to form your personality, your self-concepts, and your identity.

Interpersonal communication overlaps with sociological studies because human beings are social creatures. We are a combination of nature and nurture. Although DNA allows our physical bodies to grow and develop, our interpersonal interactions with other human beings allow our minds to grow and develop. Individuals become humanized as they are socialized and enculturated into the human family (Figure 1.3). We are told and taught what it means to be human.

Figure 1.2 Interpersonal communication is an interaction or transaction between two human beings.

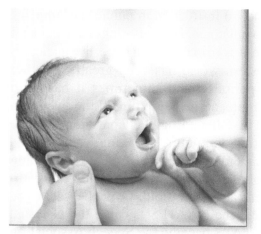

Figure 1.3 We become fully humanized as we are enculturated into the human family.

The academic field of interpersonal communication is influenced by, and owes a large debt to, humanistic psychology. Humanistic psychology is an important school of psychology which developed in the 1950s and 1960s. Two of the founders of humanistic psychology are Carl Rogers and Abraham Maslow. These psychologists are recognized as a "third wave" in the history of the study of psychology. Reacting to Freudianism (the "first wave") and behaviorism (the "second wave"), humanistic psychologists emphasize human wholeness, creativity, free will, self-determination, and self-actualization.

In 1961, Carl Rogers published his groundbreaking book *On Becoming a Person* (Houghton Mifflin Company) that revolutionized psychotherapy by emphasizing positive interpersonal interactions between therapists and "clients." Rogers believed that people could heal themselves when they were listened to and accepted with "unconditional positive regard" by their therapists. In Rogerian psychotherapy, interpersonal communication based on respect and acceptance is a crucial element of psychological health and healing.

Abraham Maslow developed several concepts similar to Carl Rogers' ideas in his theory of the hierarchy of human needs. Maslow developed a theory of human motivation and human development that is often referenced in the field of interpersonal communication. Many interpersonal communication textbooks will include a chart which illustrates Maslow's five levels of human needs: Maslow theorized that human beings must first satisfy their basic needs before they can focus on and satisfy their higher-level needs (Figure 1.4).

Interpersonal communication plays an obvious and important role as human beings progress through the levels of Maslow's hierarchy of needs. In order to become a fully developed, self-actualized person, a human being must develop the interpersonal skills that are necessary to meet physiological needs, safety and security needs, love and belonging needs, and self-esteem needs.

Rogers and Maslow (and other humanistic psychologists) contrasted their psychological perspective (and their psychological approach) to behaviorism, a school that sought to make psychology a "hard" science. Behaviorists like B.F. Skinner eschewed discussing the inner thoughts, feelings, and motives of human beings (because they could not be objectively observed or measured), and sought instead a more

Figure 1.4 Effective interpersonal communication allows a person to progress through Maslow's levels of human development.

rigorous "scientific" approach which focused primarily on external behaviors that could be observed, recorded, and analyzed.

The humanistic psychologists pointed out that hardcore behaviorists who ignored the "subjective" experiences of human beings (because these experiences were "objectively" unverifiable) were rejecting what is most important in the human experience: the inner mental life of human beings. Human beings have physical bodies that can be observed, but they also have minds that think and feel and will—this is the subjective reality that humans experience when they "introspect" and look inside themselves.

Interpersonal communication, as a subfield of human communication studies, flowered in the 1960s and 1970s, alongside humanistic psychology. It is now one of the largest divisions in the NCA. Like humanistic psychologists, interpersonal communication scholars often adopt a "soft" social science approach which focuses on the inner mental life of human beings. Interpersonal communication theories often posit or assume that human beings use their physical bodies to communicate the thoughts and feelings that are in their minds.

The transactional communication model that follows has helped communication scholars to understand and describe a human communication interaction with some clarity and precision. We will present to you some of the basic vocabulary that has been developed to describe a communication transaction, and then we will point out how this communication model emphasizes the primacy of the human mind in human communication.

A Transactional Communication Model

Communication can be defined as *a transactional process whereby two or more communicators share meaning* (Figure 1.5). In an interpersonal communication transaction, we usually think of two communicators interacting, as illustrated in the model. One **communicator encodes** a **message** and sends it through a communication **channel**. Another **communicator** receives and **decodes** this message and then sends **feedback**. While the communication transaction unfolds, the communicators must deal with communication **noise**. In an interpersonal communication exchange, multiple primary messages and feedback messages are typically sent, sometimes simultaneously. Here are some brief definitions of these essential communication elements:

Channel: A communication channel is the medium that carries a message. In face-to-face interpersonal communication, the human sensory channels most often used are touch, sight, and hearing. Interpersonal communicators primarily send messages through the auditory and visual channels, and more rarely they send messages through the tactile channel. Communicators can also use technological channels to send and receive messages.

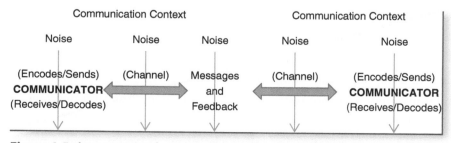

Figure 1.5 A transactional model of human communication.

Communicator: A communicator is someone who either sends or receives a message. In a face-to-face interpersonal communication situation, both communicators are sending and receiving messages at the same time. Before verbal communication is initiated, both communicators are sending and receiving nonverbal messages. When an interpersonal conversation is initiated, verbal messages are also sent back and forth between the two communicators.

Context: The inner communication context is the mental environment that exists in a communicator's mind. The more the mental environments of two communicators overlap, the easier it is for them to communicate. Conversely, the less two communicators have in common in their mental life and experience, the harder it will be for them to connect and communicate.

Decoding: Decoding is the mental process of transforming messages received back into ideas and concepts. The communication symbols used to communicate a message must be interpreted and assigned meaning. Communicators must decode both the verbal and nonverbal messages that they receive.

Encoding: Encoding is the mental process of transforming ideas and feelings into symbols (words, sounds, actions, etc.) and then organizing these symbols into a message. Often messages are consciously encoded, but sometimes interpersonal communicators send messages of which they are not consciously aware.

Feedback: Feedback is any response, verbal or nonverbal, that a receiver gives to a message. Feedback indicates to the sender whether and how the message was received and understood.

Message: A message is the content of a communication, the ideas and emotions a person wishes to share. Simultaneously with the primary messages a communicator sends, secondary relational messages are transmitted which reveal how the sender thinks and feels about the receiver.

Noise: Noise is anything that interferes with the transmission of a message. Noise can be external or internal. External noises are sights, sounds, and other stimuli that can draw attention away from the message being transmitted. Internal noises are thoughts, feelings, and physical conditions in the communicators that interfere with the communication process.

The transactional model of communication helps us understand the complexity and difficulty of interpersonal communication. There are many reasons why interpersonal communication may be ineffective:

1) a communicator may have difficulty forming or grasping a thought,

2) a thought or idea may be poorly encoded,

3) a message may be sent through the wrong communication channel,

4) a message may not be received,

5) a message may be decoded incorrectly,

6) poor feedback may be given,

7) feedback to a message may be misinterpreted,

8) internal noise may interfere with the encoding or decoding of a message, and external noise may interfere with the sending or receiving of a message.

The transactional communication model also helps us understand some important facts about communication. First, meanings are not in words or other communication symbols—meanings are in the minds of human communicators. Just because you *say* something does not mean you have *communicated* it. Your words and your nonverbal cues must still be received and interpreted by your communication partner.

Second, communication is irreversible—once you send a message (intentionally or unintentionally), you cannot *unsend* it. Once you do or say something, your communication partner will assign meaning to your actions and words.

Third, a communicator does not fully control how a message will be interpreted by another person—when you say something, your communication partner will interpret your words, and they may come up with a very different interpretation than you intended or anticipated. Interpersonal communication is a collaborative process. You must negotiate the meanings of your words and actions with your communication partner.

A Meeting of Minds

Although the transactional model of communication uses some technical scientific terms (some students might even say "jargon") to describe the basic elements of human communication, this model has a very important humanistic component: at the heart of the model are human minds. Human persons create and share meaning, it is assumed, with their *minds*.

It is the mind of a person that thinks thoughts and feels emotions that can be communicated to other human minds. It is the mind of a person that assigns meaning to human language symbols, whether encoding or decoding these symbols. It is the mind of a person that intends (or does not intend) for a message to be sent. It is the mind of a person that is consciously aware (or not consciously aware) of a message being sent or received.

Interpersonal communication allows two human minds to meet. Whereas sexual intercourse involves the joining together of human bodies, human dialogue and discourse allows two people to share their minds with one another. Whereas sexual intercourse can create physical intimacy, interpersonal communication can create intellectual and emotional intimacy. When you share your thoughts and feelings with another human being, and when that person reciprocates and shares thoughts and feelings in return, you both or creating an interpersonal relationship. The quantity and quality of these shared thoughts and feelings will determine the depth of this relationship (Figure 1.6).

A human relationship can be compared to a twin-engine vehicle. The two "engines" that power a human relationship are the two minds of the people involved in that relationship. Before committing yourself to an interpersonal relationship with another human being, it is a good idea to "look under the hood" and explore whether you are both "firing on all cylinders."

There are many ways to map out the human mind. In his 1981 book *Maps of the Mind* (MacMillan Publishing Company), Charles Hampden-Turner collects and describes (and visually illustrates in map form) 60 different maps of the most important concepts of the human mind. We will present here our own "psychodynamic schematic" of the human mind to go along with our "engine" analogy: the human mind can be compared to a V-8 engine.

There are eight major abilities or powers of the mind (Figure 1.7). The human mind has the powers of

Figure 1.6 Shared thoughts and feelings create an interpersonal relationship.

Cylinder 1: Memory: the ability to recall past events or actions.

Cylinder 2: Rationality: the ability to think or reason.

Cylinder 3: Emotionality: the ability to emote or feel.

Cylinder 4: Volition: the ability to make choices or take action.

Cylinder 5: Self-awareness: the ability to be consciously aware of oneself.

Cylinder 6: Moral awareness: the ability to make moral judgments (about what is good or bad, right or wrong, just or unjust).

Cylinder 7: Esthetic awareness: the ability to make esthetic judgments (about what is beautiful or ugly, esthetically pleasing or not).

Cylinder 8: Creativity: the ability to make new things or think of new ideas.

Figure 1.7 Human persons have at least eight important mental powers or abilities.

(1) memory, (2) rationality, (3) emotionality, (4) volition, (5) self-awareness, (6) moral awareness, (7) esthetic awareness, and (8) creativity. Each power or ability can be thought of as a "cylinder" in an eight-cylinder engine.

When you and your relational partner are using all of your mental abilities, when both human minds are "firing on all cylinders," you can experience a powerful, rich interpersonal relationship. However, if you or your relational partner are not using (or cannot use) all of your mental abilities, relational problems and difficulties can arise.

Other nonhuman animals obviously have some of the mental abilities we list to some extent, but because nonhuman animals lack the ability to use human language, we cannot know what the interior mental lives of other animals are like. Since only human beings can communicate their subjective awareness of their mental lives to one another through human language, they alone are capable of experiencing interpersonal relationships based on the verbal (and nonverbal) sharing of thoughts and feelings.

Identifying eight different mental abilities possessed by human beings also clarifies why you cannot have an interpersonal relationship with a computer. Although computers have some ability to compute or calculate, this computer intelligence is vastly different from human intelligence. Computers are not, nor can they ever be, persons. Although computers have some ability to perform operations akin to human intellection, intellection or rationality is only one power or ability of the human mind.

The V-8 analogy of the human mind is helpful (especially for people who like cars!), but all analogies break down eventually. Whereas the eight cylinders of an automotive engine are discrete, separate things, the eight mental powers of human beings are entwined together in the human mind. Human rationality and intelligence does not exist separately from human volition, emotion, self-awareness, moral awareness, and esthetic awareness. All of these powers or abilities exist in one center of consciousness (and unconsciousness) that we call a person.

Although some people think that artificial intelligence (AI) is just over the technological horizon, whatever machine intelligence is created will be vastly different from human intelligence found in human persons. Computers can process vast amounts of information and calculate at incredible speeds, but they cannot freely make choices, or feel emotions, or experience self-awareness, or make moral or esthetic judgments. They are not persons because they do not have the capabilities found in human minds.

However, we should note that computers and other communication technologies are changing the ways that human beings communicate with one another and the way that interpersonal relationships are initiated, maintained, and ended. Instead of meeting face-to-face, human beings can now communicate through audio or video transmissions using their cell phones, computers, and other communication devices.

Although you cannot have an interpersonal relationship with a computer, you can definitely carry out an interpersonal relationship using a computer. People no longer have to meet face-to-face in order to share their minds with one another. Interpersonal relationships can now be initiated, developed, and terminated online.

Although the transactional model of communication has been a standard model of human communication (especially interpersonal communication) for the past two decades, this model may need to be adjusted as human beings carry out more and more of their communication through communication technologies.

Whereas the transactional model emphasizes the "synchronous" (even simultaneous) sending and receiving of verbal and nonverbal messages during face-to-face encounters, many people are now creating and sustaining interpersonal relationships using "asynchronous" methods of communication such as emails and text messages. We further explore the effects of technology on interpersonal communication and interpersonal relationships in the final chapter of this textbook.

Let's get personal...

I know that communication technologies have expanded the ways that interpersonal relationships are initiated and maintained through the personal experience of my friend Ray. Ray was a bachelor in his thirties who wanted a wife and family, but he had never had a "serious" girlfriend. His life was changed when he received an electronic birthday card on a website for Christian singles from a woman in India.

Ray lived in Bakersfield, California, but he and his new friend from India began to send regular emails back and forth. Then they graduated to online video conferences. Without ever meeting face-to-face, they fell in love, became engaged, and set a wedding date, all in the time period of about 14 months.

The first time Ray met Sunaina in person was when he and his parents flew to India for his wedding. Ray spent 2 months honeymooning with his new bride in India, and then flew back to Bakersfield alone because Sunaina did not have a travel visa. The first year and a half of Ray and Sunaina's marriage was carried out online through emails and video conferences, until she could join him in America. They have been happily married now for almost 10 years.

— *Michael Schulmeister*

Interpersonal Communication and Other Fields of Study

When we described the development of the academic study of interpersonal communication, we contrasted interpersonal communication studies to the study and practice of public speaking: whereas public speaking focuses on the one-way, monological discourse of a speaker with

TYPES OF HUMAN COMMUNICATION

Public speaking: One-way (monological) verbal discourse of a speaker with an audience.

Interpersonal: Dyadic, two-way conversations or dialogues between two people.

Small group: Communication among persons in groups of three to twelve people.

Organizational: Communication within an organization and with entities outside the organization.

Mass communication: Communication with masses of people through technology.

Intercultural: Communication among people from substantially different cultural groups.

Figure 1.8 Interpersonal communication is one subfield in human communication studies.

a large audience, interpersonal communication focuses on dyadic conversations and dialogue between two people. However, there are other subfields in human communication studies of which you need to be aware (Figure 1.8).

The development of various communication technologies (printing, radio, television, etc.) in the last few centuries created new forms of human communication and a new field of study called **mass communication**. Mass communication is communication with masses of people through communication technologies. **Organizational communication** is the study of the way that people communicate within an organization and of the way an organization communicates with outside entities. **Intercultural communication** is the study of communication between people from substantially different cultural groups. **Small group communication** is the study of communication among people in groups of about three to twelve persons.

As you can see, interpersonal communication can be distinguished from several other types of human communication, but these subfields in human communication studies definitely have some overlap. For example, communication scholars and instructors sometimes disagree about how much stress should be put on the difference between interpersonal communication and small group communication. Some people assert that there is no substantial difference between interpersonal communication and small group communication because both types of communication involve discourse or dialogue among people, whether there are two, three, four, or more people.

However, we think it is useful and appropriate to distinguish dyadic communication between only two people (interpersonal communication) from communication that takes place among a small group of people because there is some truth to the proverb, "Two's company, but three's a crowd." Third-party observation changes the communication situation and the relational dynamics when two people attempt to communicate with one another. Interpersonal communication is a complicated process (as the transactional model of communication reveals) but small group communication is even more complicated.

Although each subfield of human communication is important and deserves to be studied, interpersonal communication is one of the most important subfields because (with the exception of public speaking) it is a part of all the other subfields of human communication. Interpersonal communication is an important component in small group communication, organizational communication, and intercultural communication. You sometimes need to communicate one-on-one with people in small groups, in organizations, and with people from different cultures. Mass communication technologies are also used to present or portray interpersonal interactions, so our notions of effective and ineffective interpersonal communication interactions are often created by mass-media products.

Interpersonal Communication versus Intrapersonal Communication

In addition to being a subfield of human communication studies, interpersonal communication also has some subfields of its own, and one of the most important subfields is the field of **intrapersonal communication**. Whereas **inter**personal communication studies the communication that occurs *between* two persons, **intra**personal communication studies the communication that occurs *within* one person.

Figure 1.9 You are a complicated person that communicates with self and others.

Human communication, you are discovering in this chapter, is complicated because it involves the complicated human mind. The mind has at least eight different mental powers or abilities, and it has at least two different levels, the conscious and the unconscious. In addition, the study of intrapersonal communication reveals that human minds are not just unified centers of consciousness that communicate with other persons: human minds are complicated entities that can send and receive messages to and from themselves.

The ancient Greek philosopher Plato describes the human soul (psyche) or mind as a charioteer trying to control two horses. Sigmund Freud distinguishes parts of the psyche which he terms the "id," "ego," and "super ego." Eric Berne developed the theory of transactional analysis (TA) that posits that each person has a "parent," "child," and "adult" inside themselves. The "you" that is involved with others in interpersonal communication is not a simple, unified "you" (Figure 1.9).

People who have never studied interpersonal communication and its subfield of intrapersonal communication often assume that most of the relational problems they face could be solved with better interpersonal communication skills and practices. They assume that if they learned to speak appropriately to other people, and if other people learned to speak appropriately to them, then most of their interpersonal difficulties would be resolved.

These people do not realize that many of their relational problems are not caused by their communication with other people, but by their negative "self-talk" that they carry on within themselves. Until they learn to send and receive positive messages to and from themselves, they cannot effectively receive the positive messages of acceptance, affection, respect, and unconditional positive regard that other persons might be trying to communicate to them. You will learn more about intrapersonal communication and positive self-talk in Chapter 2 of this textbook.

Family Communication

Another important subfield of interpersonal communication is **family communication.** Family communication studies how family members send and receive messages to and from their significant others. The family is the primary social group that enculturates human beings and that provides their welfare and belonging needs. The family is also the social group that has the largest influence on the formation and development of human personality. Most human beings are who they are, to a large extent, because of their family upbringing (Figure 1.10).

If you are a parent, your study of interpersonal communication can help you to communicate more effectively with your children. You can learn to create a warm, safe communication climate in

Figure 1.10 You are to a large extent the product of your family upbringing.

your home. You can learn to send positive relational messages that will help your children to develop healthy self-concepts and positive self-esteem. You can learn to resolve family conflicts in a way that strengthens family relationships. You can also learn to effectively communicate your parental expectations in a way that brings about desired behavioral changes in your children.

If you are not a parent and never plan to have children or a family, you should still learn about family communication and communication in close relationships. As an adult, you should recognize and appreciate the powerful effect your family upbringing has had on you, for better or for worse.

The way you relate to other people in the present is influenced by the way you were treated by your family members in the past. Much of your self-talk is the result of messages from family members or significant others that you have unconsciously (or even consciously) internalized. You may be repeating and perpetuating unhealthy family patterns, or you may be creating new relational difficulties in your present life by trying to avoid past family behaviors. You will learn more about family communication and communication in close relationships in Chapter 9 of this textbook.

A Qualitative Definition versus a Quantitative Definition

Up to this point, we have been presenting to you a "quantitative" definition of interpersonal communication. That is, we have distinguished interpersonal communication from other forms of human communication primarily by focusing on the *number* of people involved in a communication transaction. Interpersonal communication, we have asserted, occurs when *two* people are involved in a communication interaction. Two people constitute a couple, pair, or dyad, so their communication interactions qualify as interpersonal communication.

However, it is also important to recognize and acknowledge a "qualitative" definition of interpersonal communication. A communication interaction between two people can be evaluated by determining the quality of the relational messages sent between two human communicators (Figure 1.11). When two people acknowledge each other as persons worthy of respect, this is high-quality "interpersonal" communication. However, when one or both communicators do not acknowledge the humanity and personhood of the other communicator, then

IMPERSONAL ←   → PERSONAL

Figure 1.11 The quality of your interpersonal relationships can be evaluated.

low-quality "impersonal" communication has occurred.

A qualitative definition of interpersonal communication is useful because it sensitizes us to the relational messages we send to others, and it causes us to think about the types of relationships we want to develop with other human beings. You can place your relationships with other people on a continuum from very "impersonal" to very "personal."

There are several elements that figure into an evaluation of the quality of an interpersonal relationship: you need to consider (1) the amount of time

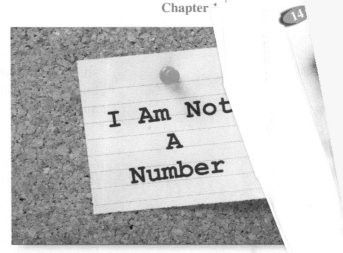

Figure 1.12 People want to be treated and respe persons.

spent with your relational partner, (2) the amount of physical touch you give and receive (3) the breadth and depth (and reciprocity) of your self-disclosures.

In addition, you need to consider whether one or both partners are in the relationship extrinsic rewards or benefits (such as money, gifts, material possessions, and prestige), or whe er the relationship itself has intrinsic value (you just enjoy each other's company). You also ne to evaluate the quantity and quality of relational messages that are sent and received by you an your relational partner both verbally and nonverbally.

However, a crucial element to consider when evaluating the quality of an interpersonal relationship is whether you treat each other as human persons. Philosopher Martin Buber points out that people can enter into an "I/Thou" relationship with one another, or they can enter into an "I/It" relationship. In other words, when two human beings interact, they can recognize that they are equally worthy of the respect owed to human persons, or they can treat each other as property or possessions or things to be used (Figure 1.12).

All of your interpersonal relationships do not need to be deep, high-quality, intimate relationships. Human relationships take time and work, and intimate human relationships take more time and more work. Therefore, it is appropriate and necessary to have some casual acquaintances that you do not know very well, especially if you are in a job or profession where you come into contact with many people. You can only divide your time and attention between so many people, so you need to carefully consider how many deep, intimate human relationships you can manage and sustain.

However, you do need to develop some high-quality interpersonal relationships for your own physical and psychological health. Human beings are social creatures that have attachment and belonging needs. They are "people who need people." As a member of the human family, you are also "needy" in this way.

The Importance of Human Relationships

The subtitle of this textbook is "Creating Successful Relationships Through Effective Interpersonal Communication," so we want to establish in this introductory chapter, and reinforce throughout this textbook, that one of the primary goals or purposes of interpersonal communication is

Figure 1.13 Human relationships are key to human health and flourishing.

Figure 1.14
A lack of interpersonal communication can lead to isolation and alienation.

the creation and maintenance of human relationships. Furthermore, we want to establish that human relationships are not just a "nice thing" for some people to have, but they are an essential requirement for human health and flourishing (Figure 1.13).

What is the worst legal punishment that we can give to a prisoner in jail? Solitary confinement. To choose solitude for a time can be invigorating, but to be forced into isolation from other people is psychological torture. Human beings can be psychologically broken and damaged by forced isolation. A brief respite from human interactions is tolerable, but separation from other human beings for an extended period of time is excruciating.

What is one of the cruelest things you can do to another human being? Call them names? Taunt them? No. Even worse, ignore them. Act like they are not there. When you ignore someone, when you act like they do not exist, you deny them what they need the most—human connection and human relationship. If you have ever been "shunned," you know from personal experience how painful it is to be ignored (Figure 1.14).

What is the height of human development, independence or interdependence? When human beings are born, they are almost totally dependent on their caregivers in order to survive. As human baby grows, we note milestones of independence: the ability to crawl and walk, the ability to feed oneself, the ability to dress oneself, and so on. Milestones of independence in childhood are sleeping over at a friend's house, going to school by oneself, and so on. The milestones of independence in the teenage years are getting a driver's license, getting a job, reaching "legal adult" age, and moving away from home (Figure 1.15).

But when a human being moves away from home, do they usually then proclaim, "Great! I am now totally alone!"? No, most human adults seek to form families of their own, and they seek to enter voluntarily into close relationships with others to fulfill mutual needs and receive mutual benefits. This is hard for some individualistic Americans to fathom, but the height of human development is not independence, but interdependence.

When people are on their deathbeds, what are they most concerned about? Most people are concerned about their relationships with friends and family members. They want to see their loved ones and they want to express their love one more time. If they have strained or damaged relationships, they often want to offer forgiveness or be forgiven in order to repair these relationships (Figure 1.16).

Your body has physiological needs for food, water, air, and so on, but your mind also has psychological needs for human connectedness, recognition, acceptance, love, and relationship. Since the mind (psyche) is connected to the body (soma), many physical illnesses are

DEPENDENCE ⟹ INDEPENDENCE ⟹ INTERDEPENDENCE

Figure 1.15 The trajectory of human growth and development.

"psychosomatic" in a very real sense: when your psychological needs are not met, both your mind and your body can suffer.

After World War II, many orphanages in Europe were flooded with babies that had been left parentless. Some of these orphanages had high standards of hygiene and excellent provisions, but for some unknown reason, a large percentage of infants were dying. When social scientists were called in to assess the situation, they discovered that although the babies were being fed and cleaned and kept warm in their cribs and incubators, the overworked nurses had little time to actually hold the infants. When the nurses followed the suggestion to hold each infant for at least 15 minutes twice a day, the infant mortality rate plummeted, and a new term for the effects of a lack of human affection was coined: "failure to thrive." Infants "fail to thrive" when they are not held and shown affection. Although their basic physiological needs may be met, if their psychological need for affection and human connection is not met, they may die even though food is in their stomach. They die because they are starved for attention and affection.

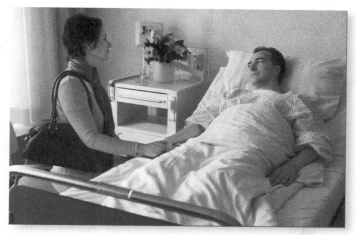

Figure 1.16 At the end of their lives, most people are most concerned about their relationships.

Figure 1.17 Human beings grow old best when they grow old in relationships with others.

Adults do not outgrow the need for love, attention, and human connection. They can also "fail to thrive" if they do not fulfill their love and belonging needs. Relational satisfaction, we are learning, is an important element of human health and happiness. If you want to live a long full life, you should eat a balanced diet, exercise regularly, and get plenty of sleep. However, you should also pay attention to the quantity and quality of your interpersonal interactions and your social relationships (Figure 1.17).

Interpersonal Ethics

Since moral judgment is one of the eight powers of the human mind, we would like to give you some ethical guidance as you interact and communicate with other human persons. You need to determine which interpersonal communication behaviors are good or bad, right or wrong. We will offer to you four observations related to the ethical dimension of interpersonal communication.

Observation # 1: Your philosophical anthropology will greatly impact the way you treat and interact with other people. By "philosophical anthropology" we mean your basic view of human beings and human nature.

For example, if you think that human beings are basically good (as Carl Rogers did), then you will be open to interpersonal relationships with almost everyone. Although we think that you should have a default setting of "trust" when initiating relationships with others, we do want to caution you that there are "unsafe," dangerous people that you would be wise to avoid. Do not let your desire for love and belonging outweigh your need for safety and security.

If you think that human beings are basically evil (as the English philosopher and social theorist Thomas Hobbes did), then you will be reluctant to enter into an interpersonal relationship with almost everyone. This misanthropic view of humanity makes it virtually impossible to build healthy human relationships based on trust, and it can also lead to self-loathing and poor self-esteem.

Consider carefully your basic view of human nature and whether it is justified. Many basic beliefs are unconscious, so you may have to do some mental work to uncover your core concepts and beliefs about human beings. Are human beings good? Evil? A mixture of good and evil? Neither good nor evil? Your basic thoughts about human nature will create your attitudes toward others, and these attitudes will drive your interpersonal behaviors.

Observation # 2: Lying can greatly damage an interpersonal relationship because it undermines trust. Be very careful about lying to people, especially to people with whom you have (or want to have) close relationships. Dishonesty is a "deal-breaker" for some relational partners. Other relational partners may be willing to forgive this particular relational transgression (depending on the frequency and seriousness of your lies), but you are undermining your partners' ability to trust you. In addition, you are also undermining your ability to trust other people. If you lie to your relational partners whenever you think it is necessary or convenient, then you will probably assume that they are behaving in a similar manner.

Observation # 3: When interacting with other people, it is helpful to remember both the Golden Rule and the Platinum Rule. The Golden Rule is an ethical maxim found in many major world religions and ethical philosophies. It suggests that you should treat other people the way that you want to be treated. This is a very helpful guide for many interpersonal situations. For example, if you are wondering whether you should tell a new romantic partner that you have a sexually transmitted disease, following the Golden Rule will help you to self-disclose this sensitive information. If they had a sexually transmitted disease, after all, you would want to know this fact.

Scholars in the field of intercultural communication have developed the Platinum Rule which goes a step beyond the Golden Rule. The Platinum Rule suggests that you should treat other people the way that *they* want to be treated. This ethical maxim has great value because it sensitizes you to the fact that other people (especially people with different cultural backgrounds) may have tastes, preferences, and values that differ from your own. If you want to demonstrate that you respect your relational partners and their personal preferences and standards, try out the Platinum Rule.

Observation # 4: Recognizing human beings as persons uplifts and ennobles humanity and encourages respect for and acceptance of other human beings. When you realize and acknowledge that other people have the same mental powers and abilities that you possess, their human dignity and worth are obvious. Human persons are rational, emotional, volitional, self-aware, morally aware, esthetically aware, and creative beings.

Human persons are able to think abstractly, feel passionately, choose wisely, and act courageously. Human persons can observe both their bodies and their minds. They can look outside themselves (at the world around them), and they can look inside themselves (within their own hearts and minds). Human persons can judge what is good, right, and just and what is evil, wrong, and unjust. Human persons can appreciate beauty and disdain ugliness. Human persons can remember the past and envision the future.

As a person, as a member of the human family, you have the opportunity to meet and interact with other unique persons. Human beings are not interchangeable widgets—they are unduplicatable persons. Every one of the seven billion human beings that inhabit our planet, and every one of the human beings that has ever lived on the earth, is or has been unique. Although human beings share a lot of the same DNA, each individual person is a unique constellation of biological, cultural, and historical influences.

We value and respect other human beings not only because we share a common humanity, but also because we recognize their unique personhood—everyone is "one of a kind." We may have our physical "doppelgangers," but no two human beings are exactly alike, not even "identical" twins. Our different personal histories and personalities result in unique individuals that are given the status of "persons" rather than "things."

Unfortunately, the fourth ethical observation we have stated above has a negative corollary: denying that human beings are persons degrades and denigrates humanity and encourages very bad behavior toward other human beings. When the personhood of human beings is denied, then it is much easier to treat them like property and to use (and abuse) them as things (Figure 1.18).

Figure 1.18 When interacting with others, get "personal" and treat them with respect.

The Importance and Value of Interpersonal Communication

I (Michael Schulmeister) began this chapter with a personal narrative relating how the study of interpersonal communication has changed my life and transformed my interpersonal relationships. At the end of this brief opening narrative, I revealed that I have a self-centered motive for teaching courses in interpersonal communication: I never want to forget the important lessons I have learned in this field of study, and I never want to lose the insights I have gained about myself, my loved ones, and our relationships.

You need to find your own reasons for studying interpersonal communication. We will help you to do this by providing a list of reasons why the study of interpersonal communication is important and valuable. As we run through this list, we will also preview the next ten chapters of this textbook.

- The study of interpersonal communication is important because it is the most common form of oral communication used by human beings. During a typical day, most of us engage in multiple one-on-one conversations with many different people. Given the prevalence of interpersonal communication in our everyday lives, interpersonal communication should be a required general education course.

- Studying interpersonal communication gives you self-knowledge. **Chapter 2 (Identity)** helps you to examine your self-concepts and evaluate your level of self-esteem. This chapter will also help you to "tune in" to your own self-talk.

- **Chapter 2 (Identity)** can also help you manage your identity and consider the way that you come across to others. You will learn to distinguish between your "private" self and your "public" self, your "perceived" self, and your "presenting" self.

- **Chapter 3 (Perception)** can help you to identify and become aware of your "perceptual filters." Since your perception is your reality, you need to consider how your family upbringing, your cultural training, and your personal life experiences influence the way you view the world and the way you perceive yourself and others.

- Studying interpersonal communication can improve your conversational skills. **Chapter 4 (Language)** will teach you how to avoid language that offends and demeans others. You will learn how to use effective and appropriate language that will enhance your interpersonal relationships.

- Studying interpersonal communication will help you to "read" other people. **Chapter 5 (Nonverbals)** will teach you to pay attention to the nonverbal messages that your communication partners are sending, and it will help you to become more aware of the nonverbal messages you send to others.

- Studying interpersonal communication can help you to express (rather than suppress or repress) your emotions. **Chapter 6 (Emotion)** will help you to identify cultural influences which create negative feelings about feeling, and it will help you to appreciate your emotions and express them appropriately.

- Studying interpersonal communication can improve your listening skills. **Chapter 7 (Listening)** will help you identify some common listening barriers and poor listening habits, and it will help you to practice active, engaged listening when you converse with others.

- Studying interpersonal communication can give you the knowledge and courage you need to open up and share yourself with others. **Chapter 8 (Self-Disclosure)** will teach you the concepts and skills you need to make appropriate self-disclosures.

- Studying interpersonal communication can help you to deepen and strengthen your interpersonal relationships. **Chapter 9 (Relationships)** will help you to more effectively manage your relationships with your family members, romantic partners, and close friends.

- Studying interpersonal communication can help you to effectively resolve interpersonal conflicts. **Chapter 10 (Conflict/Dark Side)** will give you insights into how to "fight fair" in order to resolve conflict, and it will point out some of the serious problems that can arise in interpersonal relationships.

- Studying interpersonal communication can help you develop more successful relationships by investigating the role and importance of sexual communication in your intimate relationships. **Chapter 11 (Sexual Communication)** will provide you research that demonstrates the direct connection between couples who openly engage in communication about sex and their increased relational satisfaction and longevity.

- If you work, studying interpersonal communication can help you to develop a network of acquaintances and contacts that can enhance your career.

- If you are religious, studying interpersonal communication can help you share your religious faith with others more effectively, and it can improve your interactions with people in your religious community.

- If you are sexually active, studying interpersonal communication can improve your sex life and your sexual satisfaction.

- If you are a person, studying interpersonal communication can help you make meaningful connections with other persons.

Conclusion

In this opening chapter, we have introduced you to the study and practice of interpersonal communication. You have learned that one-on-one, face-to-face communication is one of the most significant human activities, but that the academic study of interpersonal communication is only a little over 50 years old.

You learned that the field of interpersonal communication is a major subfield of human communication studies, and that it can be contrasted to small group communication, organizational communication, intercultural communication, mass communication, and public speaking. You also learned that interpersonal communication is one of the most important subfields in human communication studies because one-on-one, face-to-face communication occurs within most of these other subfields.

You have learned to describe an interpersonal communication interaction using the concepts and terms in the transactional model of communication. You have learned that a communicator encodes and sends a message through a communication channel that another communicator must receive and decode. You have learned that primary messages and feedback messages may travel simultaneously through different communication channels, and that these messages may be affected by communication noise.

You have learned that interpersonal communication is a meeting of human minds, and you have learned that the human mind has several important powers or abilities: memory, rationality, emotionality, volition, self-awareness, moral awareness, esthetic awareness, and creativity. You have also learned that the human mind has a conscious and an unconscious level. You have learned that interpersonal communication is complicated because the human mind is complicated.

In addition, you have learned about two important subfields within interpersonal communication: intrapersonal communication and family communication. Intrapersonal communication, you have learned, studies the communication that occurs within one human person, whereas family communication studies the communication that occurs among family members and significant others.

You have also learned that there is both a quantitative and a qualitative definition of interpersonal communication: interpersonal communication can be defined as communication between two people, or it can be defined as communication that treats people as persons rather than impersonal things. You have learned that human relationships are important for your physiological and psychological health.

You have learned four ethical insights into interpersonal communication, including the insight that recognizing human beings as persons encourages respect for and acceptance of others. You have learned over a dozen reasons why the study and practice of interpersonal communication is important, including the fact that interpersonal communication allows you to make meaningful connections with other persons.

You have also learned that relationships matter most. We invite you to use the knowledge from this chapter to make the most of your interpersonal relationships. We will join you in this quest. Let's get personal!

Chapter 2

Identity

By A. Todd Jones

After reading this chapter you will

- Have a better understanding of your identity
- Understand how to improve your self-esteem
- Become more aware of your self-presentation
- Know the difference between sexual and gender identity

Who am I? What makes me, me? Where do these impressions and opinions of self come from? As a full-time interpersonal communication instructor and a part-time life coach, identity and self-esteem are among my favorite topics to talk about. These concepts are so important and central to happiness in life that it deserves our attention on a regular basis. Your identity and how you feel about yourself is a topic that is not often discussed openly, but most of us think about it quite often. In this chapter, I will discuss identity, self-esteem, self-presentation, and professionalism. Andrea D. Thorson will then discuss sexuality, sexual identity, gender identity, and persons with disabilities.

Initially, your identity is developed over time based on your thoughts and interactions with parents, siblings, friends, and others. These people can be a good or a bad influence on how you see yourself. While we will take into consideration the influence others have on you, in

Figure 2.1

© Rawpixel.com/Shutterstock.com

Figure 2.2 Our identity is developed over time through our experiences and our interactions with others.

this chapter we will focus mainly on taking control of and shaping your own identity and positive self-esteem. It is important that we differentiate identity from self-esteem. Identity is your impressions of self without judgment, while self-esteem is your positive or negative evaluations of these impressions.

The terms "identity" and "self–concept" are often used interchangeably. These terms simply refer to how you see yourself. This self-view is typically stable and doesn't change quickly or that often (Hamachek 1978). Rather, it will evolve over your life time—often gradually. Identity doesn't include a judgment of good or bad. It is simply the impressions you have of your intelligence, emotions, masculinity/femininity, social skills, personality, appearance, preferences, beliefs and values, roles, interests, talents, and so on. These impressions are given to you through your interaction and experiences with others. Additional influences may include the media and popular culture. The judgment of each of these identity markers, and how we feel about those judgments, is your self-esteem (Rosenberg 1965). We will discuss that at length later in this chapter.

Central to having a better awareness of our identity is understanding the multiple roles we each play. For example, you may play the role of a student, an employee, a romantic partner, a best friend, and a family member. While these roles may not be mutually exclusive, you may act and see yourself differently as you perform the activities and interactions of that particular role. Does that mean you are

© Sofi photo/Shutterstock.com

Figure 2.3

Figure 2.4 Central to having a better awareness of our identity is understanding the multiple roles we each play.

being fake because you act differently in different contexts? Not at all. When I am in the classroom I don't play the role of a father. If I spoke to my students like I spoke to my kids, it would be awkward, and maybe a little creepy. I wouldn't communicate with my friends the same way I communicate with my students either. What roles do you play? Does your personality and communication change in different contexts? Of course, they do. You might even say that we have multiple identities (James 1890).

Our view of these roles and identities is called the perceived self. This

Figure 2.5 We try to portray a positive public image to others.

is the person you believe yourself to be in honest moment of self-reflection. This may include your opinions of your intelligence, your looks, your abilities, and so on. These perceptions of self are private and are not typically shared with many others. Our reluctance to share many of these is a reflection of the private nature of our perceived self or identity. The complete view we have of ourselves is not something that we commonly share with all we meet (Tice and Faber 2001).

On the other hand, our public self, or what we typically call our presenting self, is the image that we do share with others. Most of the time, we create an image of ourselves that we present to others for their approval. The goal is acceptance and positive interaction. We typically manage this identity differently with different people. For example, we will likely interact differently with our best friend versus the way we act with a professor or an employer. A skilled communicator will manage the self he or she presents to others based on one's perception of the relationship.

Self-Presentation and Identity Management

It's important to understand the difference between self-presentation and identity management. Self-presentation is the way we present ourselves to the world—often visually. Identity management behaviors are strategies we use to influence the way others see us, including our social interactions. Self-presentation is simply one aspect of identity management.

Self-Presentation and Making Statements

Figure 2.6

Central to the concept of our identity is our self-presentation. Self-presentation is a lot more than what we look like, how we dress, and how we carry ourselves. Self-presentation is also our personality, the music we listen to, the place we live, the car we drive, how we speak, the job we have, the way we wear our hair, and our nonverbal confidence or shyness. Each of these elements of self-presentation makes a statement of who we are and what we are about. Of course, these statements are open to interpretation from others. Sometimes these statements are strong and obvious, and sometimes they are subtle and seek simply to blend in. Some of us make statements assuming that the general public is our audience, while others make statements targeting a specific crowd. Many of us do both. However, there are times when we employ specific self-presentation strategies to impress, influence, or engage with a certain person or a more defined audience. For example, we may appear to be busy at work to impress our boss, we may appear to be humble and sorry to seek forgiveness, or we may wear our best outfit to attract a potential mate.

Figure 2.7

Have you ever been in a conversation with one of your friends and pointed out another person that you thought was hot or attractive? Perhaps your friend looked at you with a smirk of disagreement. Obviously, we each have our own idea of what is attractive and unattractive. However, positive self-presentation is a lot more than nice clothes or an attractive look. It can also be a good attitude, the way we communicate, a smile, confidence, or being friendly. Here are 10 suggestions to improve your self-presentation.

1) Improve your posture. If you are physically able, stand and sit up straight. Most of us have been told this by our parents since we were children. Slouching makes us look lazy and tired and may suggest a bad attitude. According to Yeager (2011) on Prevention.com, poor posture can cause depression, constipation, stress, increase your risk of disease, and cut off your circulation. It can also make you look heavier and unprofessional. To stand up straight, imagine a string attached to the top of your head pulling you up straight. We also need to be aware of slouching as we sit. Remember, stand and sit up straight.

Figure 2.8

2) Don't talk loudly in public; it's distracting, annoying, and tacky. Later in this chapter I tell a brief story about two people having a loud conversation in a crowded public place. Of course, if you are at a football game or another sporting events then the context is different. But in a shopping center or a doctor's office, or a place of business, and so on, being loud is inappropriate. People around you will be annoyed and unimpressed.

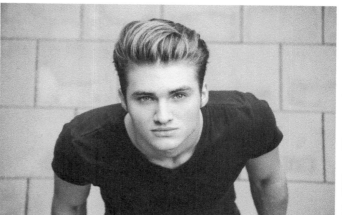

Figure 2.9

3) Avoid extreme hair and clothing styles. Evaluate your career goals and start dressing and styling accordingly. For those of you who are just starting college, this may be a new concept. (I can see you shaking your head as you read this.) Many of you are right out of high school where styles change almost yearly and are sometimes extreme. Please understand that I'm not suggesting that you wear professional clothing to school. However, I am suggesting that you evaluate your visual appearance and start aligning it with your career goals. You can do this gradually if it makes you more comfortable.

4) Dress appropriately for the occasion, season, and weather. If you're not going to the beach, the bar, or to bed, don't dress like it. Similar to rule number three, take an inventory of your visual self-presentation. I'm always a little shocked when I see a student show up to campus—in July—wearing a hoodie or a jacket. Also, revealing clothing that you may wear for an evening out is not appropriate for the classroom or the office.

© Nina Buday/Shutterstock.com

Figure 2.10

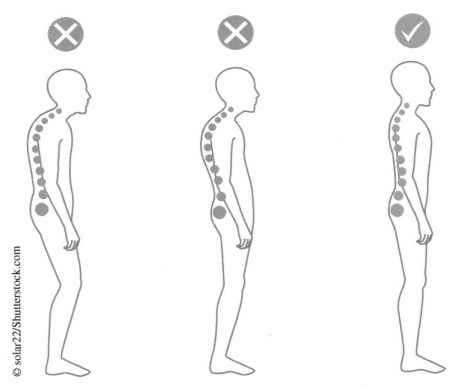

© solar22/Shutterstock.com

Figure 2.11 Correct standing and sitting posture are not only more healthy but can improve your self-presentation as well.

Figure 2.12 If you're not going to the beach, the bar, or to bed, don't dress like it.

5) Smile, speak positively, compliment others, and be happy. Nothing makes you more attractive than a smile. That combined with a good attitude and an easy-going demeanor are gold in almost any context. Look people in the eye. Be approachable and kind.

6) Always wear one or two non-neutral pieces of clothing or accessories. Avoid wearing all neutral colors—particularly all black (especially in the summer). Add a non-neutral top or bottom, a piece of jewelry, shoes, or an accessory of some kind. Don't be afraid to wear color! Wearing an accent of some kind—even a T shirt with print on it—will add personality to your appearance.

7) If you choose to get a tattoo, make sure you evaluate how it might have an effect on your career. Ask yourself these three questions: How big is it? Where is it on your body? And what is the tattoo a picture of? You may consider talking to someone who is currently working in the industry where you are planning your career to learn what is acceptable. Remember, a tattoo is forever. And whether it is fair or not, there may be judgment from those currently in your career associated with having a tattoo.

Figure 2.13

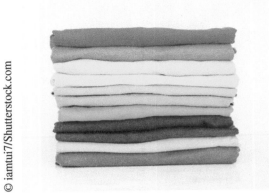

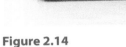

Figure 2.14

Figure 2.15

8) Be aware of your actions and behaviors and how they will affect others. A simple and regular inventory of your actions and words in different human interactions will serve you well. If you are a low self-monitor, take action to become more aware of your interactions with and around others.

9) If you are physically able, exercise! Go for a walk, play your favorite sport, go swimming, work out, go to the gym, and so on. Do something! Our bodies require cardiovascular and weight-bearing exercise three or four times a week to be healthy. Again, do something!

10) Watch what you eat. Be careful and aware of carbs, sugar, and fat intake. Practice portion control and eat more vegetables, fruits, and protein. Eat treats and junk food sparingly. In short, be the best version of you. I am not suggesting that we all become as fit as those who grace the cover of magazines. This is about health and well-being along with a positive self-presentation.

Figure 2.16

Figure 2.17

Figure 2.18 Our bodies need weight-bearing and cardiovascular exercise at least three times a week.

Figure 2.19

Figure 2.20 Eat more fruits and vegetables and fewer processed foods.

The Parade

By A. Todd Jones

Although I was raised in an area of the United States that isn't very diverse, I have lived half of my life in diverse environments and have always found myself attracted to those who are different from me. I find diversity of thought, behavior, self-presentation, culture, and background to be fascinating.

A metaphor that I have often used to describe this diversity is likening society to a parade. Sixty years ago, for example, the parade was quite narrow. There seemed to be specific expectations on how to act, who to be, and how to present yourself. If a person diverged much from these norms, they were scorned. However, as time has progressed, the parade has widened and society has become more accepting of those who are different from what was at one point considered "normal" or "mainstream." In short, these

Figure 2.21

Figure 2.22

differences become more accepted. I love the idea of the parade continuously widening. However, the parade is not all encompassing, and it is still possible to march outside of the parade—or what is typically accepted in our culture.

About 4 years ago, on the first day of class, I had a student show up to class wearing fangs. Not the typical white plastic Halloween fangs, but fangs that looked real—they matched his real teeth perfectly. As I take role the first day, I try to have fun with my students and get to know them better. As I called his name I looked up at him and saw his fangs and asked him, "What's with the fangs?" "I'm a vampire," he replied. Although I was intrigued, I thought he was messing with me. "Cool! I'm a Jedi" was my reply. He didn't seem to be joking or to take my comment with humor, so I asked him to chat with me after class.

As it turns out, being a vampire was a big part of his identity. He told me that he slept in a room painted black and that he had made his bed look like a coffin. I was fascinated and asked several questions. I had never heard of such a thing. He told me it was a version of being "goth." Even though this was completely out of my experience, it was important for me to gain his trust and for him to know that I wasn't against him.

Figure 2.23

Once the conversation became comfortable and nonthreatening, I explained to him the metaphor of the parade. We discussed where he thought being a vampire fit into this societal parade. He was a bit stumped and admitted that it probably didn't. I told him that one of the main goals of the class was to give him and all of my students the opportunity to be more employable. I then asked him not to wear the fangs to class anymore because it was distracting and made some of the other students uncomfortable. We also discussed

Figure 2.24 The reality is that we are all quirky and a bit odd.

how self-presentation is often contextual and that if he wanted to do vampire things with other people who were into being a vampire on the weekend that would be great. Finally, in the most appropriate and respectful way I could, I told him that I didn't think that others would take him seriously if he were wearing his fangs, especially an employer.

I realize that this is an extreme example. However, the reality is that we are all quirky and a little bit odd. Where do you fit into the parade? Are there some behaviors, opinions, or aspects of your self-presentation that may not be taken seriously, are too extreme, or will hinder you from getting the job in the industry that you want? Asking yourself these questions on a regular basis will serve you well socially, relationally, and professionally.

Identity Management

There are several theories and concepts that have emerged over the years to help us to understand ourselves and manage our identities. Although reality is often much more complex and messy than we realize, understanding the basics can help us to simplify and understand the complex and can aid us in understanding the detailed nuances of human behavior.

Figure 2.25 We manage our identities for several reasons.

© Monkey Business Images/Shutterstock.com

Studies have shown that there are several reasons we manage our identity. The most obvious reason is to meet, become acquainted, and possibly even start a relationship with another person Rosenfield (1997). Think about the first time you met your significant other or your best friend. You likely smiled, entered the conversation gracefully, and attempted to be charming, engaging, or funny. Your goal was to impress and to draw the other(s) closer to you, or at least to pique their interest. It is also likely that you put your best self forward in terms of dress, speech, nonverbal communication, and eye contact. Over time you may form a relationship and get to know the other person better. When this happens, we often find that we don't need to manage our identities as carefully or as strictly.

© Frederic Legrand – COMEO/Shutterstock.com

Figure 2.26

Another reason we manage our identities is to influence the behavior, opinions, or actions of others. A salesperson will dress to impress potential clients and customers. An employee will appear to be working hard to impress the boss. And politicians will say what they believe their constituents want to hear to influence their vote. When we meet people, we present ourselves in a particular way. We communicate, interact, and present ourselves in a way that we hope they will accept. This level of perceived acceptance can affect our identity and our self-esteem. We call this management of our identity

© Syda Productions/Shutterstock.com

Figure 2.27

face work. Face is how we want others to see us. We want to be accepted and respected. Part of this face management is repairing negative perceptions that others might have of our face. For example, if someone you were trying to impress were to see you in an argument with your sister, you will want to explain the situation and make yourself look good. We call this saving face.

Type A and Type B Personalities

One of the most common descriptors of identity is that of type A and type B personality. You have likely been described as one or the other yourself. A type A personality is typically driven, aggressive, a perfectionist, and has trouble relaxing. A type B personality is often more kick back, relaxed, and not easily irritated. Many of my students have claimed to be somewhere in the middle between these two extremes and have come to the conclusion that it is more of a continuum between one and the other. An extreme at either end of this continuum may describe a type A personality as impatient and irritable, and a type B person as not competitive, lethargic, or lacking passion needed to perform at peak levels. While these may describe some of us at times, most of us move back and forth a little on this continuum between type A and type B. Our personalities are fluid and subject to mood, context, and environment. Where do you see yourself on this continuum? Do you sometimes find yourself at one extreme or the other? What can you do to avoid these extremes?

Figure 2.28

Figure 2.29 There is obviously a continuum between type A and type B personalities. Where do you fit on that continuum?

Shyness

Another construct that is closely associated with our identity is our level of shyness. With so much of our communication happening electronically these days, shyness is actually on the rise (Scharlott and Christ 1995). I have had several students claim that over half of their social life is online. This along with environment and the way we were raised contribute to our shyness. Shyness is feeling insecure, embarrassed, or fear in social situations. Some may experience a pounding heart, stomach butterflies, or blushing. But the most

Figure 2.30

© Haywiremedia/Shutterstock.com

Figure 2.31 It takes effort and a certain amount of risk to overcome shyness.

© file404/Shutterstock.com

Figure 2.32

© Ivanko80/Shutterstock.com

Figure 2.33 Smile, make eye contact, and be social.

debilitating aspect of shyness is the negative thoughts often associated with shyness. Thoughts such as "I'm not an interesting person," "I'm not as skilled as they are," or "They won't like me" are dangerous and will perpetuate feelings of inadequacy. If you find yourself having these kinds of thoughts, do everything you can to stop thinking this way. Talk to a trusted friend, a family member, or a counselor to get help to change your thinking to be more positive and accepting of yourself.

There are several possible consequences of being shy. First, shyness can cause you to become overly self-conscious. The perception is that everyone is looking at your every weakness and flaw. When in reality, we all have our own things to think about. People are typically not checking us out trying to find our flaws. Second, shyness can make it difficult to meet or become acquainted with others. If we experience shyness in a social situation, we may fear introducing ourselves, thus eliminating the opportunity to gain a friend or a new relationship. Third, shyness may keep us from experiencing new things. Fourth, it can keep us from demonstrating our talents and skills in a work or social situation. In short, shyness can prevent others from getting to know the real you.

Overcoming shyness can be difficult, but it is not impossible. It's not uncommon to be shy as a child and then grow out of it as we mature. But what are we to do when that is not the case? How do we gain the confidence to put ourselves out there and become more outgoing? There are a few simple steps to becoming less shy. First, take an inventory of what makes you shy. What situations make you feel shy? Is it one on one, in groups, or in front of an audience? Once you understand the nature of your shyness, it will be easier to combat it. Second, it's all about building your confidence and self-esteem. We will discuss this at length later in this chapter.

Third, we need to improve our social skills. Smile at people and look them in the eye. If you are too shy to talk about yourself to someone, ask them about their life and interests. Remember, you don't have to be interesting; you just have to be interested. You may want to find someone who you believe has great social skills and imitate that skill. I had a friend in high school that was liked by everyone—every

Figure 2.34 Find someone who is confident and has great social skills. Then imitate those positive traits.

click and group had an affinity for Jan. How did she become so popular? I watched her and noticed that she always had something nice to say about everyone. She complimented others constantly. She was fun and approachable. I realized that her outgoing nature and compliments were what endeared her to everyone she knew. In my own way, and with my own personality, I started to imitate this skill of building others up and noticed a huge difference in the way I was treated and appreciated by others. While I wasn't shy, and I certainly didn't imitate the details of her personality, I learned a great lesson that I have used throughout my life. Who do you know with these types of people skills? How can you learn by their example?

Who Am I?

I'd like to invite you to have an experience of self-discovery. In your workbook, there is an activity that will help you to better understand the details of who you are. It will ask you to describe yourself from several different perspectives and on different topics. You will be asked to list various identity markers that are relevant to specific areas of your identity (Adler 2017).

For some of you this will be a simple, quick assignment; others will require some thought and pondering. Each of these descriptors you write down is an identity marker. An identity marker is simply one of the many ways you would describe yourself—it's a part of your identity. You may notice that some of these markers are not mutually exclusive and may show up in more than one of your lists. You may also have difficulty coming up with at least five self-identity markers for each list.

When you have finished this activity, take one last look to see if there are

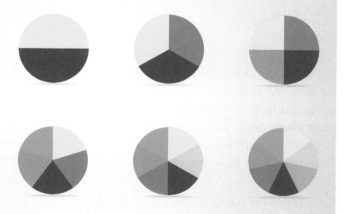

Figure 2.35 Making a simple pie chart of your most important identity markers can give you a visual representation of the make-up and balance of your identity.

any other identity markers that you may have missed. You may want to ask someone who knows you well for feedback. They may be able to add additional identity markers that you have missed. If you choose to ask for help, the other person may list items that you may not be comfortable with or relate to. This may be an opportunity to further evaluate the identity you are projecting to others as well as an outside perspective.

Once your lists are complete, take a look at all of these identity markers and choose the 10 that describe you the most and list these in order of most important on the last page of the exercise. As you make your list, assign a percentage to each of them. In other words, how much of your identity, as a whole, is each identity marker? Next, make a simple pie chart of all of these markers to give yourself a visual of your identity. What do you see? Do you believe that you have a good mix of different identity markers, or are there one or two that seem to be the majority of your identity? Is this a good thing, or do you need to consider a more balanced, well-rounded identity? What do you believe you need to do to move in that direction? What does this tell you about yourself? What changes would you like to make if any?

Now imagine that item number 10 on your list is no longer an identity marker. How much would that change you as a person? Is it difficult to imagine this not being a part of who you are? Now temporarily remove number nine and imagine and evaluate the same thing. Continue on until you have imagined that all 10 of these identity markers are no longer a part of who you are. Feel lost and dumfounded? It really is impossible to imagine, isn't it? This simple exercise further proves how deeply connected we are to our identity.

I have had several eye-opening, interesting experiences with clients and students when looking at this chart. I believe that balance is one of the most important evaluations that can come out of this exercise. Generally speaking, I suggest to you that if any of these self-identity markers are over 25 percent, you may want to take an honest look at the balance of your identity. An exception to this, among a few others, would be that of a parent taking care of small children—especially a newborn baby.

However, I once had a student list

© FamVeld/Shutterstock.com

Figure 2.36

his truck as 55 percent of his identity. After class, I asked him about it. With a smile on his face he told me that that was how he met women. We then had a conversation about others being attracted to him based mainly on his truck ownership. I also asked him if he wanted to date or marry someone who liked him just because of his truck. Of course, the answers are obvious. Balance of self–concept is important because a variety of identity markers help to create a firm foundation for how we view ourselves, as well as how we present ourselves to others.

Comparing Ourselves to Others

I often warn my students of the dangers of comparing themselves to others. The danger is that there will always be someone smarter, more talented at one thing or another, or perceived to be better looking. The list of unhealthy comparisons is endless. Although the comparison of these evaluations may be subjective, these conclusions serve no purpose and can be harmful. It is likely that someone can play the piano, play basketball, or learn geometry better than you. These comparisons can be dangerous, when in reality they don't matter at all. As I elaborate further later in this chapter, the only person you should compare yourself to is your past self. This will give you a sense of progression and the direction your life is going.

Figure 2.37 Be careful of comparing yourself to others.

However, imagine that you were born and raised in an environment with no other humans around you. You would likely have a deficient sense of self because of lack of comparison. In reality, there are some comparisons we make with other people as part of our learning process. We have a good sense of whether or not we are tall, have light or dark hair, or have a different ethnic identity from someone else Taylor, Wood and Lichtman (1983). These comparisons are relatively objective and are not based on talent or skill.

Comfort Zone

Have you ever experienced the alarm going off on a cold winter's morning? The bed is so warm and comfortable that you don't want to get up . . . ever! Have you ever felt like that in life? We are creatures of habit and routine. It is common for us to become comfortable and even complacent in our lives. We get up and go to work or school every day that it almost seems that at times we go robot. For example, do you re-member driving to school, work, or home today? Do you remember the route or what you saw while driving? Not likely. You get in your car, make

Figure 2.38

yourself comfortable, and think about other things as you drive. All of a sudden, you are at your destination without remembering what happened between the time you left and your arrival.

Does this happen in other parts of your life? Do you come home from school or work and plop down in front of the TV? What about your health or physical fitness? How is your social life? Are you socializing too much online and not enough in person? Do you order the same thing from the same restaurant every weekend? For many of us, a routine—our comfort zone—is human nature. This is not to say that all habits are bad. Many of us get up and work out every morning, eat healthy, and socialize on a regular basis. However, being in a rut may be a barrier to honest personal evaluation.

© Gustavo Frazao/Shutterstock.com

Figure 2.39

© son Photo/Shutterstock.com

Figure 2.40 Break out of your comfort zone by eating something new.

When I talk about this with my students, I challenge them to break out of this comfort zone and work on improving themselves. Specifically, I challenge them to drive to and from school and work a different route. The results are amazing and often hilarious. Some of them even get lost. I also challenge them (and you) to meet someone new. Start a conversation with someone you don't know. You don't have to form a relationship with them, but you never know what might happen. A student of mine met her future spouse by accepting this challenge. She started a conversation in the grocery store, they exchanged numbers, and they started dating soon thereafter. I realize that this may not always happen, but you never know. At any rate, you'll be happy that you put forth the effort. Other challenges may include ordering something different at a restaurant or reconnecting with an old friend.

The point is, *do something*! Mix it up a little and see what is out there that you may be missing. If you always do what you have always done, you'll always get what you have always got. Take charge of your life and make it what you want it to be.

Locus of Control

What controls your life? Are there outside forces, parents, responsibilities, bosses, friends, partners, and so on who have power over your life? What about fate? Do things just happen to you that you have no control over? Or do you believe that you have control or at least significant influence over what happens in your life? Have you ever had a goal that seemed to never get accomplished for one reason or another? Or do you believe that you have the ability to control outcomes and events in your life? The concept of locus of control suggests that we all have different ideas about what and who controls our life.

© Wollertz/Shutterstock.com

Figure 2.41

Those who feel that they have influence over the outcomes of their lives are called internals. An internal believes that they can solve problems with their own efforts, are more driven, and are often more successful in life. An external believes the opposite. Their typical outlook on life is that there is nothing they can do to improve their situation, and that "whatever happens, happens." This is a dangerous attitude because you are acquiescing control of your life. It can also create a negative perception in your mind. Our perception becomes our reality; in other words, things are what we say they are.

Your workbook has a survey entitled "What Controls Your Life?" Fill out the survey honestly and add up your score. Typically, those who score 14 or lower are seen as internals, and those who score 15 or higher are externals. Of course, as is often the case, this is more of a continuum rather than one or the other. What was your score? Does it sound accurate? What if your score indicates that you are an external? What can be done about it? If your score suggested that you are more of an external, ask yourself where these ideas came from. Are there people in your life who have influenced your thinking? Are there family patterns that have hurt you in some way? What kind of expectations have you had for yourself? Let's talk about a few strategies for taking control of your life.

We have all heard the age-old question "Is the glass half full or half empty?" Most of us would claim that the cup was half full. However, I like to suggest to my classes that if you are thinking positively about your life and feeling like you have influence and control the glass is more than half full. I once told this story to a class and a brilliant student chimed in and stated that the glass was actually completely full. This student had the right idea.

© Wollertz/Shutterstock.com

Figure 2.42

Your Script

Probably the most important way to take control of your life is to become aware of your life script. Your script is not only your story; it is your attitudes, your beliefs, your likes and dislikes, opinions, personality, and your faith or lack of faith in yourself and others. Your script is who you are and what you think about yourself, others, and things. Imagine that your life is a movie. If this were the case, who has

Figure 2.43

© Novikov Alex/Shutterstock.com

© goodluz/Shutterstock.com

Figure 2.44

© Brent Hofacker/Shutterstock.com

Figure 2.45

been writing the script? Who has had the biggest influence on you? Most likely it has been you, the people closest to you such as your family members and friends, and likely some of your teachers. Some of the scripts they have given you are positive, and others may be negative. Reflect on some of the good and bad things that others have said to you. How did these comments shape who you are today? Are you happy with your script? If you were to become the primary or only writer of your script, what would you write? What would you change and what would you keep the same? For most of us it is time to edit this script.

A story that I often tell in class is about a client of mine who owned his own Web design business. He was successful but told me that he hated talking on the phone to his customers. As his life coach, I quickly corrected him and reminded him that he hated talking on the phone because he *said* that he hated talking on the phone. We then had a discussion about how our attitudes and opinions are often formed as a product of things we say. The more we verbalize these attitudes and opinions, the more we internalize them and they become our reality.

A few weeks after I told this story, my class was talking about the different workout and exercise videos on the market and the diets that come with them. I mentioned that I didn't like eating vegetables when one of my "mom students" replied, "You don't like vegetables because you *say* you don't like them!" She was right and I committed right then and there to change my script and eat them. As a matter of fact, I just ate a plate full of broccoli! Again, our realities are altered because of the things we say and reiterate to ourselves. Our minds are much more powerful than we know. Use this power to edit your script and take control of your life.

Positive Internal Dialogue

I always get a kickout of asking my students if any of them want to claim that they don't talk to themselves. Of course, they do—we all do. The important question is what are you saying to yourself? Are you being a positive Patty, or are you being a negative Nathan? Far too many of us are having negative communication with ourselves. We are exaggerating our weaknesses and failings and downplaying our strengths. Stop it! If you want your life to move in a positive direction, you are going to have to focus and emphasize the positive. A positive internal dialogue, or talking positively to yourself, is key to success in any aspect of life. When you are about to play sports, give a speech, or take an exam, give yourself a pep talk and tell yourself that you've got this.

Figure 2.46

© boykung/Shutterstock.com

Self-Fulfilling Prophecy and the Law of Attraction

Similar to the construct of having a positive internal dialogue is the idea of the self-fulfilling prophecy. In fact, it could be argued that the positive or negative things that we say to ourselves are indeed just that—self-fulfilling prophecies (Kolligan 1990). For example, if you tell yourself that it's going to be a hard day because it's Monday, you will probably be right. Luckily, the same is true for positive thoughts. Simply put, a self-fulfilling prophecy is a statement that you make, either out loud or to yourself, that is more likely to come true simply because you have said it. Remember, things are what we say they are.

© mypokcik/Shutterstock.com

Figure 2.47

Closely related to self-fulfilling prophecies is the law of attraction (Byrne 2006). The law of attraction states that "like attracts like." When we focus on positive or negative things, we attract them into our lives. Have you ever wanted something so badly that you focused on it day in and day out? I have. I wanted to get into graduate school at Arizona State University so badly that I could almost taste it! I focused on this goal for almost a year. I pictured in my mind the day when a letter from the communication department would arrive in the mail. I pictured opening this letter and reading the first word, "Congratulations!" I imagined what it would feel like and where I would be when I opened the letter. I wasn't a bit surprised when the letter finally arrived in the mail congratulating me on my acceptance into the Arizona State University Hugh Downs School of Human Communication graduate program. Personally, I swear by this law. It has helped me to become the person I am today. I have also seen this law work in hundreds of my students' and clients' lives.

Figure 2.48 Arizona State University is the home of the Hugh Downs School of Human Communication.

Figure 2.49

Online Identity Management

A few years ago, the subject of online identity management came up in one of my interpersonal communication classes. As an example, I asked if anyone was willing to pull up their Facebook page and show the class. At first a few hands cautiously went up, but then I heard comments like, "Oh, wait. No." And "I forgot about . . ." As these hands slowly went down, I was intrigued. I asked what they were embarrassed about. Issues like too many party pictures, foul language, and pictures on the beach came up. These pictures,

Figure 2.50

according to my class, weren't appropriate for the current context—the classroom. They were right; identity management is contextual. We act and present ourselves differently depending on our audience. I then reminded them that their coworkers, their boss, instructors, and even future employers had access to the pictures and posts online (Walther et al. 2008). Managing an online identity is just one part of self-presentation—which we will discuss later in this chapter.

Self-Esteem

Now that we have defined and discussed identity, let's look at self-esteem and how it works in our lives. Your judgment, evaluation, and opinions of your identity or self–concept is what we refer to as your self-esteem (Rosenberg 1972). Do you like yourself? Why or why not? What do you like about yourself, and what would you change if you could? Similar to self–concept, our self-esteem doesn't change quickly or very often but will gradually evolve throughout our lives. This evolution can be sped up through counseling, having a life coach, having an awareness of our thoughts, or reading and pondering a self-help book. You can also be negatively influenced by your thoughts and evaluations of life's circumstances and the words and actions of others. A person with a high or healthy self-esteem generally likes and has generally good feelings about oneself. I hope that most of you who are reading this have a healthy self-esteem. Unfortunately, that isn't always the case and so many of my students struggle with this. Sometimes I think it is an epidemic. What can we do to improve our self-esteem? Here are several strategies for improvement.

Take Control of Your Thoughts

Take control of yourself and your life. Easier said than done? The first thing that has to change is the way you talk to yourself. What kind of messages are you sending? Are you building yourself up, giving yourself a pep talk, or are you cutting yourself down or doubting your abilities? If you are sending yourself negative messages, stop it! Far too often you can become your own worst enemy. You have to change the way you think.

© bizvector/Shutterstock.com

Figure 2.51

Have Confidence in Your Abilities

Think of the word "confidence." What does it mean to you? What does it feel like when you are confident? Those who have control of their lives have confidence in their abilities that lead to expected outcomes. For example, as you sit down to take an exam, do you have confidence that you will understand the questions, concepts, and theories in this exam? Do you expect to get an A? Do you expect others to respond positively to you in social, academic, and professional contexts? Do you expect to like others when first meeting them? You should. Having confidence in your ability to perform at peak levels

Figure 2.52

is key to your success. Obviously, academics is not the only area of your life that will improve as your confidence does. Confidence can improve your social life, your professional life, your athletic ability, and almost any other area of your life. It can also help you to recover from adversity. The key here is to believe that you are in control of your world and that you are capable of accomplishing great things. You will have to start to see yourself as a confident person. Visualize yourself confidently interacting with others and performing the tasks of the day. To visualize yourself being confident, ask yourself what it would feel like. How would you stand, speak, and act? See yourself the way you want yourself to be. With confidence, you can expect yourself to be successful.

Let Go of Your Past!

Remember that stupid thing you did that one time? How could you? What were you thinking? Many of us have a stupid past where we have made mistakes. The unfortunate part is that some of us allow that mistake to define us as a person, sometimes to a debilitating level. Stop it! Give yourself a break. You are human and are allowed to make mistakes. Dismiss this mistake and the guilt and get on with your life.

A better way to look at it is to evaluate what lessons you might have learned from this experience. What behaviors, words, and situations do you need to be aware of and avoid in the future?

Don't Compare Yourself to Others

It is human nature to compare ourselves to others. The unfortunate perception is that we don't measure up or that we aren't good enough. There will almost always be someone more talented, or intelligent, or stronger than you are. That is the reality of being human! Focus on the good that makes you the person that you are. The only person you should ever compare yourself to is your past self. This comparison will allow you to evaluate the direction of your life and set goals, and is often less threatening. How are you doing socially, physically, spiritually? Are you more educated or fit than you were a year ago? What do you need to do to accomplish the goals that this comparison might suggest? While this self-assessment is usually a great tool to move your life in a better direction, we need to remember that some things do not necessarily get better with age. For example, a 60-year-old man may not want to compare his level of physical fitness to himself when he was 25. Make sure these comparisons to your past self are based on logic and reality.

Face Your Weaknesses

It's not our weaknesses that drag us down; it's the way we overrate them in our minds. Stop using extremes when looking at your faults. Avoid saying things like, "I never do well on a test," or, "I'm always late." Look at things as they really are when your mood is level and you can evaluate yourself objectively. Find exceptions and focus on your strengths. Define yourself by your strengths rather than your mistakes and weaknesses.

Seek Support

In my opinion, 50 percent of us need counseling right now, today. Yes, half of us! I also believe that everyone needs counseling at least once in their lives. Counseling and seeking advice from a trained professional, parent, close friend, or a religious leader helps us to combat our problems. You are not crazy, you are not losing it, and you are not damaged. In fact, those who seek help are smart and responsible. Those who take life into their own hands sometimes realize that they need help sorting through this issue or that problem. You are normal; go and get the help that you might need.

Figure 2.53

© Stock-Asso/Shutterstock.com

Not Everyone Is Going to Like You 100 Percent of the Time

About once a year I look at one of those "rate my professor" sites that so many of you look at to find an instructor that you would like. Out of curiosity, I look myself up. While an overwhelming majority of my former students have said nice things, and recommended me, there are a few who have been nasty or didn't like the class. What? How could they not like me or the class? I'm so fun and nice! Isn't it funny that we notice and focus on the negative evaluations of others even when most of them are positive? The reality is that we all need to accept that not everyone is going to like us. There is nothing wrong with being a people pleaser as long as you are true to who you are first. Give yourself a break!

Figure 2.54

© dotshock/Shutterstock.com

Make Time to Have a Social Life

Happy people put forth the effort to have friends. They reach out to others and make time to socialize and interact. Human beings function better and at a higher level when we are involved with others. Get out of your house or apartment, get off of your phone and computer, and meet people. Go to dinner, a party, or a sporting event.

Keep a Journal

Is there a problem or situation in your life that you are dealing with? Writing down your feelings can be quite cathartic. Putting your thoughts into a document allows you to unload and to get it off of your chest. For many, it feels as if the document itself is "carrying" this burden for you. Another benefit of journaling is the ability to write, walk away from it, and then revisit it a day or two later. If you type this document into a computer, you have the ability to return and edit your original document. It's not only the journal entry that is important; it is ability to clarify your thoughts and wishes through the editing process.

You should have an exceptionally healthy self-esteem. Life is too short to feel badly about yourself. Loving and appreciating yourself is key to happiness, success, and rewarding relationships. People who like themselves are easy to like because they are happy and compare themselves to others much less. Think of how this attitude will influence others. I can't imagine a better inheritance that you can pass on to your children than a realistic love of self.

Professionalism

One of the main goals for our students taking this class is to give you the tools to be more employable. Your employer will train you to use their equipment, inform you of their policies,

Figure 2.55

Figure 2.56

Figure 2.57

and how they do things. But they expect you to show up acting and looking professional. We often hear how this company or this person was so professional, or that a person or organization handled a situation unprofessionally. Defining professionalism is somewhat difficult because there are so many definitions. Professionalism is contextual. What is a lawyer expected to dress like in the city where you live? If the lawyer is male, it is likely that he will wear a suit with a white shirt—very conservative. However, picture a male lawyer in Texas. It is likely that he could get away with wearing cowboy boots. Is the same true in California or New York? Not likely.

Figure 2.58 Your employer will expect you to show up for work presenting yourself in a professional manner.

How does your professor dress? Here in California, where I teach, it is considered acceptable to wear anything from a suit and tie to jeans, shorts, and even T shirts. My colleagues in Boston and other eastern areas of the United States consider the way some of us dress in the California classroom to be inappropriate and unprofessional. What about an artist, or a musician, a construction worker, or a police officer? Each industry and region has different expectations for professional self-presentation.

That being said, here are several examples and descriptions of being professional.

1) Behave in socially accepted way such as having appropriate manners, appropriate language, and people skills.

2) Be a team player, cooperative, open to learning, and willing to mentor others.

3) Embrace change and be flexible.

4) Look people in the eye. Shake hands with just the right amount of firmness. Avoid a weak fish handshake, as well as a grip that is too firm.

5) Be enthusiastic and proud of your company, product, or service.

6) Participate in setting and achieving goals. Be motivated.

7) Have integrity and be honest. Choose the ethical course of action. Show that you can be trusted.

8) Don't be lazy or just do the minimum to get by. Go the extra mile and do more than is expected.

9) Avoid gossiping or complaining about the company, your job, or others.

10) Gain knowledge and understanding of your industry and product so that you can appropriately discuss business with colleagues, clients, and customers.

11) Be dependable, accountable, and responsible for your actions. Do what you say you will do when you say you will do it.

12) Make sure your self-presentation is appropriate for the job. Be aware of expectations such as hair style, clothing or uniform, personal hygiene, and visible tattoo policies.

13) Carry yourself with an air of confidence with the ability to handle conflict and stress appropriately and gracefully.

Professionalism Outside the Workplace

Figure 2.59 We should also act appropriate in our social, public, and personal lives.

Figure 2.60

We most often associate professional behavior with the workplace. However, acting appropriately and professional in our social, public, and personal lives deserves to be mentioned here as well. Many of the items listed above could also apply to our time away from our jobs. Have you ever been in public and noticed another person's inappropriate behavior? My kids and I were in a big warehouse store a few months ago in line to get a bite to eat. There were four or five lines that were serviced by as many windows. The lines were long and there were several people bunched together in a small space. Soon after we got in line, a woman at the front of one line started having a loud conversation with another woman at the back of a different line. They were basically yelling over at least 30 people. It was tacky, annoying, and inappropriate. Finally, someone in the line asked them to stop yelling. We all need to be aware of how our words, actions, and behaviors are affecting others. This not only applies to the work place; it also applies to social, public, and relational contexts as well.

The above example may seem a little extreme, but we have all seen people act as if no one else is around. I love it when students participate in class making comments and asking questions. However, about once a semester I have a student who treats my lecture like a one-on-one conversation. When I speak to them in private after class about this, they are often unaware of their continuous comments. These people are what we refer to as low self-monitor. Self-monitoring is the level of awareness of how appropriate ones' actions are based on the context of the interaction (Snyder and Campbell 1982). A low self-monitor will rarely modify his or her words and behaviors to fit the situation. On the other hand, a high self-monitor is aware of the rules of their surroundings and will act accordingly. Do you see yourself being a high or a low self-monitor? If you tend to lean toward being a low self-monitor, I encourage you to become more aware of the context with which you are interacting. Be cognizant of people and situations around you. Be respectful and aware of the needs and comfort levels of others. Being a high self-monitor will not only help you in your personal life but in your professional life as well.

Culture, Race, Ethnicity, Nationality, Religion, and Gender Identity

The difference between sex and gender

> Biology
> Male
> Female
> intersex
> Masculine
> Feminine
> Androgyny
> A gender
> Transgender
> Cis gender

Sexual Identity

> Gay, straight, bi-sexual
> Pan, scolio (list and explanation of various sexualities)
> The difference between sexual identity and sexuality
> Vocabulary list of sexual identities

Key Terms

Identity: It is your impressions of self without judgment, how you see yourself.

Identity Management: Behaviors and strategies we use to influence the way others see us, including our social interactions.

Law of Attraction: States that "like attracts like."

Perceived self: Our view of roles and our identity. This is the person you believe yourself to be in honest moment of self-reflection.

Public Self/Presenting Self: The image of self that we share with others.

Script: Your story, attitudes, beliefs, likes and dislikes, opinions, personality, and your faith or lack of faith in yourself and others. Your script is who you are and what you think about yourself, others, and things.

Self-Esteem: Your positive or negative evaluations of your impressions of yourself. Your judgment, evaluation, and opinions of your identity or self–concept.

Self-Fulfilling Prophecy: A statement that you make, either out loud or to yourself, that is more likely to come true simply because you have said it.

Self-Monitoring: The level of awareness of how appropriate ones' actions are based on the context of the interaction.

Self-Presentation: The way we present ourselves to the world—often visually.

Type A Personality: Typically driven, aggressive, a perfectionist, and has trouble relaxing.

Type B Personality: More kick back, relaxed, and not easily irritated.

Identity Class Discussion Questions

1. In what ways do we manage our identities in different contexts?
2. What is your view on extreme hair and clothing styles? How do you think your future job will expect you to present yourself? What kind of rules will exist?
3. What do you think of the analogy of the parade?
4. Do you believe that shyness is triggered by the use of social media and being on our phones so much? Why or why not?
5. What do you believe are the dangers and benefits of comparing yourself to others?
6. Who are the influences and writers of your script? Do you need to edit your script? If so, in what way?
7. Do you have an example of a self-fulfilling prophecy?
8. Would anyone be willing to show their Facebook page to the class right now? Why or why not? What do you think of a potential employer looking at your Facebook page before they make a decision to hire you?
9. What does professionalism mean to you?
10. Do you believe we have an obligation to act professionally and appropriately with others outside of the workplace? What does that mean to you?

Surveys and Web sites

1. IES Survey is beneficial to see how we interact with individuals of other cultures. More and more individuals from other countries are infusing and growing our own culture; this assesses how we will interact and areas we can improve on. This survey can go both ways; it can also benefit a student who is trying to expand his or her communication skills with U.S. citizens. It does have a fee around $12

   http://www.kozaigroup.com/intercultural-effectiveness-scale-ies.
2. This is a self-identity survey conducted by Ohio University with a consent form.

   https://www.surveymonkey.com/r/9ZJJY9N.
3. Tattoo survey sites

   https://blogs4bytes.typeform.com/to/XsbLEl—Debunking the tattoo taboo https://www.surveymonkey.com/r/VYXL6XC—Body piercing and tattoo questionnaire

https://www.surveymonkey.com/r/Tattooresearchproject—tattoo research project

4. This site has three different shyness surveys: ShyQ questionnaire, Estimations of Others Scale Questionnaire, and Social Interaction and Technology Use questionnaire.

   http://www.shyness.com/resources-shyness-surveys

5. Locus of Control & Attributional Style test is on this Web site; it will take about 15 minutes.

   https://www.psychologytoday.com/tests/personality/locus-control-attributional-style-test.

6. Law of Attraction surveys

   https://www.surveymonkey.com/r/YDN3JSQ—very short survey

   https://www.surveymonkey.com/r/ZCLQKT8—10 questions, mostly fill in, students will need some familiarity with the law of attraction.

7. Online identity survey—Questions pertaining to "digital identity," would you change a relationship because of someone's online behavior, and so on

   https://www.surveymonkey.com/r/?sm=1BnzWedjGpuwFm3jbOUH%2Fg%3D%3D.

8. Posture Survey

   https://www.surveymonkey.com/r/6SVRGBF—questions steer toward corrective brace.

9. Facebook Self-Presentation Survey—brief questionnaire about Facebook activity and how a person wants to be perceived

   https://www.surveymonkey.com/r/C6DTX68.

10. Self-Esteem Surveys

    ***Printable Survey—PDF with 10 questions.

    http://www.djj.state.fl.us/docs/jjdp-performance-measurement/self_esteem.pdf?sfvrsn=0

    https://www.psychologytoday.com/tests/personality/self-esteem-test—15 minute self-esteem test

11. Personality Tests/Survey

    https://www.16personalities.com/free-personality-test

    http://www.humanmetrics.com/cgi-win/jtypes2.asp

12. Professionalism

    https://www.dol.gov/odep/topics/youth/softskills/Professionalism.pdf *This site is a PDF with activities for examining an individual's professionalism in the workplace

13. Fitness survey

    https://www.surveymonkey.com/r/Q3YRLRY *This survey asks basic fitness and nutrition questions.

Movies and TV shows

Hidden Figures (Movie) 2016

Before a computer became an inanimate object and before Sputnik changed the course of history, before the Supreme Court case *Brown v. Board of Education* established that separate was in fact not equal, and before the poetry of Martin Luther King Jr.'s "I Have a Dream" speech rang out over the steps of the Lincoln Memorial, a group of black women working at the Langley Memorial Aeronautical Laboratory in Hampton, Virginia, were helping America dominate aeronautics, space research, and computer technology, carving out a place for themselves as female mathematicians who were also black, black mathematicians who were also female. *Hidden Figures* is their story. (http://www.hiddenfigures.com/)

Fences (Movie) 2016

Troy Maxson makes his living as a sanitation worker in 1950s Pittsburgh. Maxson once dreamed of becoming a professional baseball player, but was deemed too old when the major leagues began admitting black athletes. Bitter over his missed opportunity, Troy creates further tension in his family when he squashes his son's chance to meet a college football recruiter.
    http://www.imdb.com/title/tt2671706/plotsummary?ref_=tt_ql_stry_2

Harry Potter and the Soccer's Stone (Movie) 2001

This is the tale of Harry Potter, an ordinary 11-year-old boy serving as a sort of slave for his aunt and uncle who learns that he is actually a wizard and has been invited to attend the Hogwarts School for Witchcraft and Wizardry. Harry is snatched away from his mundane existence by Hagrid, the grounds keeper for Hogwarts, and quickly thrown into a world completely foreign to both him and the viewer. Famous for an incident that happened at his birth, Harry makes friends easily at his new school. He soon finds, however, that the wizarding world is far more dangerous for him than he would have imagined, and he quickly learns that not all wizards are ones to be trusted.
    http://www.imdb.com/title/tt0241527/plotsummary?ref_=tt_ql_stry_2

Star Wars the Force Awakens (Movie) 2015

A scavenger (Daisy Ridley) and a renegade stormtrooper (John Boyega) enlist the help of legendary smugglers/freedom fighters Han Solo (Harrison Ford) and Chewbacca to transport a droid carrying information regarding the whereabouts of long lost Jedi Master Luke Skywalker to General Leia Organa of the Resistance before it falls into the hands of Kylo Ren and the First Order.
    http://www.imdb.com/title/tt2488496/plotsummary?ref_=tt_ql_stry_2

Danish Girl (Movie) 2015

A fictitious love story loosely inspired by the lives of Danish artists Lili Elbe and Gerda Wegener. Lili and Gerda's marriage and work evolve as they navigate Lili's groundbreaking journey as a transgender pioneer.
    http://www.imdb.com/title/tt0810819/?ref_=nv_sr_1

Bridesmaids (Movie) 2011

Annie (Kristen Wiig) is a maid of honor whose life unravels as she leads her best friend, Lillian (Maya Rudolph), and a group of colorful bridesmaids (Rose Byrne, Melissa McCarthy, Wendi McLendon-Covey, and Ellie Kemper) on a wild ride down the road to matrimony. Annie's life is a mess. But when she finds out her lifetime best friend is engaged, she simply must serve as Lillian's maid of honor. Though lovelorn and broke, Annie bluffs her way through the expensive and bizarre rituals. With one chance to get it perfect, she'll show Lillian and her bridesmaids just how far you'll go for someone you love.

http://www.imdb.com/title/tt1478338/?ref_=nv_sr_1

Devil Wears Prada (Movie) 2006

In New York, the simple and naive just-graduated in journalism Andrea Sachs is hired to work as the second assistant of the powerful and sophisticated Miranda Priestly, the ruthless and merciless executive of the Runway fashion magazine. Andrea dreams to become a journalist and faces the opportunity as a temporary professional challenge. The first assistant Emily advises Andrea about the behavior and preferences of their cruel boss, and the stylist Nigel helps Andrea to dress more adequately for the environment. Andrea changes her attitude and behavior, affecting her private life and the relationship with her boyfriend Nate, her family and friends. In the end, Andrea learns that life is made of choices.

http://www.imdb.com/title/tt0458352/plotsummary?ref_=tt_ql_stry_2

What's Eating Gilbert Grape (Movie) 1993

After his father's death, Gilbert has to care for his mentally disabled brother, Arnie, and his morbidly obese mother, which is suddenly challenged when love walks into his life.

http://www.imdb.com/title/tt0108550/?ref_=nv_sr_1

Legally Blonde, 2001

Elle Woods, a fashionable sorority queen, is dumped by her boyfriend. She decides to follow him to law school. While she is there, she figures out that there is more to her than just looks.

http://www.imdb.com/title/tt0250494/?ref_=nv_sr_1

Will and Grace (TV Show) (1998–2017)

http://www.imdb.com/title/tt0157246/?ref_=nv_sr_2

Several **Disney Movies** explore identity issues as well

References

Adler, R. B., and R. F. Proctor. 2017. *Looking Out, Looking In.* 15th ed. Boston, MA: Cengage.

Byrne, L. 2006. *The Secret.* Hillsboro, OR: Atria Books, Beyond Words Publishing.

Hamachek, D. E. 1978. *Encounters with the Self.* 2nd ed. New York, NY: Holt, Rinehart, and Winston.

James, W. 1890 *The Principles of Psychology.* Vol 1. Cambridge, MA: Harvard University Press.

Kolligan, J. Jr. 1990. "Perceived Fraudulence as a Dimension of Perceived Incompetence." In *Competence Considered*, edited by R. J. Sternbeg and J. Jr. Kolligan. New Haven, CT: Yale University press.

Rosenberg, M. 1965. *Society and the Adolescent Self-image.* Princeton, NJ: Princeton University Press.

Rosenberg, M. 1972. *Society and the Adolescent Self-image.* Princeton, NJ: Princeton University Press.

Rosenfield, P. 1997. "Impression Management, Fairness, and the Employment Interview." *Journal of Business Ethics* 16: 801–808

Scharlott, B. W., and W. G. Christ. 1995. "Overcoming Relationship Initiation Barriers: The Impact of a Computer Dating System on Sex Roles, Shyness, and Appearance Inhibitions." *Computers in Human Behavior* 11: 191–204.

Snyder, M., and B. H. Campbell. 1982. "Self-monitoring: The Self in Action." In *Psychological Perspectives on the Self*, edited by Suls, Vol 1, 185–230. Hillsdale, NJ: Lawrence Eribuam.

Taylor, S. E., J. V. Wood, and R. R. Lichtman. 1983. "It Could Be Worse: Selective Evaluations as a Response to Victimization." *Journal of Social Issues* 39: 19–40.

Tice, D. M., and J. Faber. 2001. "Cognitive and Motivational Process in Self Presentation." In *The Social Mind: Cognitive and Motivational Aspects of Interpersonal Behavior*, edited by J. P. Forgas, K. D. Williams, and L. Wheeler, 39–156. New York, NY: Cambridge University Press.

Walther, J. B., and B. Van Der Heide, D. Westerman, and S. T. Tong. 2008. "The Role of Friends' Appearance and Behavior on Evaluations of Individuals on Facebook: Are We Known by the Company We Keep?" *Human Communication Research* 34: 28–49.

Yeager, S. 2011. "Don't Be a Slouch: How Exercise Can Improve Your Posture." *Prevention.com.* http://www.prevention.com/fitness/strength-training/exercises-improve-bad-posture

Scholarly Journal Articles

Improving Self-esteem and Body Image Promoting a Healthy Body Image in the Classroom

Jacklin Barreira, Stella Chu, & Virginia Dos Santos

Summary Body distortion is when a person sees his or her body shape and size in an inacurate fashion. Self-esteem is one's perception of himself or herself as a whole. Self-esteem is something that is developed over time. We wrote a proposal to the New Jersey Board of Education to incorporate awareness of body image, self-esteem, and the effects negative body image and a negative self-esteem can have on an individual. Our goal is to create awareness of our issue.

file:///C:/Users/Mr.%20and%20Mr.%20Jones/Downloads/rutgers-lib-37905_PDF-1.pdf

Becoming Somebody!

How Arts Programs Support Positive Identity for Middle School Girls

Debra L. Holloway, Margaret D. LeCompte & Debra L. Holloway

Pathways for Positive Identity Construction at Work: Four Types of Positive Identity and the Building of Social Resources

Academy of Management Review, 2010

Jane E. Dutton
University of Michigan

Laura Morgan Roberts
Georgia State University

Jeffrey Bednar
University of Michigan

In this paper, we organize research on work-related identities into a four-perspective typology that captures different ways identities can be "positive." Each perspective on positive identity—virtue, evaluative, developmental, and structural—highlights a different source of positivity and opens new avenues for theorizing about identity construction. We use these four perspectives to develop propositions about how different forms of positive work-related identity construction can strengthen employees through building social resources.

> http://amr.aom.org/content/35/2/265.short

The Power of Positive Identity

Emma Violand-Sanchez, & Julia Hainer-Violand
Educational Leadership, v64 n1 p36–40 Sep 2006

By 2050, Latinos will account for 25 percent of the U.S. population. Despite their increasing numbers, many children of immigrants consider themselves members of a minority group in a way that negatively affects their behavior, school performance, and social integration. Educators need to develop a better understanding of the culture and issues that affect the well-being of Latino English language learners because these issues will ultimately affect the future of the United States. Addressing the needs of Latino students means acknowledging and capitalizing on the cultural and linguistic strengths that students bring to the classroom. Schools should foster a positive ethnic identity by viewing bilingualism as an asset and immigration as a source of pride, empower Latino students through leadership roles within the school and community, and encourage student voice by having students speak and write from experience.

> https://eric.ed.gov/?id=EJ745631

Narrative Identity Processing of Difficult Life Experiences: Pathways of Personality Development and Positive Self-Transformation in Adulthood

Jennifer L. Pals
First published Journal of Personality: 2 May 2006

Difficult life experiences in adulthood constitute a challenge to the narrative construction of identity. Individual differences in how adults respond to this challenge were conceptualized in terms of two dimensions of narrative identity processing: exploratory narrative processing and coherent positive resolution. These dimensions, coded from narratives of difficult experiences reported by the women of the Mills Longitudinal Study (Helson 1967) at age 52, were expected to be related to personality traits and to have implications for pathways of personality development and physical health. First, the exploratory narrative processing of difficult experiences mediated the relationship between the trait of coping openness in young adulthood (age 21) and the outcome of maturity in late midlife (age 61). Second, coherent positive resolution predicted increasing ego-resiliency between young adulthood and midlife (age 52), and this pattern of increasing ego-resiliency, in turn, mediated the relationship between coherent positive resolution and life satisfaction in late midlife. Finally, the integration of exploratory narrative processing and coherent positive resolution predicted positive self-transformation within narratives of difficult experiences. In turn, positive self-transformation uniquely predicted optimal development (composite of maturity and life satisfaction) and physical health.

> http://onlinelibrary.wiley.com/doi/10.1111/j.1467-6494.2006.00403.x/full

What is me online? Insights into how users manage digital identity.

Sebastian Schnorf & Martin Ortlieb
UXPA 2013

This talk provides comprehensive and up-to-date insights about how users manage identity-related aspects online. We gathered 100+ user stories from four countries as well as 1,000+ survey responses in the United States and the United Kingdom. We will illustrate how people present themselves in profiles, manage devices, as well as set up and share accounts. Furthermore, we will show how users curate different audiences using social networking sites, if and how users selectively disclose information to others, and how users perceive and deal with identity conflation situations. Finally, I will discuss some implications for the development of identity- and privacy-related features.

https://research.google.com/pubs/pub42459.html

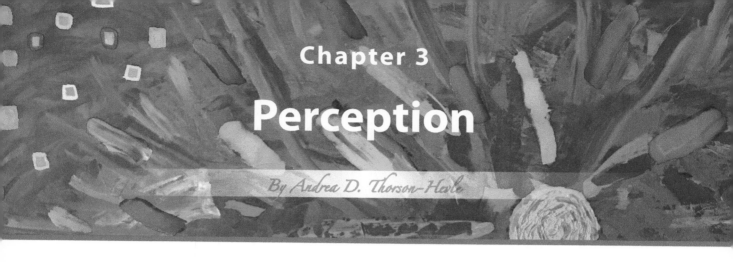

Chapter 3

Perception

By Andrea D. Thorson-Hevle

Let's get personal. . .

As a mother of three toddlers I'm always reminding myself to give my boys positive reinforcement when they behave well, use good manners, or speak well.

It's so easy to get in the "no, no" mode and only use verbal language to address negative behaviors. For a couple weeks I forgot this important lesson and every time my son, Sebastian, would forget to say "please" or "thank you," I would reprimand him and ask him to say it politely, but overall he wasn't improving as much as I would like.

When I started constantly using the positive affirmations, telling him how nice he was talking, and how I liked how he said "please," or "you're a nice boy for saying that, thank you," he started improving within about 3 days. Positive language choices have a beautiful effect on kids; they soak up compliments and positive attention. It affects each of them differently, but all of them positively.

My 4-year-old Monty responds immediately to positive language, he appreciates being noticed for his good behavior and smiles right away. A sense of great pride comes over him. If you watch him you can see his shoulders go back, his chest comes out, and his head is held higher.

If I could recommend only one tip to you and your families, it would be to use more positive affirmations with the children and adults in your home. It is powerful and can be far more effective in changing behavior than negative language. Tell them when they do good things, not just bad things, even if it's little.

— Andrea D. Thorson-Hevle

You need to read this chapter

- To understand how perceptions change the way you view others.
- To identify ways to reduce your biases.
- To learn what factors contribute to perceptions.

Perception

Perceptions play a critical role in interpersonal communication. We tend to think there is an ultimate truth about people that we can access, but this is skewed thinking. We can never really know someone 100%, all we can know is how we perceive them to be. Our perceptions are based on many things. Things that contribute to perception are cultures, experiences, and prejudice. **Perception** can be understood as the process of observation and interpretation using senses. It allows us to capture information from a given stimuli.

When we talk about perception we tend to think about how we perceive other people. But, perception has an equally important role in our lives. The ways in which others perceive us can have a direct effect on our self-esteem, how we treat others, how we craft our identity, and more. In this chapter we will dissect the concept of perception in two fundamental ways: the ways in which it can affect others and the ways in which it can affect us. To begin we will cover some fundamentals of perception, then work our way to conversations about culture and others, and finally end with a conversation about how perception influences us. Several theorists have crafted slightly different ways to define the perception process. Many categorize it in three or four categories. I like to address them in these categories: attending/selecting, organizing/recognizing, interpreting, and retrieving.

Figure 3.1 The Perception Process

Perception Phase 1: Attending and Selecting

The first stage, attending and selecting, involves making a choice as to what stimuli to focus on and which ones to ignore. In other words, we need to decide what we pay attention to. In any given situation, there are a number of things going on, people, situations, elements, experiences that you could focus on, we must select one to focus on or our minds will overload.

The *selecting* part of the perception process makes sense and must be done. But, what requires a bit of conversation is how we end up making that selection to begin with. Because we are overwhelmed with stimuli at any given point in time, our minds allow us to select "important" information to save us from a breakdown. But how exactly do we select? Well, there is something called "selective perception." Perhaps you have heard of it.

Selective perception happens a lot more than we would like to admit. It is the act of selecting specific things because they align with our beliefs, values, and attitudes, fulfill our wants and needs, or highlight our own interests and goals. For instance, research has demonstrated that people who align with a certain political party will tend to select and attend to messages that reinforce their beliefs and values, while ignoring chances to pay attention to information that shows an alternative perspective.

One thing some of us do is focus on the negative instead of on the positive. For instance, one summer my husband, a high school teacher and coach, had the summer off and I had to work. I was working full days 4 days a week and working on writing this book and a rhetoric book. I was really busy. While I was working, he took care of our three young boys and the home. He'd never been in charge of doing most of the laundry, cooking, and cleaning. In the past he had of course helped with the cooking, and cleaning, and done some laundry, but there is a huge difference between helping and being the person in charge of those things 4 days a week all day without help.

The first weeks were hard on him. He couldn't manage the laundry and the cleaning let alone keep up with the children's lessons and fun time. The house was a mess. But then he got the hang of it and managed his time. I came home one day to the house looking fabulous. The carpets were vacuumed (he hadn't used that vacuum before), the floors swept and mopped, the kid's toys picked up, and the dishes pretty well tended to. I told him what a great job he did and how wonderful the house looked. I told him it felt so good to come home to a clean house and how I remember trying so hard to get the house in order before he came home from work during the regular school year. I gave him a hug and a kiss and showed honest appreciation.

Then I noticed the vacuum was sitting on top of the basin of water. Our vacuum is a water vacuum that sucks dirt into a bowl of water to decrease dust in the air. If the vacuum is in the "off" position, it must be taken off the water or it will ruin the motor. He knows this, as I have mentioned it often. He was there for the salesperson's instructions, and I mentioned it to him just a few days earlier when he said he might vacuum. I yelled, "Oh no! How long has that been on there?" I ran to the vacuum, he looked at me, "uh, I don't know." I said, "Of course you do, when did you stop vacuuming? We might have broken the machine!" He was frustrated with me. Here he had cleaned the house and now all I was doing was focusing on the one thing he didn't do well. My one negative comment had more power than all the other positive comments combined.

Side Note: In hindsight I should have thought before reacting. It was a $2,000 machine so I was scared. But if it hadn't been running for over an hour it was dead anyway. I could have waited for him to turn around, went over and lifted the water basin from the machine, and given him a reminder later on. I should have let the great stuff be the only stuff right there in that moment.

Similarly and more simplistically, if someone were to give you compliments on how you looked, mentioning how you look fit, your hair looks shiny and smooth, your face is glowing, and then mentioned, "Oh you have freckles, I never noticed that before." If you have any insecurity about your freckles you might attend to the freckle comment more than any other comments.

Perception Phase 2: Organizing and Recognizing

It makes sense that we categorize. We have to. Every moment of every day we are bombarded with stimuli. It is impossible to process everything one by one and with great examination; so our minds deal with this constant flow of information by using **heuristics**. *Heuristics* are basically mental short cuts that help us understand, find solutions, learn, and predict. We need these to help us get through life without being stuck on every little thing we encounter, but they can be problematic and lead to stereotyping or even prejudice. So, it's important that we be careful.

Let's look at eight of the various types of *heuristics*. Please note there are a great many *heuristics*. I won't be able to touch on them all, but will discuss several herein.

1) **Availability heuristic**: A quick way to help humans make judgments based on past examples.

2) **Representative heuristic:** A quick way to make judgments when trying to make a decision about the probability of an event.

3) **Affect heuristic:** A quick shortcut that allows humans to make discussions and craft solutions quickly in situations of fear, emotion, surprise, and pleasure.

4) **Contagion heuristic:** A quick way to make a judgment about whether something is contaminated or bad and thus should be avoided.

5) **Effort heuristic:** Is a rule that makes humans assign value based on the amount of effort that went into obtaining or creating the item.

6) **Similarity heuristic:** Is a way of being highly productive by means of repeating experiences that were positive and avoiding experiences that were negative the previously.

7) **Simulation heuristic:** A mental strategy to determine the probability of something happening based on our ability to imagine it.

8) **Peak-end heuristic:** A rule that leads people to feel a certain way about an experience based on its most memorable/intense moment and its end, instead of considering the entire experience in total.

While these heuristics are helpful because they allow us to act quickly based on past experiences they also leave the door open for negative outcomes like *stereotyping*. **Stereotyping** is used to categorize a group of people based on a hyperbolized generalization, which isn't altogether accurate. *Stereotyping* is a generalization about someone based on a group they are perceived to belong to regardless of the true reality. Sometimes stereotypes have a small bit of truth to them, but not usually. The harm in stereotypes is that they are often the precursor to bias, prejudice, and discrimination. Because categorization occurs in our mind, often without much consciousness, we need to make conscious efforts to avoid stereotyping.

For instance, I remember being in a discussion with a co-worker about same-sex marriage. This person said that they were against same-sex marriage because if "they wanted to be straight they could, it's a choice to be gay. If they were actually born that way and couldn't change then I would feel different, but that is not the case."

Knowing that this was not true, I provided the person with facts about various studies and research that shows scientists have discovered a genetic marker in the DNA of gay men. This person hadn't heard this information before, but knew that I was a credible source.

They said, "Really, so they can't help it?" I replied, "Nope, they have found the genetic marker—so just like you can't chose the color of hair or eyes, your sexuality is not choice based either. And same-sex attraction and sex naturally occurs in more than 1,500 mammal species." Just then a student walked by and said, "yeah, but we shouldn't be like other mammals, we are humans, so we should be able to change."

The student's assertion was not founded in research. It was less logical, and even irrelevant to the argument at hand. But, that information is what my colleague listened to and used to back her own argument. She basically ignored the evidence I presented. Now, remember she had said if it wasn't a choice then she would support same-sex marriage. I provided scientific evidence that it wasn't a choice and a random 19-year-old boy provided an opinion that we should be "better" mammals. My information was clearly more credible, but my friend selected and attended to the boys remarks because his comments aligned with her base attitudes and believes about same-sex couples. It became clear that my colleague wasn't just against same-sex couples marrying because she thought it was a choice, she was prejudice against them in general.

Most people deny being prejudice, bias, or being involved in stereotyping others, but statistics say otherwise. Most people are bias and have some prejudice. We aren't born that way; our environments influence us. We absorb the hate and misinformation, the stereotypes and negative biases, from our families, friends, religions, and other cultures. One thing I have noticed over time is that a lot of stereotypes, which often leads to prejudice and discrimination, are excused away with "but, it really is true." A lot of people really believe their stereotypes about people are true.

I'd like to set a few commonly articulated stereotypes to rest:

1) **"Women are the worst drivers"—UNTRUE**
   a. Men are by far the worse drivers in the United States. Men are involved in 80% of crashes that kill or seriously injure pedestrians.[1]

---

[1] http://www.thedailybeast.com/articles/2011/12/31/america-s-worst-drivers-the-states-genders-with-the-most-accidents.html (2014)

b. According to the Social Issues Resource Center report, which analyzed numerous studies on male and female driving differences concluded: "In all studies and analyses, without exception, men have been shown to have a higher rate of crashes than women."[2]

Figure 3.2 Men are by far the worse drivers in the U.S.A.

Figure 3.3 The stereotypes out there about who abuses and sells drugs are simply not true.

2) **"Black/African American men are the most likely to use and distribute drugs."—UNTRUE**

a. In fact, African Americans represent "12% of the total population of drug users, but 38% of those arrested for drug offenses, and 59% of those in state prison for a drug offense.

b. Five times as many Whites are using drugs as African Americans, yet African Americans are sent to prison for drug offenses at ten times the rate of Whites."

c. In 2002, Blacks constituted more than 80% of the people sentenced under the federal crack cocaine laws and served substantially more time in prison for drug offenses than did Whites, despite that fact that more than two-thirds of crack cocaine users in the United States are Whites or Hispanics.[3]

3) **"Boys and men always want and have more sex than girls and women."**

a. Teenage girls are 6.5% more sexually active than teenage boys.[4]

---

[2] http://abcnews.go.com/2020/story?id=3148281 (2014)

3 http://www.naacp.org/pages/criminal-justice-fact-sheet (2014)

[4] http://www.thedailybeast.com/articles/2010/07/20/sex-statistics-who-does-it-the-most.html (2014)

b. "Women want sex just as much as men do, and this drive is "not, for the most part, sparked or sustained by emotional intimacy and safety."[5]

Were you surprised by any of these myth busting findings? If you were, it is probably because society has bombarded you with endless movies, commercials, images, biased new reporting, and rhetoric about these myths. Regarding number 3, women and sex, this is always shocking to my students when I quote research that shows, most of the time, women want sex just as much as men do. Why are they so shocked? Well, probably because their whole lives they have been told about "horney" men and that women say, "I've got a headache." You've also been told how women only have sex if they can connect and it's always an emotional experience. Research shows the difference between men and women actually isn't all that much. The "emotional connection," well that is a myth so far reaching some women feel obligated to feed into it. Yes, emotional connection is important to women, but recent findings show it is just as important to men and unimportant to women under certain circumstances.

Ways to Diminish Stereotyping

1) Recognize that what you might call "intuition" or "a gut feeling" may be a deep-seated stereotype.

2) Be honest about what prejudices you have and how that might be affecting your relationships. Then think before you speak and really investigate the truth of these negative thoughts.

3) Don't make assumptions about people based on appearances.

4) Recognize that when you are experiencing negative emotions (anger, frustration, fear) you are more likely to rely on stereotypes.

5) Avoid making decisions until you have all the information or have collected information from valid sources.

6) If someone has told you that you hold bias beliefs about a certain culture of people, consider it. Reflect on what made them feel that way. Next reverse the people in the situation or replace them with a culture you don't have a bias against and see if your perspective changes.

7) Don't make assumptions about people based on groups they belong to.

8) Don't treat people poorly just because you have had a prior bad experience with someone of the same culture.

Perception Phase 3: Interpreting

Once we have organized and recognized the information, we must make sense of it. The interpreting phase of the perception process accomplishes this. Sadly, as you have seen previously, we often have biases that affect the ways we perceive information. So when we get to

---

[5] http://www.theatlantic.com/sexes/archive/2013/06/turns-out-women-have-really-really-strong-sex-drives-can-men-handle-it/276598/(2014)

this stage, not much is different; including misinterpretation of language use and nonverbal cues as well. Chapters 4 and 5 will discuss the implications of these variables more fully.

Figure 3.4 Reading between the lines can cause problems if you are not careful.

Basically, our interpretations can be affected by a number of things including but not limited to:
1) Our self-concept
2) Our self-esteem
3) Our communication competence
4) Our knowledge of others
5) Our prior experiences with specific people
6) Our prior experiences with specific cultures
7) Our cultures' teachings
8) Our prejudice/bias

Perception Phase 4: Retrieving

The final stage in the perception process is the simplest. It is the stage that you recall the information you have attended, organized, and interpreted. But, like so many other aspects of this perception concept, this stage too is riddled with potential for basis. A concept called selective retention is to blame. Selective retention is our tendency to store and thus recall information that is consistent with our perceptions and specifically dismissing or not storing information that does not.

Perception Checks

Because our perceptions are so often a reflection of our own insecurities, biases, or past experiences, it is important that we perform basic perception checks before we take big actions in our relationships. **Perception checks** help us ensure we fully understand another person's behavior or intention.

There are three basic steps to the *perception checking process*: describing, interpreting, and clarifying.

Perception Check Process

☐ Describe their behavior

☐ Interpret what you think that behavior may mean (two options)

☐ Clarify the behavior and interpretation

This process is vitally important and can even save a relationship. I'm sure you can think of an occasion in which you misinterpreted what someone else said or meant and thus reacted inappropriately because of it. Had you followed this simple process all those nasty side-effects might have been avoided.

For instance consider these potential situations:

Situation #1

A couple argues. The man storms out of the house, slamming the door on his way out. He doesn't return for 5 hours. During that absent time he doesn't answer his phone or respond to text messages from his partner.

Response (Without Perception Checking)

Partner: "I hate it when you leave like that! You are such a jerk to just abandon me. You do this all the time and I'm sick of it. I can't take it anymore. You don't respect me or love me enough to talk or try to talk things out. You don't even care about this relationship and I can see that; so I'm done. I've packed your things, please leave and do not come back. We are over."

Response (With Perception Checking and Potential Outcome)

Partner: "When you walked out of the house in the middle of our conversation and didn't come back for hours (description) I wasn't sure if you didn't care about this relationship anymore or just didn't respect me (interpretation). What exactly is going on with you when you do this? (clarify).

Situation #2

A father notices his son is being distant. He asks his son, "is everything okay?" His son replies, "Yeah, I'm fine."

Response (With Perception Checking)

Dad: "I noticed you aren't speaking much today. You look a little down." (description) "I'm wondering if you are upset because I missed your basketball game last night or if there's something else bothering you." (interpretation)

Internal Factors that Influence Perception

There are a number of things that can change the ways we see people in the interpret event. To cover them all in a little section and say I did a great job would be a lie and or a terrible joke. I can't possibly dissect all the factors that affect perception. What I can do is go over some general areas and give you some examples. It is my hope that my categories and examples will ignite your memories, inspire your mind to think of more, and allow yourself to investigate these ideas further.

Factors that Influence Our Perceptions

Our Senses

Our senses provide us a plethora of information that we use to discern and understand, to organize and interpret, and thus to craft perceptions. If you SEE someone cry, it helps you craft perceptions. If you FEEL your friends' hand shaking, it helps you craft perceptions. If you SMELL burning trees in the woods, it helps you craft perceptions. If you HEAR sirens behind you while driving, it helps you craft perceptions. Our senses are an intense and immense factor in the perception process. Can you imagine what your life would be like without all of them? How much information do you think you get from your senses?

Our Cultures

Cultures can be anything from the sex and gender we identify with, to the religion we were born into, to the education level we did or did not obtain. Cultures can be political affiliations, economic status, race, ethnicity, nationality, language, and membership oriented.

Our cultures have a significant impact on the perception process because they teach us narratives about traits, characteristics, expectations, norms, roles, and people that we later categorize during the organization phase of the perception process. So, regardless of whether or not there is real truth to ideas, our perceptions can be tainted by our cultures stories, trainings, customs, and biases.

Our Personal Experience

Experiences we have in life build heuristics, short cuts in the brain that we use the next time we encounter a similar situation. Our brain assumes that because last time something happened, when something like that happens again it will end up the same way. So, in part our brain does this, but in part we do this. What I mean is, as humans we tend to feed into myths and sometimes just plain lies about various people and cultures just because we had one or two personal experiences with a culture in the past.

Our Cognitive Dissonance

From a young age we were told things about certain types of people and those words stayed with us. And sometimes despite the fact that we have had several experiences that disprove those narratives and ideas about a culture, we still believe what we were taught was true. When we hold conflicting information about a given situation we experience discomfort. This is called cognitive dissonance. People don't like to feel uncomfortable, so we seek to reduce discomfort and restore balance as best we can.

Our Measuring Sticks

As my friend AJ would say, "Let's be real." We don't judge all people by the same set of standards. In fact we use wildly different measuring sticks depending on who we are assessing. For most part people tend to be one of two things: hardest on themselves or hardest on others. Which are you? I am definitely hardest on myself.

But what about other people, specifically the ones you love the most, do you think you see them "through rose colored glasses?" Research would suggest that you do. Studies have shown that we tend to give those we love a bit more slack than we do other people, but we do it in really interesting ways. For instance, if at a friend's house your child responds to a question with attitude and a nasty look, you determine that it is because your child is tired or having a bad day. When you see another person's child with the same behavior you most likely attribute those traits to being indicative of the child's general demeanor, not as a rare occasion or exception to the norm.

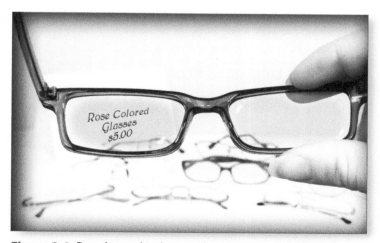

Figure 3.4 People tend to have at least one person they view through rose colored glasses. Have you even been accused of not seeing people with clear lenses?

Similarly, we sometimes categorize people as a certain kind of person based on first impressions and make our measuring sticks based on that impression. For instance, if the first time you meet someone they are in an argument with someone and they use profanity, are inconsiderate, and loud, you might assume that is there general personality style. Research suggests that you will be more likely to think that that person is generally more likely to be mean, aggressive, volatile, and harsh, than kind, gentle, passive, and considerate. This isn't necessarily true of course, but that initial encounter frames the perspective that we will use to measure future encounters.

External Factors that Affect Perception

Perceptions can be influenced by our external surroundings/environments as well. There are a seemingly endless amount of environments which influence our communication and perceptions at any given moment (classrooms, offices, restaurants, parks, movie theatres, live theatres, churches, living rooms, formal rooms, recreational rooms, dining rooms, bedrooms, etc.). Each environment inspires us to communicate differently.

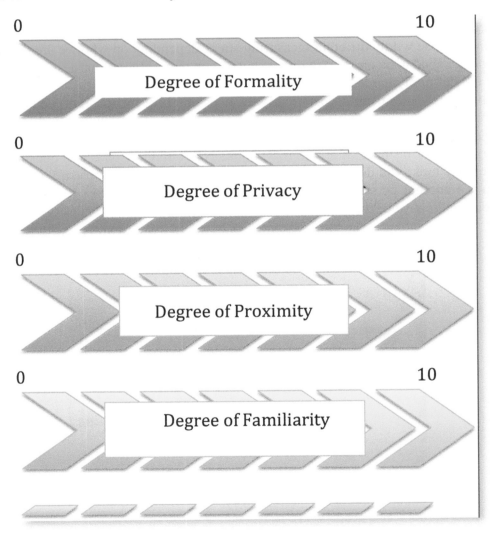

Have you ever had a conversation with someone and they told you "this is not the place to have this conversation." Perhaps you have said this to someone? This is because we tend to find certain places more appropriate to have certain kinds of conversations. Research suggests there are a few things that contribute to perception in terms of our surroundings: degrees of formality, degrees of privacy, degrees of distance, and degrees of familiarity.

Degree of Formality

Degree of formality refers to a continuum of formality that any given setting may have. If you were in trouble in school and needed to be disciplined, you were taken to the more formal setting like the principal's office, to be communicated with. If you were having a discussion with your partner in a restaurant and it escalates you might stop and say it is should be addressed later in a different, less formal place. With formality come expectations. The higher the degree of formality a setting has the more likely you are to communicate in shallow conversations, and less likely to engage in emotional exchanges, intimate self-disclosures, and displays of intimacy.

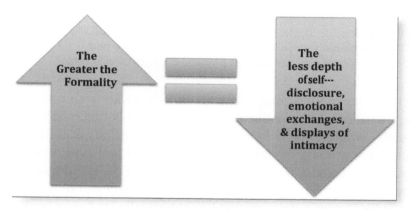

The Greater the Formality = The less depth of self---disclosure, emotional exchanges, & displays of intimacy

Degree of Privacy

Degree of privacy refers to idea that certain settings can alter perceptions based on what privacy is communicated. Have you ever been in a public restroom where you thought you were alone with your friend, having a confidential conversation and all of a sudden you hear a toilet flush? Certain settings come with clear restrictions on privacy. There are also certain things you can do with certain places that communicate a degree of privacy. For instance, you might leave the door to your office open slightly so that others know that you are in and willing to see people, but currently prefer some privacy. You might leave your door wide open to communicate you are willing to have people come right in. You might leave your door half open if you are alone with someone in your office and want to avoid any possible allegations or perceptions of inappropriate behavior taking place. I know it is common practice in our department at our college to leave the door to our office partially open if we have students in the room with us to increase the likelihood that professor/student interactions will be perceived as professional and acceptable at all times.

Degree of Proximity

Degree of proximity concerns the distance between communicators as a result of the environment. Perceptions of proximity are interesting, because they really come in two different types: physical distance and emotional distance. Physical distance in our environment can be created by any number of things including but not limited to furniture, chairs, where your room is located in reference to another, and where your home is located in relation to another. You can have a perception of being close to someone who is sitting across the table from you or across the room from you, or even someone who is in a country thousands of miles away from you.

Figure 3.5 There are two kinds of distance: physical and emotional. Can you remember a time where you had emotional distance but not physical distance or vice versa?

I know a couple who endures long segments of time away from each other. He travels for work and is gone for about 3–5 months at a time. Once he is home he usually stays for about 6 weeks. I personally wouldn't be able to endure that kind of physical distance in my relationship, because one of the primary means I communicate and feel close to others is physical distance. For this particular couple, however, it works rather well. It did take a bit of getting used to at first, but it was never devastating for them or totally unacceptable. They maintain closeness through forms of online communication, texting, phone calls, and even packages in the mail.

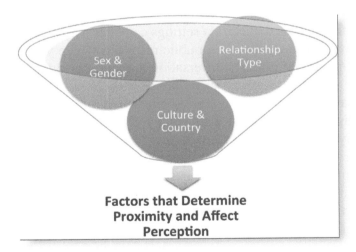

Factors that Determine Proximity and Affect Perception

Emotional distance, or as some researchers call it "psychological distance," is an interesting and a concept I am sure you can relate to. Here in the United States we have very particular standards of what is and is not appropriate in terms of how close we stand to other people when communicating with them. If fact, moving another 12 inches closer or apart communicates an entirely different relationship to the people around you. How much space you place between you and another person alters the ways in which others perceive that relationship. For instance, a person you who is your boss would stand at least arm's length away from you at all times. Most people would say they would be most comfortable with two arm lengths, unless it was necessary or the room size was small. This is because there is not an intimate relationship between the two people and no one wants it to be perceived that way (it may also be because they don't like the other person.)

If you're standing with friends you are likely standing about 30–26 inches apart. Your intimate sexual partners or someone you are romantically interested in have a much closer proximity at about 18 inches. Research shows that we don't mind those people coming much, much, much closer than everyone else. In fact sexual partners and romantic interests can be touching us when we stand to chat and that is perceived to be acceptable. This doesn't mean that that we always want our romantic partners to be elbow to elbow with us. In some cases people want to practice discretion. Perhaps co-workers are dating and haven't told anyone yet. If they wanted to keep people from perceiving them as romantically involved or interested they would keep the arm's length or greater distance. If they wanted to start letting people know they were in a relationship without actually verbally telling everyone, then all they need to do is start standing a bit closer when they speak and people will soon perceive them to be romantically linked.

Reflect on your past interactions with people you were romantically interested in. Did you tend to communicate with them at a closer proximity than other people? Did they like the closeness or did they take a tiny step back? Step backs often indicate that one person in the conversation either doesn't want to be romantically closer, or they do not want others currently in the environment to perceive them as romantically close to you. Perhaps you are the person that tends to take the step back?

Here is a table to help you understand the proximity standards we have in the United States.

4 – 12 feet	Strangers
3 – 10 feet	Co-workers/Acquaintances
18 inches – 3 feet	Family and Close Friends
0 – 18 inches	Intimate/Romantic Relationships

The last thing you want to do is make a mistake with proximity and relationships. People make all kinds of assumptions based on distance and this type of distance communicates a lot. Visit the non-verbal chapter for a full discussion of this area.

Degree of Familiarity

Degree of familiarity refers to the continuum that reflects the degree to which people have awareness and prior experience. Unfamiliar surroundings are likely to cause people to communicate in a slower and more hesitant manner. People tend to like familiar settings in part because they communicate more easily, feel more comfortable, know what to expect, where things are, and understand the degree of formalness and proximity involved.

If you need to have an intense personal conversation with a friend you are not likely going to pick a surrounding that is new. A new restaurant, bar, or lounge may be too loud or too quiet for your needs. It might be too young of crowd or too old of crowd. I remember when I moved to a new city in California, a man I was dating from New York was coming to town to visit and asked me to pick a restaurant for dinner and somewhere fun to dance after.

I didn't know many places in my new city and did the best I could. I ended up picking restaurant where the average patron was about 60 years old and they all looked at me and my guy like we were so odd in our fancy suit and shiny nice dress. It was far too quiet to talk the way we liked talking; jokes, sarcasm, and laughter.

When I became a professor I had a great number of students who confided a great many things to me. Among them were usually conflicts with their parents. Student after student wanted to assert their independence, their desire to be their own person, to make their own choices, to be respected as an adult and not treated as a child. And each and every student reported these conversations going poorly for them. My first question to these students always is, "where were you for this conversation." I usually get a look of bewilderment or irritation. Clearly I must not be paying attention to the point of their story if all I am asking about is where the conversation happened. But, where this conversation takes place is of great importance, because the surroundings communicate and it changes the way people communicate. Surroundings can alter our perceptions.

Time after time, students reported that these big conversations about not wanting to be seen as children anymore were taking place in their "childhood" homes. This is not good. I explained that if they want to have a chance at this conversation they needed to have the conversation at a place that is neutral or that gives them (the student) the upper hand. I recommend picking a place their parents did not frequent, but the students did. I recommended picking an environment that is quiet and respectful. A fast food restaurant for instance, is not a good choice, it is too informal and noisy. A restaurant they went every Sunday after church as a family is not a good choice either, this will only serve to remind the parents of their "baby" and moments of "childlessness." These are not memories you want stirred up when you are trying to convince people you are an independent, responsible adult. I often recommended quant coffee places that have a hint of sophistication, but still a hip vibe, which lets the student feel comfortable and the puts the parents in a place that doesn't constantly remind them of their "baby."

Conclusion

In this chapter we covered some fundamentals of perception, learned how to check our perceptions, and discussed the many factors that contribute to our perceptions and their inherent limitations. I hope this chapter afforded you an investigation into the basic process of perception as well as inspired you to think about how your perceptions are influenced by the world around you.

Perception checking is perhaps the most helpful little tid-bit in this chapter, please use it. Your relationships are important *and* your feelings are important, and your perceptions influence both of those things. Take control and be critical and aware of the factors that are influencing your perceptions.

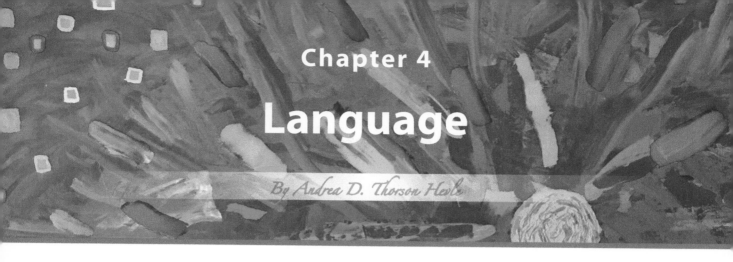

Chapter 4

Language

By Andrea D. Thorson Hevle

Let's get personal...

I am constantly reminding myself to make better language choices. When I do make positive changes I see the effects almost immediately. This is an area I do work on regularly despite the fact that I am a communication expert and this is in large part because my upbringing has had a significant impact on the ways in which I communicate and interpret the concepts of respect and values.

Growing up I was taught it was a sign of disrespect and poor character if you didn't work hard, fast, and do things right the first time. My family was not a family that recognized "effort." Our family recognized real work, output, results, ability, and will power. We were expected to do things correctly the first time and as soon as we were asked. We were taught to be proactive and fast; allowing anything but perfection was a failure. As an adult my mindset was similar.

As an adult I tended to be a perfectionist, a fast and hard worker, and determined to complete tasks as soon as I could regardless of any obstacles placed in my way. Because of this tenacity I sometimes made others feel like they weren't doing as good of job in comparison. Additionally, I have high standards and little empathy for people who put things off, don't try their hardest, or let an obstacle hinder them, and this can be evident in my language choices. I might say, "Why would you let that stop you?" or "You can always try harder." "It's gotta be done today; you'll just have to find a way." You see, I've been through a lot in my life and I have never given up, I still did all the things I said I would and do all the things others do and I managed that by saying these very same things to myself. And it works for me. But, it doesn't work for everyone and honestly, they are not the healthiest language choices.

Although I don't intend to hurt people, in fact, at the time I think I am helping them, these negative language choices can make people feel criticized and result in hurt feelings. Perhaps the people who grew up like me would respond positively, but usually the positive language choices are much more likely to get people encouraged and produce effective and efficient outcomes. Positive language choices can recognize a person's efforts and build a person up. Affirmations usually inspire people. I am a loving person and I want those around me to feel supported and loved and that means adjusting and recognizing the moments I am allowing my past to dictate my future. This is a lesson I have learned pretty well, but I can always improve it. A few of the principles you will learn in this chapter have helped reshape my communication and I hope you find them helpful too.

— *Andrea D. Thorson Hevle*

You need to read this chapter

- To appreciate the importance of language.
- To understand how language can bring us closer to others.
- To identify oppressive language.

Language

The words we choose to use in our everyday interactions with partners, friends, co-workers, and family can make lasting impressions. They can create long-term consequences and benefits and, as such, should be chosen very carefully. Language has the power to reinforce ideas and it has the power to dispel them. Language can paint a vivid picture in the mind of your audience, or it can erase an image that had been in the mind for years. It has been used for some of the most memorable and wonderful moments in history, as well as the most devastating and horrific.

As children I'm sure you can remember words being used to hurt. It isn't too hard for you to recall hurtful words as an adult either, is it? Words can harm, but they also have the ability to heal, rebuild, and support. In interpersonal relationships language is huge. You simply must understand the power of your words and the relationship between language and meaning and people and power.

Language as Symbolism

In order to discuss language we need to first clarify what language is. **Language** is any system of expression that uses words, gestures, motions, pronunciation, enunciation, and articulation to create a meaning. It is often referred to as symbol making. Sometimes we use symbols to communicate an idea or feeling.

Language is not just the spoken or written word. Many cultures rely on gestures to add meaning to words and even the culture of sign language uses movement to communicate language. Language is also symbolic because words and gestures represent meanings; they are symbols for more concrete things and abstract ideas as well.

For instance, when I say, "I saw a woman," the word "woman" conjures up a series of images that the listener associates with "woman." Consider the term "accomplishment." When you define accomplishment what does it mean? Is that the same as the way your best friend, parents, siblings, teachers, or people much older than you would define it?

Of course not. I know what Type A friends define as accomplishment is quite different from Type B friends conception of accomplishment is.

Understanding that there is no answer key to language is important—what one word or concept means to one person can have totally different meanings to someone else. Meaning is not actually found in words, it is found in people. This chapter helps you navigate the more complicated terrain of language choices as it pertains to you, as well as how your language choices

affect others. Specifically, this chapter discusses language and meaning with regard to your interpersonal relationships with a focus on how to use language to improve our relationships.

Language and Meaning

Denotative Meaning versus Connotative Meaning

The history of language is built in categories and ways of thinking. Language is fundamentally a learned and accepted process. There are detonative and connotative meanings to language; each of these types adds a dimension of power to a word.

Denotative meaning reflects the dictionary definition of the term or concept. **Connotative meaning** reflects the attached meaning and commonly associated emotional intent of the word. For instance, the denotative meaning of childish is "childlike." The connotative meaning can be anything from immature, selfish, and so on. If you are trying to communicate that someone is immature or selfish, then "childish" is a good language choice. If, however, you were trying to point out someone is free, young at heart, and happy, the term "youthful" would be better because it has fewer negative connotations.

In interpersonal relationships you must consider what someone's connotation for that word might be before you decide to use it. I remember when I moved from a small town in Montana to a large city in California; it was common for students to greet each other saying, "yo, what up, fool!" For me, the word "fool" did not come with the connotation of "friend." In Montana "fool" was synonymous with "idiot," "moron," or worse. Being called a "fool" was disrespectful in my culture. I had a hard time making friends for a while because I thought people didn't like me, were being rude, or trying to pick a fight.

In 1923 a model was created to communicate these same ideas; it is called the Semantic Triangle of Meaning (Ogden and Richards). The Semantic Triangle of Meaning helps demonstrate how language choices can be understood. The triangle begins in the lower left corner with symbol. In this case, symbol refers to the specific term, word, or phrase that a speaker uses. The next part of the triangle is the lower right referent. Referent refers to the denotative meaning of the word—what the symbol (word) represents. The final area is the reference or thought. Reference refers to the connotative meaning of the word or phrase and/or its historical representation. The reference can hold emotional and physiological responses as well.

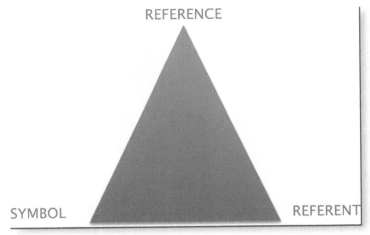

Let's say we use the phrase "an act of terror." In America before September 11, the phrase, "an act of terror" didn't hold much value to us beyond the denotative meaning. Now, after September 11, 2001, when Americans hear the phrase, "an act of terror," there is a great emotional and physiological response by many Americans. Some people will have a flashback to that day, others will feel anger and fear, and still other people will equate that phrase to a particular group of people. The triangle demonstrates how although we may all understand the denotative meaning of the word we may not have the same connotative understandings.

For example, we may have different emotional and thought-based reactions to hearing the terms based on our own personal and historical connections to a word or phrase. Consider using the semantic triangle when you encounter a term you are questioning using. Try to determine what possible reference your partner, friends, family, or co-workers (your audience) may have for that term before using it.

Using Language to Get Closer to Others

This section will provide you some discussion on various language choices you can make while communicating with your partners, friends, family, co-workers, and so on.

These language strategies are helpful for all of your interpersonal relationships and can be broadly applied. These are some of the greatest tools you can have in life, so pay attention and do some self-reflection as you are reading this section. Try to be honest and evaluate your communication patters to see if you participate in any or all of the negative language choices. If you do, don't feel bad. Well, maybe you should feel a little bad. But, then you need to snap your straps and start figuring out how to implement the positive language choices. I've broken this section down into several categories and pitted the bad language choices against the good ones. I've tried to provide you with examples and some personal examples of my own in hopes to clarify the difference between the concepts. Here we go; take notes.

Concrete versus Vague Language

It is very important that you use concrete instead of vague words in most situations of interpersonal communication. **Concrete** words are simple, to the point, and they tend to have less chance to have connotation issues. **Vague** language (often termed abstract language) is ambiguous language that is less clear in what it is referring to. It is generally expected that you use more concrete terms to avoid misunderstandings or unintended interpretation. You can see in the chart that as language becomes more concrete it becomes clear what the speaker is really trying to say. Reflect on your last few exchanges with others in which hurt feelings occurred and misunderstandings caused hurt.

Were you using vague or concrete language? Would it have helped had you used more specific words?

"I" versus "We" versus "You" Language

"We" versus "I" to Communicate Cohesion

In 2010 *NBC News* reported that couples who say "we" instead of "I" tend to be happier and have less stress in their marriages. It was discovered that this was especially important in times of conflict. "We found more 'we' language in older couples and in happier couples," said Robert Levenson, the study's senior researcher at the University of California, Berkeley (NBCnews. com, 2010). At the next opportunity, while talking to others/your partner, make an appropriate and accurate choice to use the inclusive "we." "We" language makes people feel like they belong in a special group; it communicates cohesion and respect and value. All of these are positive in a relationship, so we need to practice them more. You discussed something about you and your partner. Did you say "we" or did you say "I"? If you can't remember, next time pay attention or better yet ask your partner if they feel you use "we" or "I" language. The chances are they will remember far more easily than you and have plenty of examples to back it up. "We" language shares responsibility and pressure, and it also tells others that you are one with your partner. Using "I" language communicates that you are separate from, diminishing your connection with, and or not valuing your partner.

Consider the following examples.

1) I love this restaurant. Mia does too. Versus. We love this restaurant.
2) I'm happy in my marriage. Bob is happy as well. Versus. We are happily married.
3) I went to that movie last week! Versus. We went to that movie last week!

"You" versus "I" and "We" Language to Take Responsibility and Diffuse

In other situations "I" language is actually a good thing. When you don't have an opportunity to make a claim about something that includes both of you (this is when "we" is actually the word that should be used), but instead allows you to take responsibility for something, then you should use "I" language. This rule is generally good if you are saying "you" in a sentence that may come off as accusatory or threatening. "You" language is an expression of judgment of another which can cause problems for many reasons. "You" language can also be hurtful and problematic because "you" language is accusatory. Accusatory language often sets up a defense mechanism in people that is very hard to disarm.

For instance consider these "you" statements:

1) You need to do the bills tonight.
2) You have issues because all you do is yell when we disagree.
3) You are so rude!

4) You're always getting on me.
You never listen to me.

I am definitely guilty of number five on that list. Yep, even communication experts make mistakes. Relationships are hard and making sure our language choices are consistently good takes effort. Writing this chapter has reminded me that I need to stop saying "You never listen to me" to my wonderful husband, because the truth is most of the time he does listen to me.

Sometimes he doesn't listen, but that isn't actually what I'm trying to tell him when I say that. What I am trying to say and doing a terrible job of saying is,

> "When I talk to you about important things, and you respond to me like you heard then later don't recall anything I said, it makes me feel like you don't care about what I think is important or how I feel. I don't know if you are side-tracked or tired at the end of a day, but it hurts my feelings. The more this happens the more I start to pull away from you and not want to talk to you."

But it takes a lot more effort to say all of that, doesn't it? Well, it is more effort, but my relationship is worth it, and so is yours. So, how can we start removing the "you" language? Follow these simple steps and you will be on your way to exterminating that ugly "you" language.

1) **Recognize the actual problem:** The first step you can take is to be honest with yourself about what you are really upset about.

2) **Identify the action/behavior causing problem:** Then distinguish what the other person is doing that is contributing to that problem.

3) **Verbalize your feelings and thoughts:** Then verbalize how that behavior makes you feel and think.

4) **Address side effects:** Finally, address what possible side effects will result if this behavior continues or is already present because of it.

Let's practice

Bad You Language: You never give me compliments anymore.

Good Language: I've been distant lately and avoiding intimacy because I don't feel close to you anymore. Over the last few months I have tried to dress nice and even sexy at times to get your attention, but you haven't said I looked "nice" or "attractive" or "pretty" in 3 months. It makes me feel sad and rejected and unattractive. So, when you want to get intimate I feel like it's because you have a need, not because you actually want "me." That's why I've been avoiding intimacy lately and probably will have a hard time with it until I feel like you are attracted to me again.

Changing our language and using more positive choices is important, but our nonverbal language is as important if not more important. Be sure to control your facial expressions and body language when you are talking. If your language is non-accusatory and fair, but your body and face are saying otherwise, your partner will become defensive or shutdown, neither of which is a good thing for communication. Studies show that humans tend to believe nonverbal communication is a more accurate reflection of how other people feel than their verbal communication. If you give mixed signals, your partner will not trust you and that is not a place you want to be. I know that this all seems like a bit much to you right now, but please trust me: this stuff works;

it really does. It will take some getting used to and it will require that you make a conscious effort to think and process before you speak, but as I said before, your relationships are worth it!

Confirming versus Disconfirming Language

Confirming responses are constructed of language that demonstrates you care for the person, value the relationship, and care about what they are feeling and thinking. Confirming responses create a supportive communication climate because they make people feel like they matter and are valued. You should have a great deal of confirming responses in your day-to-day communication. **Disconfirming** responses on the other hand, are responses that create a defensive communication climate because they make people feel less valued. Disconfirming responses can negatively affect a person's sense of worth and demonstrates you don't care about the person or care about what they are feeling and thinking.

Sieburg and Larson identified these two different types of responses. Their work has yielded to our understanding seven disconfirming responses and five confirming responses. Over the years more have been added to our understanding of this kind of language. There are also nonverbal ways to be confirming and disconfirming to your partner, but that is discussed in the nonverbal chapter.

Disconfirming Language

The following **disconfirming language should** be avoided in your interpersonal communication because it creates a defensive communication climate in which people feel devalued.

1) **Impervious responses:** Speakers do not acknowledge in any way that someone else has just spoken. They are "impervious" to the preceding remark, and they proceed with their own remarks as if the previous speaker had made no comment at all.

2) **Interrupting responses:** Speakers "barge in" while another person is still speaking. Instead of waiting for a person to complete his or her thought, they cut the person off in order to present their own thoughts.

3) **Irrelevant responses:** Speakers respond to a remark by introducing a totally unrelated topic, or by returning to a topic that they had introduced before. They act as if they are unaware of the conversation that has just occurred.

4) **Tangential responses:** Speakers acknowledge a comment, but then they quickly take the discussion in a different direction. After briefly acknowledging a remark, they "go off on a tangent."

5) **Impersonal responses:** Speakers talk in vague generalities or clichés, and they act as if they are addressing no one in particular. Their responses lack first-person "I" statements, and they are filled with impersonal, abstract discourse removed from the people sitting around the table.

6) **Incoherent responses:** Speakers give responses that lack any apparent coherent meaning. They speak in garbled, incomplete sentences, or their responses ramble with much backtracking, side comments, and verbal clutter.

7) **Incongruous responses:** Speakers give verbal responses that are out of synch with or contradict their nonverbal cues. These incongruous verbal and nonverbal messages create confusion and uncertainty.

Confirming Language

In contrast to the seven disconfirming responses listed above, the five following confirming responses can help to create a supportive communication climate in which people feel acknowledged and valued.

1) **Direct acknowledgment:** Speakers respond directly to a previous remark. They acknowledge that the remark was made, and their responses directly relate to the remark.

2) **Agreement about content:** Speakers verify that they understand the content of a previous remark. They may not agree with the remark, but their response demonstrates that they fully comprehend what another group member has said.

3) **Supportive responses:** Speakers attempt to empathize with, support, or encourage another group member. Their responses indicate good will and positive regard for the person who has just spoken.

4) **Clarifying responses:** Speakers try to clarify the meaning or intention of a previous remark. Their responses may include requests for more information, prompts to expand the original remark, or paraphrases to check for understanding.

5) **Expressions of positive feeling:** Even if they disagree with a previous remark, speakers express positive feelings about the discussion that is occurring or the people who are involved in the discussion.

Description versus Evaluation Language

This category and the next few are really inspired by Dr. Jack Gibb who focused for several years on general defensive and supportive behaviors that serve to create a supportive or defensive climate. **Evaluation language** is any language that evaluates another person's ideas, thoughts, or contributions. Examples of evaluation language might be if you are in a conflict with your friend and you say, "You are so stupid!" or you are communicating with your partner and say, "You're totally incapable."

Evaluation language is critical and often mean. The speaker is not always intending the remark to be hurtful, but it doesn't matter the intent; hurt is hurt and being criticized doesn't feel good.

Instead of using evaluative language, use **descriptive language.** Description-based language removes the nasty remarks and likelihood that others will feel attacked and criticized. Instead of saying, "you are so stupid," describe what you think the person was saying in your own words (paraphrase), and describe how you feel instead of evaluating them. Instead of saying, "you are totally incapable," perhaps say, "When I come home and nothing was done like we discussed, I feel like I'm not important or valued."

Problem Orientation versus Control Language

Some people like being in control, and they also use language that asserts power.

Controlling language can be any language that asserts someone is more powerful or has more say in the relationship. This is very dangerous. Language that demonstrates control can be hurtful and make others feel unimportant, insignificant, less valued, and even afraid.

Examples of control-based language are as follows:

1) "I expect this to be done by 2 am."
"I did not feel okay with them sleeping in my house. You will not be doing that anymore."

Instead of using control-based language, consider a problem orientation approach. Problem orientation is inclusive language that communicates to others that their perspective is valued and their participation is their choice. Instead of saying the examples above consider saying, "what do you think about us getting things accomplished by about 2 pm?" or " It makes me feel uncomfortable when the guys are over after 2 am. I'd like to discuss having some basic boundaries for our friends and stay overs." Problem orientation language takes more effort, especially when we are angry or upset, but do your very best to try it; it makes a world of difference.

I remember a situation where a friend of mine was in a relationship with a man who consistently used controlling language with her. He would say things such as, (1) When I come home I expect dinner to be on the table and hot; (2) We are leaving now; (3) You won't be going to that if you don't get ... done.

She tried to tell him how it made her feel and he never quite got the message. The controlling language made her feel devalued and fearful even, because controlling language can often feel like a threat. She left him eventually and is now happily married to a man who uses language that shows her that her opinion matters. I remember being at a dinner party and he turned to her and said, "What time do you think you want to be home by? I was thinking about 11, but what do you think?" My girlfriends and I all looked at each other and smiled. We were so happy to see her with a man who valued her and didn't order her around. They had a conversation about what time they should be back home instead of one person dictating the time without regard for the other person's feelings and needs.

Empathetic Language versus Neutral Language

Empathy is perhaps one of the most useful and beautiful things we can develop as humans. When we are empathetic, others feel supported and understood, or at least that you are legitimately trying to be supportive without judgment or pity.

Empathetic language is most often useful when an interpersonal relationship is at a point where someone is self-disclosing. When someone discloses something of significance to you, it is important that you respond with words that reflect you are listening, that you care, that you are trying to understand, and that you feel for them. For instance, if your friend tells you they have just been diagnosed with an incurable illness, you should respond with concern and care.

Neutral language is appropriate and useful sometimes, but it is not the best choice when a friend or partner is disclosing something personal. If you appear neutral or indifferent when someone has disclosed to you, you will likely hurt their feelings, make them feel devalued, and decrease the chances of that person disclosing to you or others about that topic in the future.

I remember when I was diagnosed with a life-long illness recently; it was shocking and devastating to me. I didn't tell many people, in fact only three at the time. One night I decided to tell a friend about my diagnosis and recent pain and physical struggles. I did so with tears being pulled back, and his response to me was, "Oh, that's not that big a deal; I have lots of friends with that. They are fine; you can't even tell. You're fine." This was hurtful to me because I had already told him about some of my visible symptoms and how it was affecting my life. His dismissive comments made me feel like he didn't care about me. He had not one shred of empathy for my situation. Being a mother of three young children, I expected my friend to be more supportive and understand why this diagnosis would be so devastating for me and my family.

I didn't need tears or a hug, but some basic empathy instead of neutrality was needed. I decided to never to disclose anything deeply personal to him again and this is not an uncommon response when some feels a friend/partner has been neutral instead of empathetic. So, be empathetic not neutral when communicating, people want and need to feel understood and loved; empathy is a great big step in that direction.

Now, that we have discussed some of the basics of language communication, let's get a bit more in-depth about language and its power over our lives.

Language and Power

Language should be the bridge that brings people together; it should not be used to divide or dehumanize. To **dehumanize** refers to the degradation of another, the oppression of and diminishment of a particular person or culture. In order to avoid dehumanizing and harmful language, we must recognize we are limited by our own experiences, which means we need to consistently understand that our words have consequences. One example of this is the use of ethnocentric language. Ethnocentric means someone who thinks their culture is superior to other cultures. This chapter focuses on the role of effective language in public speaking. Specifically, we discuss how to create concise language, discuss how our language is reflective of our culture, understand how it affects other cultures, and finally examine strategies that can be used in your relationships (Figure 4.1).

When communicating with others you need to adhere to making appropriate language choices and recognize that your words reflect who you are to people around you (Figure 4.2). The first amendment of the constitution protects speech, but it does not protect hate language, slander, or defamatory language. As an ethical communicator it is your obligation to understand what words and phrases are not protected and are hurtful to certain individuals or cultures. This section of the chapter helps you understand why some terms should be avoided and why others are preferred. We specifically examine sexist language, language surrounding sexual orientation and gender, ethnic language, and language regarding the disabled community.

Oppressive Language

It has been found that more than half of Americans use oppressive language every day and do not recognize it. It's very important that you understand what is considered oppressive language and learn strategies to diminish your use of it. **Oppressive language** is any word or series of words

Figure 4.1 Intolerance is most evident in our language choices. Intention to harm others irrelevant the fact that your words cause harm is.

that uses an identifier of a person or a certain group as a negative or undesirable characteristic (class, race, sex, gender, ethnicity, sexual orientation, ability, etc.). It is usually used to suppress and belittle, whether intentional or unintentional. It is considered a form of verbal violence.

Oppressive language begins with some form of bias. Bias is communicating or treating someone differently because of their connection. Cultural myths and stereotypes usually don't match the facts to a given culture. This includes such cultures as age, ethnicity, sex, gender, disability, race, political affiliation, hobby-based groups, social affiliation, marital status, occupation, religion, and sexual orientation.

Bias usually stems from one or more places:

Figure 4.2 Language is powerful and hurtful. Words can be remembered forever. Know the power of your words and use them to bring others up, not down. In all these examples the hurtful language results in similar nonverbal results: slumped shoulders, hanging head, weakened posture, and a generally weakened sense of self.

1) A lack of information or correct information about a culture

2) A fear of a culture

3) Hate of a culture

4) Stereotypes and prejudices about a culture

5) **Ethnocentrism**—is a belief or feeling that your (or one's culture) culture is superior to other cultures.

Bias is the breeding ground for hate crimes and should be avoided at all costs. Using any oppressive terms when communicating furthers the acceptability of the term, desensitizes others from the word, incites negative emotion, and reinforces stereotypes. In order to avoid biased language you need to first recognize the ways in which you are currently biased and your own use of oppressive language. This is not a fun process. It means you have to admit you hold negative and typically untrue ideas about different cultures of people based on totally irrelevant, inaccurate, or unimportant information.

Furthermore, you must recognize that those beliefs have the power to physically and emotionally harm others. Once you have accomplished your self-reflection, it is time to assess your language and make adjustments.

Take, for example, World War II when Hitler led Nazi Germany. Hitler gave a great number of speeches aimed at convincing his audience that a certain culture or cultures were bad and should be eradicated. Think about that for a minute. How powerful must language be to persuade you that not only should a certain culture be eradicated, but also convince you to take part in the process? Really think about that. Language must be one of the most powerful tools on Earth because all Hitler had to do to convince others to slaughter children, women, and men was choose his words carefully.

Hitler never called Jewish people just "Jewish." When he referenced Jewish people he added descriptive prejudice language in an attempt to incite and create a negative connotative meaning in the mind of his listeners. He would say "vermin" and refer to them as a "disease" that was infecting the country. We know that language is learned and that connotative meaning is very powerful. If you hear something often enough and that is the common way it is expressed, soon you will begin to accept it as truth. This is exactly what Hitler accomplished with his language choices and what ultimately lead to the Holocaust where millions of Jewish people were killed.

You can also reference the history of the United States. When settlers came to the United States, they invaded a country of what are now called American Indians. The language strategies that were used referred to native people as "savages." Savage has an entirely different connotative value to it than native. Savage implies a brutal, violent, and dangerous meaning. This could easily incite feelings of protectiveness and defensiveness. Native implies they were the first to inhabit and thus may be the rightful owners. It is far easier to kill a person or take something from someone who you think of as an intruder or dangerous than to take something from someone who is defending their home from you. Words are powerful, and they can have lasting effects on people and cultures, which is why it is very important you get rid of oppressive language that you use, even if you don't think the people around you are from the culture you speak of, and if you belong to the culture you are putting down.

Today the phrase, "that's so gay," is commonly used. Those who use this phrase often say they are not intending to hurt any culture or even talk about gay people. So why is it a problem? Because intentions are irrelevant; the outcome is relevant. The outcome is that phrases like "that's so gay" are used every day to dehumanize, hurt, oppress, and even inspire suicide in the gay and lesbian community. This phrase is also one of the most common forms of hate speech used in America today and has been linked to a significant number of hate crimes.

The bottom line is that phrase is not being used to applaud or support the gay and lesbian community; it is used to suppress them. When you say that phrase, are you saying it say something is great or are you communicating that something is bad or someone is less valuable? It's the latter. If you aren't using phrases about different cultures to communicate something good, then don't use it.

Oppressive versus Proper Ethnic Language

Ethnically proper language is language that considers the culture's preferred way of being addressed. In the United States there have been numerous transitions and rules about how to address certain co-cultures. There is a history of oppressive terms that people of certain ethnic groups have been called and there have been the more acceptable forms. For instance, in the last several years scholars and activists have pushed the term "people of color" when addressing non-white groups. This has been widely preferred over the standard quantified "American" such as Asian American, Mexican American, and African American.

The problem that was addressed is that the terms characterize the culture first by being something other than American. The extra terms bring attention to a specific culture that may not accurately reflect that person. "People of color" is most commonly the more acceptable term to use. Martin Luther King Jr used the term "citizens of color" and that is where the phrase originated.

"People of color" is meant to be a better option than "minority" as well. It is thought that "minority" has a connotation that implies someone one is less than another. In fact, in America, people of color are the majority so much of the time it actually doesn't make sense to say "minority" unless you are referring to white (Caucasian) people. In general, "people of color" is preferred over terms like "minority" or "non-white." Yet this term is still not a perfect choice in all situations. It is important to understand some people have strong opinions on different labels and, if possible, it is best to use the language they prefer.

General rule for using ethnic language:

- Use the specific culture, not a general term. Many cultures are very different and prefer not to be recognized as part of other cultures. For example, the term "Asian American" can be insulting to Pacific Islanders and any of the Asian cultures that wish to be recognized by their particular culture's name (Japanese, Filipino, North Korean, South Korean, Chinese, etc.).

Other common oppressive terms include "Oriental" or "Hispanic." There are no such "oriental" people. If you are referring to people who are Japanese, Chinese, or Korean, for instance, you must call each culture by those specific names not an overarching name like "Asian." Oriental is considered highly offensive and racist. Some states like New York and Washington have banned the word from appearing on any documents. The term began during a period in history in which the United States instituted exclusion acts to keep people from entering the country. The term began as a way to communicate a group of people were inferior. Given this alone we shouldn't use the term, but perhaps the most compelling reason to avoid this term is that it has never been a widely accepted term used by any "Asian" culture. We should always refer to people in the way they prefer to be identified. Allowing other people to create terms for other cultures is simply not a good thing.

"Hispanic" is problematic because it attempts to classify Spanish, Cuban, and Mexican people in the same group. These are wildly different cultures, with very different norms, lives, values, and so on. To lump them together is unacceptable and insulting to some. If someone wants to be identified as "Hispanic," then you can use that term, otherwise refrain from using the term. The general rule is to call a person or a culture by its specific name, do not lump cultures together—doing so diminishes the independence and uniqueness of their cultures. It can also make people feel like you don't understand them and their culture. A good friend or partner would not use language that creates distance and hurts, we use language that brings us closer together and reflects that we love and respect others cultural affiliations.

Common ways people communicate their bias is through assumptions, jokes, or offensive or stereotypical examples. The table of language options is here for you to consider. The list is not comprehensive; if you encounter a word you want to use, but think it may be problematic, do not use it.

Oppressive Language Has Been Linked to:
Stigma: an undesirable mark of disgrace associated with a person or group of people, quality, or circumstance.
Stereotype: misjudgment of a person by assuming that they belong to a certain group or that belonging to that group means they have a specific set of characteristics.

(continued)

Oppressive Language Has Been Linked to:
Prejudice: preconceived judgment based on opinion.
Hate language: any speech, gesture, conduct, or writing that may incite violence or prejudice against an individual or group.
Hate crime: crime directed at an individual or group of people based on their affiliation with certain groups or characteristics including race, religion, ethnicity, or sexual orientation.

Sexist Language

Sexist and gendered language is the most common type of oppressive language. Speakers who fail to use gender neutral and inclusive language run a great risk of being seen as uneducated and lacking empathy and credibility. One of the most common examples of sexist language today is the use of "you guys" when referring to an audience of men and women. "Guys" is a term that recognizes the male sex; it does not include the female sex. If someone uses "you guys," they are ignoring or diminishing the presence of the women in the room. Consider using a word like "everyone" when addressing a group.

Before I can continue this explanation we need to establish the difference between sex and gender. **Sex** refers to the biological sex of an individual such as male, female, or intersex (having both sex organs). Sex considers specific chromosomes, sex organs, and hormones as a means of identification.

Gender refers to the degree to which a person confirms, identifies with, and/or adopts specific social roles; specifically we can break gender up into expression, identity, and roles. **Gender expression**, for example, refers to the ways people tend to communicate their gender externally. This may come in the form of clothing, jewelry, tattoos, hairstyles and color, and even the sounds of their voice. **Gender identity**, on the other hand, refers to how people perceive themselves and how they prefer to refer to themselves. **Gender roles** refer to the various expectations, roles, and behaviors that have been assigned to men and women based on the idea that men should be masculine and women should be feminine.

Gender is understood as encompassing two main concepts: masculinity and femininity. It is important, however, to comprehend the scope of gender. There are not two categories; rather, gender can be mapped out on a continuum with femininity at one end and masculinity on the other. The space exactly between the two is called androgyny. **Androgyny** is a mixture of feminine and masculine traits. Research has shown that most people have developed their gender by the time they are about 3 years old.

Masculinity is commonly associated with men and femininity with women, but this is not an accurate assumption. **Femininity** is associated with certain characteristics and masculinity with certain characteristics. Between these two is androgyny, which is a blend of the two ends of the gender continuum, where a person can have some masculine traits and some feminine traits. Research has found that most people have a combination of masculine and feminine traits regardless of their sex.

When you talk to men, do not assume they only relate to masculine traits, and when speaking to women, do not assume they only respond to feminine traits. Doing so can insult the person that you are talking to as well make you look ignorant. For instance, I once was in a group made up completely of women. The person giving a presentation noted that we were all females from the start and from that point on every example that person provided was relevant to cheerleading, mothering, cooking, or shopping. More than half the women were irritated by the sexist assumption and several women left.

Over the decades we have tried to make right the biased language that fundamentally ignored the presence of women. At one time, it was commonly accepted to refer to anyone and anything that wasn't established to be a woman or girl explicitly as "he." For instance, if a person spoke about seeing a cute baby whose sex they did not know they would have said, "He is such a cute baby." Then society determined we should also allow women to be addressed and so it became proper to say, "He or she is such a cute baby." This is also where the "his/hers" and "him/ her" became common. Although the "his/hers" method did finally allow women to exist in language, it is still problematic. Read the difference between those sentences again. The one where "he or she" is written is more distracting. By this I refer to the fact that some of the attention from the sentence is now focused on the sex language rather than the point of the sentence.

	Sentence by . . .	
"No man shall stand in our way."	Neutral words	"No **person** shall stand in our way."
"A student who takes their test will remain in **his** seat until everyone else is finished or until **he** is asked to leave."	Plural words	"**Students** taking the test will remain in **their** seats until everyone else is finished or until **they** are asked to leave."
"The group meeting summary is collected by the secretary each day and until **her** report is filed you cannot move onto the next step."	Definite article	"The group meeting summary is collected by the secretary each day and until the report is filed you cannot move onto the next step."
"Every student must pay all fees and holds before **he** can obtain **his** diploma."	"they" "them""themselves " "their"	"Every student must pay all fees and holds before **they** can obtain **their** diploma."
"Any trainee who struggles with the fitness test must learn and train to finish it **herself**."		"Any trainee who struggles with the fitness test must learn and train to finish it **themselves**."
"If the parent of the child is satisfied with the level of accomplishment of **his/ her** child then we are too."	Repeating the noun	"If the **parent** is satisfied with the level of accomplishment of the parents' child then we are too."
"If the officer finds there is reasonable suspicion, then **he** should investigate further."		"If **the officer** finds there is reasonable suspicion then **the officer** should investigate further."
"The teacher may add a student after the deadline if **she** determines there are circumstances that warrant **her** making the accommodation and if her class has enough seats available that it won't make **her** classroom too full."	Rewrite	"The teacher may add a student after the deadline if it is determined that circumstances warrant the accommodation, seats are available, and the class won't be overcrowded as a result."

It is also problematic for gendered reasons. By saying "his and hers" you are indicating there are only two choices of gender or sex which fundamentally ignores the presence of other groups of people. Your language should always strive to be as inclusive as possible. So, today, in order to be inclusive it is recommended that we remove any distinguishing sex or gender terms and replace them with neutral terms. For instance, "that baby was so cute!" or "it was one of theirs," instead of "it was his or hers." As a general rule, you will want to limit the use of pronouns altogether.

To avoid sexist/gendered language:

1) Use neutral words.

2) Use plural words.

3) Replace any possessive pronouns with a definite article.

4) When referring to singular indefinite nouns (his, he, hers, she) replace it with "they," "themselves," "them," or "their."

5) Repeat the noun.

If none of the above will result in a usable sentence, you must reconstruct the sentence to eliminate the pronoun entirely.

Another distinction that you should be aware of is any language that brings attention to the rareness of something being done by a certain sex (this is often a perception of rareness not actual rareness). For instance, "the male nurse said I should take the pills twice a day." This sentence unnecessarily draws attention to the fact that the nurse was male, and thereby reinforces the idea that men shouldn't be nurses or rarely are nurses, even though this is not the case. This is problematic because the more a culture reinforces ideas about what each sex should or can do or become, the younger generations buy into those beliefs. The same can be seen for female examples like, "the lady engineer will meet with us tomorrow." Again, the unnecessary word placement of a person's sex in front of a given occupation reinforces the ideas and stereotypes that are associated with it. In this case the idea is that women can't be engineers. If you say male or female terms as a qualifier to any given occupation, you are engaging in sexist language that oppresses certain groups. The following table provides examples to guide you.

Say This	Not This
Salesperson	Salesman
Mail carrier	Mailman
Nurse	Male nurse
Doctor	Female doctor
Firefighter	Fireman
Supervisor	Foreman
Server	Waiter/waitress
Performer	Actor/actress
Fisher	Fisherman

Say This	Not This
Assistant	Male assistant
Humans or humankind	Mankind
Be stronger/Buck up/Try harder	Man up
Chairperson	Chairman
Homemaker	Male homemaker

Sexuality/Gender

Sexist language is not the only kind of non-inclusive language that can end up insulting, demeaning, or dehumanizing your partners, friends, coworkers, acquaintances, and so on. You also want to consider the effects of other oppressive language especially because it will have a direct effect on your how you are perceived by others. People who are not aware of the basic rules surrounding various cultures will find people quickly label them as incompetent, untrustworthy, racist, prejudice, sexist, homophobic, rude, or inconsiderate. This is in part because of the concept called linguistic relativity. **Linguistic relativity** asserts that language shapes the way we see the world and what a culture or person values. So, if a speaker uses sexist or culturally oppressive language, the receiver(s) will interpret that to mean the speaker doesn't value that culture. If the receiver is a member of that culture, then you have just created a hurtful event and damaged that relationship.

Sexual orientation is often used inappropriately with relevance to sex and gender, and it is a culture that is frequently oppressed with unintentionally and intentionally oppressive language choices. **Sexual orientation** is not something that is based on sex or gender; instead, it is based in two primary concepts: those who are attracted to the opposite sex, which is termed "straight," and those who are attracted to the same sex, which is termed "gay" or "lesbian." However, those are not the only categories and, in fact, there are not necessarily categories at all.

Similarly to the gender continuum, there is a continuum of sexuality. The sexuality continuum is measured on a scale of seven—one being the most "straight" and seven being the most "gay/lesbian" on the scale. In the 20th century, Alfred Kinsey's research found that most people were not straight or gay/lesbian, and that they were somewhere in between. The research also showed that people who identify themselves as "straight" actually rate as a one to three on the sexual orientation scale when they answer a series of questions relevant to sexuality. Findings also discovered that most people who identified themselves as gay or lesbian were consistently ranking in the range of three to five.

What this research demonstrates is that in fact most people are a little bit in between straight and gay/lesbian. Terms for this middle area have changed over the years, but the most commonly used term in research is bisexuality. An easy way to remember the difference between gender and sex and other ideas is:

1) gender expression is how someone expresses their gender to the world around them
2) sexual orientation is how someone feels about a certain sex or sexes in terms of sexual attraction.
3) sex refers to the sexual organs a person has
4) Identity is how someone prefers to be identified by others.

It is important to recognize that sexual orientation is irrelevant to sex and gender. Sex, gender, and sexual orientation are not related or dependent on each other at all. In relationships, you have a responsibility to use language that is accurate and doesn't perpetuate misinformation and the use of hate terms. You also have a responsibility to show respect to those you love and those around you.

One of the more common mistakes happens with regard to the LGBTQ community. LGBTQ refers to several communities of nonexclusively heterosexual cultures: lesbian, gay, bisexual, trans-gendered, and queer individuals. Although I recognize that most people will say they know what those terms mean I am going to provide much needed clarification anyway. The term lesbian refers to women who are sexually attracted to other women and refer to themselves as lesbian in sexual orientation. The term gay refers to men who are sexually attracted to other men and identify them-selves as a gay in sexual orientation. Bisexual is term used to identify people who are attracted to both sexes. The degree to which they are attracted to one over the other is not important.

Transgendered refers to individuals who exhibit behaviors and tendencies that reject the con-ventionally and socially taught gender roles of their sex. The label transgendered doesn't com-municate a preference for sexual orientation. Queer refers to gender minorities that either don't directly identify as heterosexual or who are questioning their sexuality. Some LGBT members reject the Q and the "queer" term entirely whereas others embrace it. Some who reject it feel that because "queer" was a hate term that had been used to oppress gays and lesbians at one time, it should not be used even if it is redefined.

Those who embrace the term queer believe that the LGBT community should embrace all cultures that are not heterosexual regardless and they should be inclusive no matter what. Queer is a term that is not always included, but I have included it here in an effort to teach you the dif-ferences and reasons why you should consider your language choices for these communities.

Now that we know the exact meanings behind these terms, we can use them more correctly and cognitively. One common and insulting language choice made often in America is referring to lesbian women as "gay."

For instance, a speaker might say, "in talking to the gay community, I learned that oppres-sive language has historically promoted inequality and prejudice." In this sentence the speaker is only referring to men who are gay; they are fundamentally ignoring the presence of the lesbian community. Now, if the speaker only spoke to gay men and was only referring to men, then using the term "gay" would be acceptable. If they are in any way including women in that state-ment, then the statement is problematic and considered oppressive language. The proper way to say that sentence in an inclusive way is to say, "In talking with the gay and lesbian community, I learned that oppressive language has historically promoted inequality and prejudice." Do you see the difference?

Another common mistake is calling any member of the LGBTQ community "queer." As dis-cussed before, queer refers to only those people in a state of question or in a non-heterosexual state. Equating that status to gays and lesbians, bisexuals, and transgendered people is insulting and ignores a significant part of their identity. Additionally, you may have noticed I did not use the term "homosexual" to define people who are lesbian or gay. For years it was deemed appropriate to call gay men and lesbian women homosexual. That is no longer the case necessarily. Many in the gay and lesbian community rejects that term because when the term homosexual was first created it was considered a mental illness (by the way, so was menopause back in the day). Now, of course, we recognize it is not, (at least in the United States), Given its history and the fact that the community largely prefers it not be used, the term homosexual should be generally avoided. The LGBT acro-nym is preferable if you must refer to an entire community.

Disability Language

Language regarding the disabled community has changed many times. In recent years the terms have been the final and best choices for the community, but always be aware that the terms for any community may change with time and it is your responsibility to ensure you are using the proper language. You must be aware of the connotative meanings of the words you use when talking about or talking to the disabled community, especially if you have friends and loved ones with a disability—you don't want to unintentionally hurt their feelings or perpetuate oppression.

There are three different types of disabilities that we need to understand: physical, sensory, and intellectual. There is a long history of terms used to define intellectually disabled persons, and there are certainly oppressive terms that are used to define a person with a physical or sensory disability as well. This section tackles those terms and provides you with more acceptable and culturally sensitive options.

Physical Disability

Physical disability refers to a person who has a disability that affects the body. It is important to always address the person first and the disability last when speaking of them, not vice versa. You want to be sure the disability does not define the person in total. "He is a disabled person." This is a sentence to avoid. Notice how the word "person" is after the "disability." Thereby, you are communicating that he is first and foremost defined by his disability.

Figure 4.3 The language you use to address a person with a disability is very important and reveals more about you than them. Learn how to communicate effectively and without diminish the changes that you will oppress others.

There are several terms that have been used to address this community that are problematic and should always be avoided. Even if you hear members of that community using any of the problematic terms, it does not give you the permission to use them. In your relationships, you set standards of what is acceptable; you also have the power to influence and create norms, so your responsibility is great. Terms to avoid are listed in the figure for you.

Terms to Use
Hard-of-hearing
A person who is deaf
Visually impaired or blind—depending..

Terms to Avoid	Terms to Use
Cripple	Physically disabled
Wheelchair-bound	Person with a mobility disability
Lame	Person with a physical disability
Physically incapable	Physically disabled
Physically challenged	Physically disabled
Handicapped	Physically disabled

Ways to better communicate with a person who is blind:

Figure 4.4 Never touch people without their permission, but a willingness to communicate effectively can be greatly appreciated.

- Use person first language.
- Use directional language instead of pointing or vague language.
- Identify yourself when you enter the room.
- Address the person by their name when you are speaking to them since they can't see that you are looking at them.
- Treat them like they are as capable as others because they are, don't use language that makes them feel pitied or less valued.
- Mention when there are steps coming or a door that's partially opened.

- Don't ask their parents or partner what they want or need; ask them; they are blind not incapable.
- Don't touch them without permission. Grabbing their arm to assist them seems nice, but it's rude to touch someone without asking and startling for a person who is blind.
- Don't talk down to them or in short sentences.
- Use descriptive vivid language.
- Don't ask them to tell their "blind story." They have told it a million times and they have lots of other stories to tell.
- Don't apologize for saying words like "see" or "watch."
- Feel free to offer assistance, but listen and don't get offended when the offer is declined.

Intellectual Disability

Intellectual disability (ID) refers to a person who has a disability of the mind. These individuals were once and are sometimes referred to with names I'm certain you are aware of. This terminology is unacceptable and should be avoided at all times. These terms are demeaning and oppressive in nature. In its conception the term "mentally retarded" referred to any person with an IQ below 70 and before the age of 18 it was apparent they had a limited ability to adapt to surroundings. The term mentally challenged is now considered politically incorrect. Using this term will also insult, demean, and dehumanize your audience

Figure 4.5 When discussing someone's specific condition, be sure to use the specific name of the disorder as opposed to using an overarching category. Disorders are very specific and when you show you understand the name it can actually go a long way to demonstrating you care and are trying to understand.

and subsequently negatively affect your ethos. These terms also result in the audience believing you think negatively about the disabled community.

It is important to note that there are other types of disabilities that often get lumped together but in fact are very separate and distinct. There are various emotional disturbances and behavioral disorders. It is generally expected that you use the specific type of disorder unless you are referring to multiple kinds then you can use the overarching terms of emotional disturbance or behavioral disturbance. For instance, instead of saying emotionally disabled you would specifically refer to bipolar disorder, anxiety disorder, or multiple-personality disorder.

Avoid	Use
Emotionally disturbed	Emotionally disabled
Unstable	Person with an emotional disability
Schitzo	Emotionally disabled

The bottom line is your words reflect your values, attitudes, and beliefs. Your words also perpetuate or discourage prejudice, oppressive, or hateful language that serves to harm others. Because of this, during any scenario in which you address the intellectually disabled community, you will use the term intellectually disabled (ID) and for all others you will use the specific name of the condition (e.g., cerebral palsy, autism, Down syndrome, and bipolar disorder). The only exception is if you are in fact referring to a broad range or you don't know the specific condition, in which case you will use the term emotional disturbance.

In the end you must be educated about language choices, and you must consider how those language choices will make others feel, especially with regard to your interpersonal relationships. If you have diverse friends and family members, this is a wonderful thing. I encourage that, and I equally encourage using language that is inclusive.

Conclusion

This chapter was all about helping you deconstruct the verbal communication you are using in your relationships and helping you makes positive language choices for the future. You learned about the foundation of language and meaning and the ways in which you can craft more concrete and affirming language that helps you have successful happy relationships. We also discussed how powerful language is and how oppressive and hurtful it can be, and thus why it is important that we choose our words wisely. I hope you really processed this chapters and took the time to understand the concepts and the reasoning. If you can accept and implement these language choices your relationships can't help but improve.

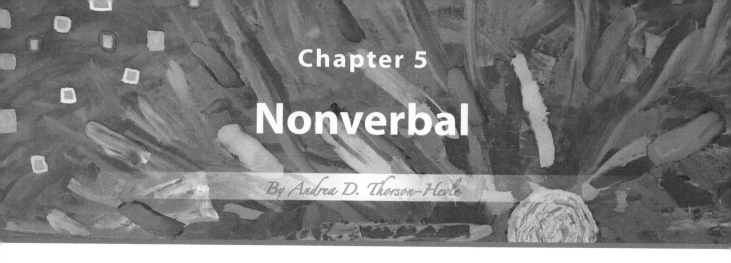

Chapter 5

Nonverbal

By Andrea D. Thorson-Hevle

Let's get personal. . .

When I was in my twenties, I had a wonderful friend, let's call her Abigale. Abigale was fabulous. She was funny, and cute, smart, and dramatic. We got on very well, except for one little thing. She liked to be very close to me when we spoke.

I thought it was odd at first, then I thought perhaps it was because she couldn't hear me well. So I took a step back and spoke much louder. But without missing a beat she took a step toward me. I tried walking with her side by side, but even then she was too close, her arm was touching mine. I would move my arm subtly as to provide some space, but Abigale would with seamless ease collapse that space and we would once again be touching.

I couldn't manage any way to keep her from me when we spoke. I took a step back; she took a step toward me and sometimes two. Abigale liked being about 8 inches from me when we spoke, and I preferred at least an arm's length. My exception to this rule was of course the occasional whispers that friends might want to hide from others, which is by the way what I would have thought she was doing all the time had she not been so very loud when she talked.

Eventually, I found myself avoiding her or placing tables and desks between us. Finally, one day I decided I had to talk to her about it. I did, and she said others had told her the same thing before. I asked her why she hadn't changed that habit.

She said, "I don't realize I'm doing it at the time. I like being close when I talk I guess, I don't know why. I feel like I'm just not very close to people if I'm not actually close to them." It was interesting, she could only feel closeness emotionally if she felt it physically and it felt so normal to her, despite being told by several people the behavior was problematic.

You need to read this chapter

- To understand how nonverbal communication functions in our lives.
- To learn the difference between verbal and nonverbal communication.
- To understand the different nonverbal channels.
- To identify ways to improve nonverbal skills.

Nonverbal Communication

There are many ways nonverbal communication serves to function in our relationships. Nonverbal communication alters the way in which we perceive and thus communicate with people, it provides us information that is contradictory or similar to verbal communication, and it allows us a way to distinguish the degree to which we should trust and believe people. Now, unfortunately, nonverbal communication isn't always communicated with 100% precision, nor is it decoded correctly all the time. So, there are a lot of opportunities for things to go wrong. This chapter will focus on nonverbal communication; specifically, how it functions in your relationships, the types of channels we have in the nonverbal communication realm, how it differs from verbal communication, and how we can improve our nonverbal skills.

Figure 5.1 Nonverbal communication can tell us a great deal about what people are thinking.

The Functions of Nonverbal Communication

Research in the field has distinguished six basic functions of nonverbal communication (Figure 5.1):[1]

1) To accent
2) To contradict

---

[1] Burgoon, J. Guerrero, L., & Floyd, K. (2010). *Nonverbal communication* (Boston: Allyn & Bacon). Burgoon, J. K.. & Bacue, A. E. (2003). Nonverbal communication skills. In J. O. Green & B. R. Burleson, J. K. Burgoon, & A. E. Bacue (Eds.), (2003). *Nonverbal Communication Skills*. In J. O. Green & B.R. Burleson (Eds.), *Handbook of Communication and Social Interaction Skills* (pp. 179–220).

3) To compliment

4) To control

5) To repeat

6) To replace

Figure 5.2 Nonverbal communication can tell us a lot about what other people are thinking, doing, or have done. Humans tend to believe nonverbal cues are more accurate indictors of truth than verbal cues.

Nonverbal Communication as Accent

Often we use nonverbal signals as a means of emphasizing what we are saying. Nonverbal communication as an accent means we emphasize a specific part of the message we are constructing and delivering with a specific nonverbal communication, which has an impact on meaning and significance. For instance, when I was recently coaching a client for a speech she was going to be giving publically, I had to remind her to accent her speech. We went evaluated sentence by sentence through the speech, highlighting the words or areas that she thought were most impactful and important—those parts that must be emphasized in order to affect the audience. For these parts we added a nonverbal accent. In one area she said, "It must start with us." I told her to add a nice powerful hand gesture. I had her move her hands out for "It starts" and in and crossed over the chest on the word "us." This display accented the word "us," making it more emotional and full of impact with one simple gesture.

Nonverbal Communication that Contradicts

Some nonverbal communication is contradictory to the communication a person is sending. When this happens the encoder can get mixed messages, feel they are being tricked, perceived to be dishonest, or not trustworthy. Sometimes we contradict ourselves on purpose. For instance, to be funny you might tell your friend, "Yeah, that shirt is super cute!" but give her a raised eyebrow, raised lip, and shake your head back and forth (signal for "no").

Nonverbal Communication that Compliments

Nonverbal communication isn't just meant to contradict; one of the most important functions is to compliment. The function of nonverbal communication as compliment was confusing to me in college because it seemed an awful lot like accent. I was less than pleased with my college professor's ability to distinguish between the two, so I hope I do better job here for you, but if I don't, by all means ask your instructor.

Compliments are much like accents, but instead of adding impact and significance, they reinforce what is already being done; it's a bit more subtle than an accent. For instance, in the example I gave you for *nonverbal accents*, I mentioned the powerful gesture that was an accent. Now, a compliment would be the slight turned up sides of the mouth she had when she said "us." A slight smile was a subtle compliment to the word "us" because she said the word "us" with hope and happiness, positive communication, and the turned up smile compliments that message.

Nonverbal Communication that Controls

One very cool function of nonverbal communication is its ability to establish control during a communication. Note, I don't recommend you overly use or abuse this. But, I do hope you learn to use this wisely, because although it can be used for bad, it can be used for good as well. Nonverbal communication functions to control because it allows us to communicate that we want to alter the communication in some way.

People show signs of trying to control a conversation by leaning toward others, making movements with their mouth, which clearly signal certain messages, and the ones we all know best, the hand movements that clearly communicate someone is trying to take control of the conversation.

In my graduate school years, there was a guy who always used his hands to communicate control. His voice was not as powerful as some of ours and he had a smaller frame than others, so using nonverbal displays of control were something he used to get peoples attention and take control of a conversation. He would literally raise his hand up and out when someone was speaking or about to say something he clearly didn't want to discuss at that time. His gesture would often quiet the other person and soon he steered the conversation in a new direction.

I know I use this nonverbal function when speaking with someone in my life who constantly interrupts. This person interrupts everyone she communicates with. She will actually ask a question of someone and as they are in mid sentence to respond she will interrupt them with a statement, question, or totally change the topic. It is so very rude and some people avoid conversations with her altogether because it is so frustrating. I have grown tired of asking her to stop interrupting, since doing so makes me interrupt myself or others as well. I also noticed when anyone specifically verbally addresses her behavior she gets defensive, dramatic, and ends up taking all the attention again. Whoever was in the middle of a story still doesn't ever get to finish it. Now, I use a nonverbal signal to indicate the conversation will be staying where it is (with the person currently speaking) and her comment is useful, but better used at a different time. I said all that with just a kind, soft, but direct flick of my hand; how wonderful.

Nonverbal Communication as Repetition

Repetition as a function of nonverbal is another favorite of mine. I love this one because I use eyebrows as a major part of my communication. Those things are flying all over my face when I talk and they serve a very distinct purpose, to help get my message across! Repetition in nonverbal communication refers to the fact we can do certain things nonverbally that says the exact same thing we said vocally.

Take for example, my husband has a tendency not to listen the first time I talk to pretty often. I'm not sure why, I think it's his upbringing actually, now that I think of it, his parents are like that too. I'm sure he will love that I disclosed that in a book. Anyway, he doesn't listen well, and after I ask him something and say, "What do you think?" I usually wait and stare at him and then raise my eyebrows up and put my mouth is an odd "u" shaped position to indicate, hey I asked you a question. "What do you think"? I basically repeat what I say, without actually repeating it. This is an example of nonverbal communication that is used as repetition.

Nonverbal Communication to Replace

Literally replacing words with movements is the lazy person's favorite nonverbal function. So, those of you who hate talking might just love this function of nonverbal communication. It is pretty great. Think of all the things you can communicate nonverbally and if done effectively ensures you don't have to actually speak a word. I can think of a few:

"What's up"—simple head nod
"I'm fine"—shrug the shoulders
"Okay"—not sure how to explain it but you know the sign
"Good"—thumbs up
"Bad"—thumbs down
"I don't really like you at all"—middle finger
"Eh, so so"—hand flat and shake it
"No" and "yes"—shake your head accordingly—you know the drill

So as you can see nonverbal communication serves many functions in the realm of communication and each one is a bit different. Which one do you like the best and use the most? Which one drives you a little bit bonkers? Which one do you need to improve your use of? Luckily for you, you're reading this book. We can help.

Nonverbal versus Verbal Communication; Understanding the Difference

	Verbal Communication	Nonverbal Communication
Vocal Communication	Speaking words and sentences	Laughing, grunting, sighing paralanguage: voice rate, volume, pitch, etc.
Nonvocal Communication	Writing, texting, and signing	Body position and posture, body movement, facial expressions, eye contact, etc.

Figure 5.3 There is perhaps no more universal symbol of care than the heartfelt touch of hands in this specific manner.

In an effort to fully understand nonverbal communication it is important we understand what it is not and what other kinds of communication entail. Please consult Figure 5.3 for a visual representation of what I will discuss herein. You have always heard of verbal and nonverbal communication, but you might not have heard much about vocal and nonvocal communication. There are in fact four components to communication, not just two, and they are all important to understand. Two of those components are considered nonverbal communication and will be discussed in this section. But, I would also like to lightly discuss the other two types (vocal and verbal communication) as well, in an effort to give you a rounded understanding of communication and to also set you up for better understanding the coming chapters.

Vocal versus Verbal Communication

Vocal communication is communication expressed through voice, but is not actual words. It uses our diaphragms, vocal chords, and mouths. Examples of vocal communication include, but are not limited to, laughter, scoffs, grunts, purposeful clearing of the throat, "ohh" and "ahh." For instance, a sigh when you are tired is a vocal nonverbal communication or a grunt when your child is irritated that you asked them to do a chore. Nonverbal vocal messages can be anything from your rate of speech, to your tone of voice, pitch, to your projection, and volume levels. Nonvocal nonverbal communication uses your senses and surroundings, your posture, touch, body movements, hand gestures, and so on.

Paralanguage: Paralanguage is component of communication that alters meaning and is often seen in pitch, tone, and volume and differs from culture to culture. It is conducted consciously and unconsciously all the time. Usually used to refer to nonverbal elements of speechmaking, but it can be used in other forms of communication,

Figure 5.4 Sign language is a form of verbal communication.

Words are the most commonly thought of **verbal communication**. Any communication expressed in human language is considered verbal communication, which means written, spoken, and signed language. This means that sign language is also considered a form of verbal communication.

Nonverbal Channels

Kinesics

Kinesics is how humans move and the meaning associated with the movement. It is often referred to as gestures. Kinesics is also the term used by social scientists to describe body language. Ekman and Friesen were the scholars who laid the foundation for these areas and they established five functions of kinesics.

1) Adapters
2) Affect displays
3) Emblems
4) Illustrators
5) Regulators

Adapters

Adapters are displays of nonverbal communication which people perform unconsciously a lot of the time. Adapters are nonverbal displays that are not usually purposefully communicated as part of the intended message, but rather a communication which occurs as the person adapts to the communication environment. Most of us find that adapters provide us subtle hints as to what the person is really thinking and feeling, despite what they might be saying.

There are three categories of adaptors: self-adaptors, alter-adaptors, and object-adaptors. Self-adaptors refer to adaptions we do to ourselves like rubbing our neck. Alter-adaptors refer to adaptions directed at others like moving a strand of hair from your friend's shirt. Object-adaptors are behaviors directed at items like tearing the sticker off a glass bottle.

Examples of adapters include the following:

Tapping of feet
Fixing someone's tie
Rubbing your ear
Pushing up glasses needlessly
Twisting hair
Pulling eyebrows
Doodling
Rubbing nose
Shredding a paper cup
Rubbing your face
Scratching
Tapping

Figure 5.5 Twisting your hair and doodling are examples of adapters.

Affect Displays

Affect displays are nonverbal indicators that the body and face communicate. These displays are usually emotional in meaning or communicate affective states of some kind. These displays are more conscious than adaptor communications, but they are sometimes spontaneous. These tend to reinforce your verbal messages purposefully, but sometimes may occur without your conscious thought. Affect displays tend to reflect emotions. For instance do you remember seeing a movie where an angry person was rubbing their hands not saying a word? That was an affect display.

Examples of affect displays include the following:

Smiling
Frowning
Rolling up sleeves
Placing hands in a steeple position
Shrugging
Bouncing around
Pounding fist in the air
Slouching
Folded arms in the front of the body

Emblems

Emblems are nonverbal communications which reflect actual words without saying them. The "okay" sign or the "thumbs up" and "middle finger," all of these communications are considered emblems. Like with so many things you have read in this book so far, emblems are highly tainted by cultures. Meaning, what is a direct translation in one culture is not in another. For instance the middle finger in the United States is not a positive gesture, but in other cultures it means nothing at all. In some cultures holding your little pinky up is the equivalent to the U.S. middle finger. So, before you choose emblems be aware of any cultural differences which might exist; there may be better ways to communicate. In some ways emblems are really unique. Emblems have the ability to bring groups of people together, to enforce a bond through a shared symbol making gesture. For instance, think about all the gangs out there. Do they all have one kind of hand shake or greeting? No, not at all. They all have their very unique way of greeting one another and that shared emblem helps create a sense of unity and pride. It seems silly, but it really works.

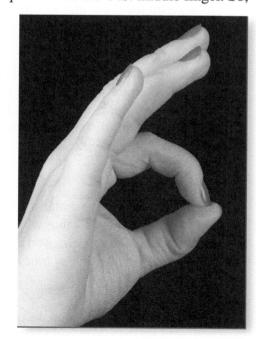

Think back to elementary school. Did you have a special friend who you practiced special handshakes with or did you see some students who did? Then you saw how this bonded the two people together. A shared emblem is a very powerful device.

Those of you who are sports fans might have a special place in your heart for emblems. If you ever rooted for a team with a mascot that had any kind of attribute that was made into a nonverbal gesture to symbolize you were with that team? It was likely an emblem. For instance, if your team was the "steers" and you held your fingers up on your head like horns, this would be an emblem.

Examples of emblems include the following:

Thumbs up
Thumbs down
Okay sign
Peace sign
Pointing in a direction
Waving

Illustrators

Illustrators are nonverbal symbols that reinforce a verbal message. Hand gestures are illustrators when they are used to reinforce a verbal message. For instance, if you said, ". . . and I could see again." I might use my hands to gesture over my eyes and then uncover them and bring them out broadly—this would reinforce what I was saying, I was able to see again.

Regulators

Regulators are nonverbal cues that control the communication flow. Regulators are wonderful little signals that tell people when to talk and when not to talk. If they are used properly they can make for an efficient conversation. If they are used with malice or abused, they can generate a climate of irritation, negativity, and anger.

Examples of regulators include the following:

Holding your finger over your lips "shh."
Putting your hand out to indicate someone should "stop."
Putting you hand out and gesturing your fingers back toward you to indicate "continue."

Proxemics

Proxemics is a category of nonverbal communication defined as observations and theories about human's use of space as a reflection of culture. The study of proxemics has been conducted for a very long time, but a man named Edward T. Hall was especially influential to interpersonal communication. Hall distinguished two specific subcategories of proxemics: personal space and territory.

Personal Space

We discussed something similar to this in the previous chapters, the idea that we have a certain amount of space around us that we need other people to respect. If we violate people's personal space rules, we risk being perceived as wanting a certain kind of relationship or being seen as threatening. Hall specifically defines four areas of personal space:[2]

---

[2] Hall, E. T. (1966). *The hidden dimension*. Anchor Books. ISBN 0-385-08476-5.

1) Intimate
2) Personal
3) Social
4) Public

These four categories serve as guidelines, and you might see them as more or less true for yourself. Hall does note in his studies that there are differences when people are sitting versus standing, in relationships versus strangers and so on. Culture always plays a significant role in these rules. The numbers you were given in the diagram are numbers generally reflective of our culture, but are certainly not reflective of all cultures. Some cultures like to stand very close to one another when they speak, they think it's respectful. There are even some cultures that stand so close they can smell the other person's breathe. In the United States, members of its culture would grimace and take a step back.

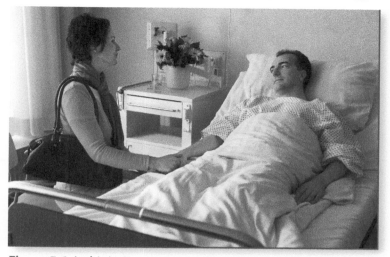

Figure 5.6 Is this intimate, personal, social, or public display of personal space?

How close you stand to someone when you communicate with them communicates quite a lot to them. If you are interested in someone romantically, think about how you showed them that. One of the ways was likely proximity—you likely closed that gap and merged closer and closer to the "intimate distance."

Have you ever been to a doctor's office and sat in a chair that was surrounded by empty chairs, then someone comes in and instead of selecting a seat several empty chairs away from you, they sit right next to you! Why? My goodness, why would someone do that? You didn't love that, did you? Of course not. Well, perhaps it was a very attractive member of the sex you prefer and you saw it as an opportunity… I digress. My point is this per-

Figure 5.7 This couple is in a committed romantic relationship. They are displaying communication through proximity. What does this nonverbal communication tell you?

son broke a rule, a very clear cultural proxemics rule. *Do not sit next to someone when there are clearly other empty seats.* The reason that violation feels so much like, well, a violation, is because they broke the rule. When you sit in a chair next to someone, you are in intimate space and it doesn't make people feel comfortable.

Similar situations may have happened to you on an elevator. Have you ever been on an elevator when someone got in and instead of them leaning on the wall opposite you, they stand right next to you or lean on the same wall you are leaning on? Awful isn't it?! Now think back, did your parents

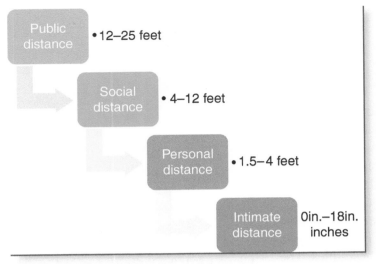

Figure 5.8 Personal Space in the United States.

teach you that rule? Did your parents have the "elevator talk" with you? "Now, Ben, when you get on an elevator and someone else is on it, always select a position as far away from the other person as possible as to not make the other person think you are a total creep!" No, that didn't happen. You weren't sat down like a seventh grader getting the sex talk. You were in fact enculturated into the rule. You picked it up. And you think everyone should have picked up that same hint from society. I agree and I wish it were true.

Figure 5.9 How close we are physically to others communicates how close we are to them in other ways. The boys in this picture are friends and are showing that through close proximity and touching.

Territory

There are four types of human **territory** according to proxemics theory. The first is called **body territory,** which is the space immediately around us. It was discussed previously to some extent.

There is the **home territory,** which is the area a person has control over on a consistent basis (like their home). Then there is the **interactional territory**, which is an area where people informally meet and interact (office or lunch room). And finally, there is **public territory,** the area where anyone can come and go as they please, and no one has true ownership. However, public territory is a difficult concept because it's not always as black and white as it seems. For instance, gangs and drug distributers often "own" certain "public territories."

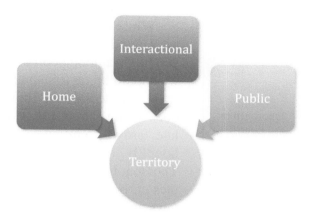

Chronemics

Chronemics refers to the study of how time affects human communication. The way we use time can communicate things to people about how much you value them and respect them. In the Western culture, time is a huge part of our culture. Being "on time" is a very important practice in our culture. We have been taught that if you are late it reflects you are lazy, poorly managed, disrespectful, rude, and/or inconsiderate. None of these things are positive. If you are going to be late, our culture teaches you that you should notify people in advance and apologize. This is not the case in every culture. In fact some cultures don't value time much at all. In some cultures if you say you will meet someone at 3 and show up at 4 it is acceptable and no one will feel jilted or hurt and they won't judge you as inconsiderate, disorganized, or rude.

Let's Get Personal...

Growing up as a child and even now as an adult, going to the movies with my father was an experience. Don't get me wrong. I loved going to the movies with him. In fact, I wish we did it more, but if we didn't get to the movies, I mean in our seats, at least 15 minutes before the previews started, we were "too late." We would literally have to walk out if the previews had started before we sat in our seats.

I remember wanting to see a movie so bad one day and in the truck on the way there, my dad looked at the clock, and said, "Nope, we are gonna be late. Next time we will just be on time" and we turned around and went home. My dad's definition of "on time" was very different from mine. I hated previews so if I got to the theatre right when the

> movie started I was happy. Neither of us was right, but if we wanted to have a good relationship we needed to understand and communicate about what "on time" meant to each of us.
>
> — *Andrea D. Thorson-Hevle*

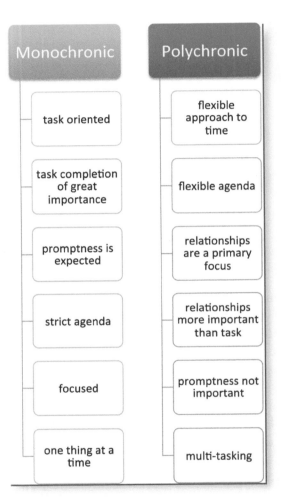

Monochronic	Polychronic
task oriented	flexible approach to time
task completion of great importance	flexible agenda
promptness is expected	relationships are a primary focus
strict agenda	relationships more important than task
focused	promptness not important
one thing at a time	multi-tasking

While there are some basic norms we have in the United States for time, there are mostly large variations among people. Yes, as a culture we know we should be on time and respect time, and understand that to be late shows disrespect. But, what does being "late" really mean? Define "late." Is late, tardy by 5 minutes, 10 minutes, 30 minutes, an hour? If you asked my father, the wonderful James Thorson, he would tell you, "If you are not 15 minutes early you are late." On the other hand, my in-laws are on time if they arrive somewhere within two hours of the planned time and they are pretty understanding if anyone else is late by an hour or so. You can imagine that when I had to merge cultures what a transition it was for me.

Facial Expression

Facial expressions are one of the first ways we know how someone is feeling. We use our faces to communicate emotion in ways no other form of communication can. In fact, facial expressions are one of the only forms of communication that are cross-cultural, meaning they possess the same meaning in all cultures. A baby doesn't get taught to smile, a baby knows to smile when it feels happy. A child doesn't learn to frown, the child instinctively frowns when they feel sad. We have seen this throughout cultures around the world. Research has shown that the emotions for surprise, fear, anger, happiness, sadness, and disgust are nonverbally expressed the same across all known and explored cultures! That is amazing, because as you have noticed by now, most of our communication is crafted and regulated by cultures.

Facial expressions can communicate the true nature of a person at any given point and time, but they can also conceal. If someone gets good at performing, they can use their facial expressions to trick others into the believing they are experiencing certain emotions that they are not actually experiencing. I myself am quite good at this. I'm in a great deal of pain most days, some days my feet feel like there are a thousand bees stinking them and my legs and back are always in pain because of my herniated disks and other medical condition. But who wants to be around someone who is always in pain? Many people say they wouldn't care, they wouldn't want their friend or partner to pretend to feel good when they don't. To these people I ask if they have ever known someone who is actually in constant pain every moment. The answer is consistently "no." Oh now, don't lie. No one wants to be around someone in pain all the time. People who are in pain have facial expressions that show they are sad, angry, frustrated, moody, and sometimes they are crying. I certainly do not want to be that person, so I choose to put on a different face. Some days, by the time I get home I'm exhausted from my days' performance. My husband looks at me and knows of course, because eventually I had to let him in on the truth. But I lie even to him much of the time and do it not through words, but through my facial expressions. Instead of showing the pain on my face I smile a lot. That's how you know I'm in pain, I smile too much. People who know me very well can see the difference in my smiles. How do you conceal through facial expressions? Have you ever received a gift you hated, a proposal you didn't want?

Masking facial expressions isn't always done for the betterment of others or so that others won't totally hate you, like in my case. Sometimes, people try to conceal and alter their facial expressions in an effort to purposely trick others, like when someone is showing false sincerity. Have you ever been in a conversation with someone and they seemed into what you were saying, they were empathizing and then for one quick moment you saw them look away and raise their eyebrows in exasperation? This is a true emotion they were concealing. Researchers call these "micro-expressions." I recommend paying attention to these, you will learn who your friends are much more effectively.

Eye Contact

Eye contact is very important in nonverbal communication. In the United States we have been raised to show respect by looking each other in the eyes. Failure to look at someone when they speak to you is a blatant display of disrespect and if you are in a relationship with that person it is likely to hurt their feelings. While maintaining direct eye contact is very important in Western culture, it is not that way in all cultures. In some cultures, like Japan, you should not make direct eye contact with people who are considered superior to you.

Let's Get Personal...

My best friend in college, Shoko, was from Japan. She was able to assimilate to the U.S. culture in all ways except for eye contact. She simply couldn't bring herself to look her professors in the eye when they spoke to her. In our communication theory class, she was regularly being asked questions and she would consistently answer them with her head down and her eyes diverted. This enraged our professor. Finally one day, I went to his office and explained that Shoko had only been in the United States for a year. I explained that eye contact was still very difficult for her. He said she was being disrespectful and didn't much care for my intervention. I went home to speak to my friend. I explained how important it was here to look people in the eye and after about 30 minutes she finally understood. She did a lot better after that and started making a lot more friends.

— *Andrea D. Thorson-Hevle*

In interpersonal relationships it is very important that you establish eye contact when communicating. Failure to look at someone when speaking with them makes them feel devalued and disrespected. I can't tell you how many times students have reported their relationships ending because their partner refused to look at them when they had conversations. In recent years video games and online activity have seemed to be the most prevalent causes for distraction. For example, someone is playing a video game, but their partner wants to talk. The person playing says they can listen and play at the same time. Perhaps this is true, but is it the same? No, of course not. To the person talking it feels like their partner doesn't care about them, doesn't feel what they have to say matters, or is showing disrespect. This example often happens with parents and children and between friends too. If you are playing a game and looking at something other than me, you are not really interested in me—that is the impression you are giving your partner. Once this perception is formed then all the other assumptions start to come ... my partner doesn't respect me, care for me, listen to me, care what I think is important, want to be in this relationship ... the list will go on. So, don't open that can of worms in your relationship. Give your partner and other relationships full attention and eye contact.

Can you recall a date you went on and the person continued their conversation with you while texting a friend or trolling the internet? Most people have had this experience more than once and it is unfortunate. Technology is taking over and even if you can manage to have a conversation while texting, you shouldn't. Give people respect and show them that they are valued by looking them in the eye when you talk to them.

In the United States, people who avoid eye contact are perceived as:

1) Dishonest
2) Rude
3) Disrespectful
4) Fake
5) Mean
6) Hurtful
7) Incompetent
8) Unintelligent

Personal Appearance

The way we dress and things we wear communicate things to other people. Certain items of clothing can signify you belong to certain groups (Hells Angels Jacket, Christian religious cross, star of David, tattoos, piercings, etc.). The truth is these indicators of groups you belong to are not always reflecting the truth, but when we get dressed in the morning or get a tattoo or a piercing we must consider what groups others will perceive we belong to because of it. Now, I'm not saying you should hide any of your identities, heck no. But, I am saying if you are thinking about applying for a job as an executive assistant at a conservative company who only seems to hire people without piercings, getting that ear plug or nose ring might be something you think twice about.

Today's companies are becoming more and more accepting of diversity in appearance with regard to piercings and tattoos, but assumptions about people with these items is still generally the same; they are alternative, dangerous, lower class, and/or like pain. After seeing the research that suggest this, I decided to do a totally nogeneralizable random sample of the culture around me. So, I surveyed 123 college students and faculty sure enough people commonly associated

Figure 5.10 The way we present ourselves can alter the ways in which people view us. What does your appearance say about you? Do you dress and groom in ways that reflect the person you want to be seen as?

tattoos, non-ear piercings, and plugs with assumptions of the person being "lazy, a criminal, from a lower class background, and unintelligent." Older generations seem to hold the most judgmental views on these choices, but it was notable across all generations.

Personal appearance is a factor in interpersonal attraction. Different people are attracted to different types of appearance. Your clothing and grooming choices are among the most influential in the "attraction" process, but accessories seem to be fairly important too, especially for friendships. This is likely because friends like to have things to bond over and share things they have in common. Accessories give people a means of expressing their individuality or style and if other people like that or dress similarly they might be attracted to you.

In romantic relationships there are often preferences for how your partner appears physically as well as expectations regarding their grooming habits. Some people like men with big long bushy beards, while others would never date a man with a beard. Would you? Some people prefer their partner to have shaved legs and shaved armpits, while it's not as important to others. For some people they want their partner to dress in clothes that reflect a certain gender and are uncomfortable with anything else. There is no right or wrong for your appearance, only what is good for you and your relationships. Think about your appearance. What do you think the way you dress and groom yourself says about you to other people? Are you happy with that?

Improving Your Nonverbal Communication Skills

If you want to improve your nonverbal communication skills the first thing you need to do is start paying attention. Ha-ha. Yes, well, you are already starting to do that by reading this book. Here are a few other tips to help you on your journey toward more successful relationships.

1) Be aware of what your body language is telling people. How are you standing, where are your arms?

2) Be aware of what your face is telling people. Are you thinking about your facial expressions? Do you get asked if you are mad a lot—but you aren't ever mad? You need to be more aware of your facial expressions and make them reflect how you feel.

3) Control your negative facial expressions. Facial expressions can be just as painful as words.

4) Consider what your gestures are doing and whether or not they are actually helping you. Are you using accents? Try them!

5) Look at people when they speak to you. Put down everything else and just engage in the person you are with. The relationship in front of you is worth far more than a video game, a Facebook update, or a text message.

6) Consider what "on time" means to the people who are important to you and negotiate a norm for your relationship. Have an honest conversation about time and agree to a set standard for your interactions, this will help avoid feelings of hurt and even breakups in the future.

7) Consider what that outfit is telling the world about you! Are you dressed to attract the kind of people you want to attract? Are you dressing in a way that communicates accurately who you are and how you want to be perceived?

8) Consider the possibility that someone else's nonverbal communication may not be an accurate reflector of what they are feeling, so ask them. Talking doesn't hurt ... much.

Conclusion

This chapter showed you the many ways nonverbal communication functions. This chapter focused on nonverbal communication; specifically how it functions in your relationships, the types of channels we have in the nonverbal communication realm, how it differs from verbal communication, and how we can improve our nonverbal skills. I hope you use this chapter to reflect upon your own practices and improve them. Communication is a skill, which means it can be improved with practice and work. Good luck to you!

[3] Hall, E. T. (October 1963). "A system for the notation of proxemic behavior." *American Anthropologist* 65(5): 1003–1026. DOI:10.1525/aa.1963.65.5.02a00020.

Chapter 6
Emotions

By Michael Schulmeister

Let's get personal. . .

Fifteen years ago, I remember making fun of my colleague and the interpersonal communication course she taught at Bakersfield College. At the time, I was the speech and debate coach, and I prided myself on teaching the most intellectually challenging course in our department—critical thinking. When I heard her students crying or getting emotional in her classroom or office, I would tease, "What are you doing in that 'touchy-feely' interpersonal class? Your students are a mess. I will never teach that course!" In return, she would get under my skin by asking me, "Michael, how are you feeling?"

It was a very humbling experience for me when I learned that my adult children and I had some psychological deficits because I had trained my family members to suppress and repress their emotions. After going through counseling and studying the importance of emotional expression, I began teaching interpersonal communication. Learning to appreciate and express my emotions more fully has transformed my life. I want my students to experience the same psychological liberation I experienced when I got in touch with my "touchy-feely" emotions.

— Michael Schulmeister

You need to read this chapter

- To identify the sources that may cause you to suppress or repress your emotions.
- To appreciate the benefits and positive aspects of emotional expression.
- To understand how to express your emotions appropriately.

Human beings possess several important psychological powers or abilities. Figure 6.1 lists three of these abilities: (1) volition, the ability to decide or to act, (2) rationality, the ability to think or reason, and (3) emotionality, the ability to emote or feel. Therapists working with young children might describe these abilities as "your doer, your thinker, and your feeler."

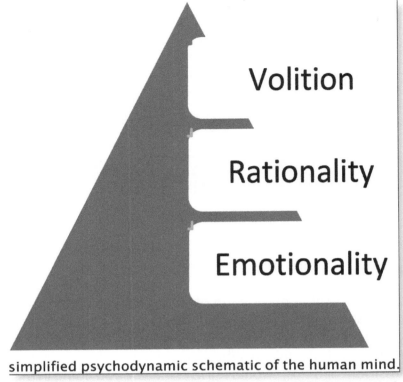

Figure 6.1 A simplified psychodynamic schematic of the human mind.

To begin this textbook chapter on emotions, we will ask you to choose which power of the mind is most important. If you had to choose between these three powers or abilities, which do think is most important for human flourishing? What is most important for human beings, their ability to make decisions and take action, or their ability to reason and think, or their ability to feel emotions and care deeply?

Good arguments can be made for the pre-eminence of each of these psychological abilities. You could argue that your volition is most important because you have the power to *choose* to think and feel or to stop thinking and feeling. You could argue that your rationality is most important because human *thoughts* are the generators of most human emotions. You could argue that emotionality is most important because your *emotions* drive your decisions and behaviors.

However, we have asked a "trick" question because human volition, rationality, and emotionality are interconnected, interdependent psychological abilities. Human minds are centers of consciousness that should be viewed holistically: although we can analyze and label the powers of the human psyche separately, in reality, they work together to create the human experience.

Whether or not emotionality is the pre-eminent power of your mind, emotional expression is a crucial component of interpersonal communication, important enough to merit an entire chapter in this textbook. In order to have successful relationships with other people, you need to be able to identify and express your emotions, and you need to be aware of the emotional states of your interpersonal communication partners.

In this chapter, you will learn the reasons why human beings sometimes suppress or repress their emotions. You will then learn the benefits and positive aspects of emotional expression. Finally, you will learn how to appropriately express your emotions, and you will also learn how to respond appropriately to the emotional expressions of others.

Emotion Defined

You will learn in this chapter that Western culture has focused much more on human rationality than human emotionality. For the past two millennia, people in Western cultures have carefully studied and discussed human thought. As a result, there is a rich vocabulary in the Western world related to human thought and intellection. It is only in the past two or three decades, however, that we have begun to focus our careful attention on human emotionality. Consequently, the academic vocabulary related to human emotion and feeling is not as developed, so it is more difficult to define emotion accurately.

The definition of human emotionality is also somewhat controversial because the exact status and nature of human beings is controversial. As we pointed out in Chapter 1, hardcore modern materialists claim that individual personhood is an illusion and that human experience is best understood from a purely physical perspective. Your subjective "inner" human experiences are best understood as objective physical brain states, and your emotions are best understood as physical states of the body.

Traditional dualists, on the other hand, view emotions as mental states originating in the mind and then manifesting themselves in the physical body. Both materialists and traditional dualists can agree, however, that emotions have a definite physical component. We define **emotions** as affective states of consciousness (distinguished from cognitive and volitional states) often accompanied by physiological changes and influencing human motivation and behavior.

Although some people make a distinction between "emotion" and "feeling," I will use these terms interchangeably in this chapter. Another term related to emotion is "mood," which often signifies a more general emotional state rather than a specific emotion. "Affect" is the technical, most encompassing term used to refer to feelings, emotions, and moods.

Emotions can be communicated both verbally and nonverbally. The nonverbal, nonvocal cues that communicate emotion most obviously are posture and facial expression. Facial expressions are the main nonverbal cues of the internal emotional state of a communicator (Figure 6.2).

Unlike other nonverbal cues (such as hand gestures) that vary widely among different cultures, facial expressions seem to have some universal similarities in all people groups. At least six basic emotions seem to be communicated with similar facial expressions in all cultures: (1) happiness, (2) sadness, (3) disgust, (4) fear, (5) anger, and (6) surprise.

In addition to being either verbal or nonverbal, emotional communication can also be conscious or unconscious. The nonverbal expression of emotion is often unconscious. People may be unaware that their posture and facial expressions are communicating their emotional state to others. Obviously, the verbal communication of human

Figure 6.2 Facial expressions are the primary nonverbal cues of emotion.

emotion is almost always conscious. When we give labels to and speak about our emotions, we are aware of our emotional state, and we are also making others aware.

It will be useful to distinguish emotional expression from both **emotional suppression** and **emotional repression**. Although the terms "suppression" and "repression" are often used interchangeably, we will use the phrase "emotional suppression" to refer to the conscious concealing or masking of emotions, especially in relation to nonverbal cues. People often suppress or hide their emotions by consciously controlling their physical bodies.

We will use the phrase "emotional repression" to refer to the unconscious stuffing of emotions. Psychoanalytic theory and therapy uses the term "repression" in this way. When people are "repressed," they may be totally out of tune with and unaware of their own emotions. When people continually suppress their emotions, they may eventually become emotionally repressed. Both emotional suppression and emotional repression can cause psychological and physical harm, but emotional repression is the more serious problem.

Reasons for Emotional Suppression and Repression

A unique characteristic of human beings is that, unlike other life forms on earth, we have emotions **about** our emotions. Pet owners are aware that their domesticated pets have first-level feelings (Figure 6.3). For example, for several years my wife and I were the proud owners of a toy poodle named "Sassy" who was obviously very happy to see us whenever we came home because she would perform a joyous "happy dance" when we walked in the door. Sassy would also become very jealous if we didn't give her our full attention, and she would become distraught and despondent when she realized that we were getting ready to leave her at home.

However, our poodle Sassy did not have second-level feelings about her feelings: although we may have sometimes been guilty of treating Sassy as if she were a human being, we never imagined that she was ashamed of her jealousy, or that she took pride in her enthusiastic displays of affection. Only we self-aware humans have the ability to feel good or bad about whatever emotions we are feeling.

Surprisingly, a large number of people do not have good feelings about their feelings. Many are afraid or ashamed of their emotions (especially strong emotions), and many become annoyed or angry with themselves when they "get emotional." As my personal story at the beginning of this chapter reveals, 12 years ago, I was one of these

Figure 6.3 Other nonhuman animals experience first-level emotions.

people. For the first four decades of my life, instead of feeling good about my feelings, I often suppressed and repressed them.

In the next section, I present a dozen different forces I have identified that cause people in modern Western societies to downplay, denigrate, or deny their emotions. As you read through the following list, I want you to consider whether these forces have shaped your attitudes about emotion and whether they have affected your ability to experience and express your emotions.

Forces Hostile to Emotion

The Dirty Dozen

1. Greek and Roman Philosophy:

Our modern culture has two influential ancient strands: the Judeo-Christian strand and the Graeco-Roman strand. Generally, ancient Greek and Roman philosophy elevated human reason and denigrated human emotion. A deep and long-standing bias against emotion was generated over 2,300 years ago in ancient Greece when Zeno of Cyprus established the school of philosophy labeled "stoicism." Stoic philosophy reached its zenith in the first and second century A.D. in Rome when it was popularized by the famous Stoics Seneca, Epictetus, and Marcus Aurelius.

According to James Mannion's guide to *Essential Philosophy* (David & Charles, 2007, p. 35), "The Stoics ... saw the passionate side of human nature as evil and something to be eradicated." The Stoic ideal was to feel nothing, especially pain and suffering. Peace of mind was to be gained by not feeling or caring. Just as we have inherited our calendar and many other cultural elements from the Romans, we have also inherited the Stoic bias against emotion. I remember when I learned the term "stoic" as a teenager. I immediately thought of my father: it seemed like he could bear almost any difficulty without giving any indication that he was hurting. I determined then to be "stoic" just like my dad. Stoicism is alive and well in modern America—it is the "tough guy" approach to handling problems. If you act like nothing bothers you, or if you think it is admirable to feel no pain no matter how difficult your situation, you are a modern-day Stoic.

2. Religious Teaching and Training:

America is often characterized as a Christian or Post-Christian nation because the Christian religion has played an important part in the formation of American culture. Although the Judeo-Christian scriptures are full of emotional expression (see the Psalms, e.g.), some Christian theological traditions denigrate emotion. The Christian theological doctrine of *impassibility*, for example, teaches that God is free from emotion and not subject to passions.

The notion of divine impassibility, the notion that God does not have emotions or passions, arose first among the Greek philosophers. Since the Greek philosophers elevated reason and rationality, they developed the concept of the divine being as an immaterial force that was pure intelligence. In an article in the April 1984 edition of the academic journal *Themelios* (*Themelios* 9.3, pp. 6–12), Professor Richard Bauckham explains how the Greek idea of divine impassibility entered into the early Christian church through the church fathers: "The idea of divine impassibility (*apatheia*) was a Greek philosophical inheritance in early Christian theology .... virtually all the Christian Fathers took it for granted, viewing with suspicion any theological tendency which might threaten the essential impassibility of the divine nature."

People from Christian traditions that teach the impassibility of God will most likely suppress and repress their emotions if they desire to be conformed to the divine being. However, Christians from other traditions may also be taught or trained to suppress or repress only certain emotions. For example, some Christian teachers may claim that the emotion of fear indicates a lack of faith in God or that the emotion of anger is sinful or unholy.

In addition to Christianity, other religions can send negative messages about emotions and emotional expression. As a young boy, one of my favorite television shows from the 1970s was "Kung Fu." In this show, the main character, a Buddhist monk named Kwai Chang Cain, wandered the American west. I admired Cain for two reasons: first, he had some really cool Kung Fu moves that he used to "take out" the bad guys; second, he almost always remained calm and serene, even when bullied by hooligans and ruffians. The television show "Kung Fu" implied that Buddhist training and meditation could help people eliminate strong emotions from their lives. Thirty years later, I still see many people influenced by this Americanized version of Buddhism. If you buy into the "Kung Fu" ideal of calmness and serenity at all times and in all situations, you have been influenced by the Western "pop culture" version of Buddhism.

3. Western Science and Scientism:

Christianity was the primary cultural influence in Europe until the rise of modern Western science in the 16th and 17th centuries. Over the past 350 years, modern science has played a larger and larger role in Western culture. Science has brought us astonishing knowledge about the natural world, and it has also produced some truly amazing technology, but the popular notion that effective scientists are dispassionate, "objective," purely rational people has further lowered the status of human emotion.

Even worse, the success of Western science has led to "scientism," a philosophy that holds up the scientific method and scientific knowledge as the only valid or reliable truth source. Knowledge based upon objective scientific observation is thought by some to be superior to other forms of "subjective" knowledge tainted by things like emotion. The idea that science is a purely rational field of knowledge devoid of emotion is largely untrue, but you may have been influenced by this myth of scientism.

4. The Enlightenment:

Many philosophers of the 18th century embraced modern science and rejected traditional Christianity. At the same time, they embraced reason and rejected emotion. They thought that emotion and religious enthusiasm had played a large part in the devastating religious wars of the 16th and 17th centuries, and they believed that a new age of progress would be ushered in if people turned away from traditional Christianity (which stirred the passions) and trusted instead in human reason.

French philosophers dubbed their time period "The Enlightenment." They felt that science and dispassionate human reason was inaugurating a bright new age in human history, the "Age of Reason." When the French Revolution occurred in 1789, the common people demonstrated how vigorously they bought into enlightenment philosophy: they toppled many of the religious statues in Notre Dame Cathedral and erected instead a statue of the goddess "Reason."

We are descendants of the Age of Reason. The modern world has adopted many enlightenment principles and ideals, including the mistaken notion that pure reason must be separated from passionate emotion. If you have ever told an emotional person that they needed to "be reasonable," you have expressed an enlightenment thought.

5. Higher Education:

Although there are a handful of college classes that emphasize the importance of emotion and emotional expression, the majority of college classes, and the majority of college instructors, seek to develop the ability to **think** rather than the ability to **feel**. Although critical thinking is often stressed and evaluated, there is no general education requirement for passionate feeling. Unfortunately, thinking and feeling are often presented as if they were at odds with each other.

Too often, college students are given the impression that feeling emotion will get in the way of thinking clearly. I have spent over 25 years in higher education—10 years as a college student and 15 years as a college instructor—and I can testify that there is a strong bias against emotion in most college classes. As a critical thinking instructor, I have (in the past) promoted this bias, often characterizing arguments that contained emotional appeals as "fallacious."

If college students express strong emotions verbally or in writing, they are often sent the message that they have not carefully thought through the issue at hand. They can easily pick up the idea that critical thinking must be free from emotion. If you have attended college, you have probably been exposed to this educational bias against emotion.

6. Certain Schools of Psychology:

Although human emotion is a primary focus in the field of psychology, not all schools of psychology promote positive views of emotion. Freudian psychology, for example, has little to say about positive, healthy human emotions. Sigmund Freud was one the most famous and influential psychologist of the 20th century. Even people who have never studied Freudian psychology have had some exposure to Freudian concepts such as the "Id," the "Ego," and the "Oedipus Complex."

Modern society owes a great debt to Sigmund Freud because he pointed out the importance of the unconscious mind. However, Freud had a very negative view of the drives and emotions that were contained in the unconscious mind. Freud presents human beings as creatures driven by unhealthy, socially unacceptable feelings and primal urges that must be repressed. If you are reluctant to examine your emotions, if you are afraid to look inside yourself because you suspect that you are driven by harmful primal urges, then you have probably been influenced by Freudian psychology.

Evolutionary psychology is another psychological school that can promote negative feelings about feelings. If *Homo sapiens* are distinguished from "lower" life forms by a capacity for rationality that results from a more highly evolved brain, then emotions can be viewed as leftover, primitive survival mechanisms. Lower animal life forms first developed basic emotions to aid the animal processes of territoriality, predation, and reproduction, and human emotion is just an evolutionary refinement of these basic animal emotions. Some evolutionary psychologists claim that when you are enraged, for example, you are being influenced or sabotaged by your "lizard brain."

Let's get personal. . .

I remember the anxiety that my son and I both experienced when we realized that we would need to seek psychological counseling for our suppressed and repressed emotions. As we sat on the street curb near our house, my son said to me, "I don't want to see a psychiatrist. What if I discover that I have terrible things inside of me?" "I know," I replied, "I am afraid too. Perhaps we will discover that we have murderous rage, or something worse, inside of us." Obviously, Freudian psychology had a strong influence on our thoughts and feelings about psychiatric therapy.

— *Michael Schulmeister*

7. Ethnic and Cultural Conditioning:

When we are born into this world, we are born into a particular culture and a particular ethnic group. Different cultures and different ethnic groups react differently to the expression of emotion. Some cultures and ethnic groups encourage emotionality and emotional expression, whereas other cultures and ethnic groups discourage emotionality and displays of emotion.

In the early 2000s, Mitchell R. Hammer developed an intercultural "conflict management styles" chart that recognizes four conflict management styles. The four conflict management styles he identifies and describes are determined by two variables: first, whether a person prefers to address a conflict directly or indirectly; second, whether a person prefers to address a conflict with emotional restraint or with emotional expressiveness.

The two conflict management styles that encourage and expect emotional expression are called the "engagement" style and the "dynamic" style. People who use the engagement style want to address conflict directly, but they also expect the people involved in a conflict to become emotionally engaged. A strong display of emotion, they believe, demonstrates that a person cares about the matter at hand. The engagement style of conflict management is the dominant style in Greece, Italy, and many Latin American countries. (It is also the dominant style of African Americans in the United States.) Many Greeks, Italians, and Latin Americans value direct discourse that is animated and punctuated by strong emotional displays. They are willing to "get in your face" in order to make their point, and they expect you to be just as passionate when you express your viewpoint or position (Figure 6.4).

People who use the dynamic style avoid the direct discussion of conflict, but they also expect people to express strong emotions. Their interest in strong relationships causes them to avoid

	Preference for Emotional Restraint	Preference for Emotional Expressiveness
Preference for Directness	Discussion Style (Country: US)	Engagement Style (Country: Italy)
Preference for Indirectness	Accommodation Style (Country: Japan)	Dynamic Style (Country: Saudi Arabia)

Figure 6.4 Hammer's four conflict management styles.

conflicts which may threaten these relationships, but they want to signal sincerity and commitment to their principles through the strong display of emotions. The dynamic style of conflict is the dominant style in Saudi Arabia and many other Arab countries. Many Saudis and other Arabs avoid "spelling out" the precise issues or concerns that they think may destabilize their political or social relationships, but they value animated, emotional verbal discourse and nonverbal displays.

The two conflict management styles that discourage and avoid emotional displays are the "discussion" style and the "accommodation" style. People who use the discussion style prefer to address conflict directly, but they avoid the open display of emotion. They want to "talk things out" in a "reasonable" manner. The discussion style of conflict management is the dominant style in England and the United States. Many British and American people value frank, direct discourse and cool, calm deliberation. They like to address problems head-on, but they may get uncomfortable if a conversation gets heated or emotionally charged.

People who use the accommodation style do not like to address conflict directly, nor do they like strong displays of emotion. They prefer to address conflict indirectly in order to "save face," and they strive to maintain a calm, "inscrutable" demeanor that reveals little of their inward state, especially if they are angry or upset. The accommodation style of conflict management is the dominant style in Japan and many Southeast Asian countries. Many Japanese people and other Southeast Asians value verbal discourse that appears harmonious, and they expect people to pay attention to subtle nonverbal signals which indicate disagreement and dissatisfaction. They often find it very difficult to express an opinion that contradicts the opinions of others in their group, and they also find it very difficult to display an emotion that they think may threaten the cohesiveness of their group. My last name is Staller, so I have a German ethnic background. Germans, like Americans, prefer the discussion style of conflict management that avoids displays of strong emotion. My German-American cultural conditioning helps to explain, in part, my reluctance to communicate my emotions to others. You need to consider your own cultural background and conditioning when thinking about your attitude toward emotional expression.

8. Masculine Stereotypes:

Psychotherapist Marvin Allen worked with many men who had totally "numbed out" their feelings—these men were unable to feel any emotion at all, even though they knew they should. These men had consciously *suppressed* their emotions so often that these emotions were eventually *repressed*: like a spring of water gone dry, these men were no longer capable of experiencing any emotion at all. When Allen asked why emotional repression was more common in men than in women, he discovered a host of societal messages that conditioned men to shut down their emotions. Marvin Allen shares his insights about masculine conditioning and masculine stereotypes in his book *Angry Men, Passive Men* (Ballantine Books, 1993).

According to Allen, men in American society are assigned three traditional roles—providing, protecting, and procreating. In order to fill those masculine roles, especially the first two, little boys must learn to repress more of their emotions than little girls. I would like to share an insightful passage from pages 6 and 7 of Allen's book:

"Our culture maintains—and rightly so—that men are more efficient workers and warriors when they are not inconvenienced by tender feelings. To this end boys are raised according to a masculine code, a complex set of beliefs that influences how they think, feel, and behave. The masculine code is not taught through institutional or formal means. Boys learn how to be men by absorbing the thousands of messages about manliness that filter down to them through parents, siblings, peers, ministers, teachers, scout leaders, comic books, cartoons, TV shows, action movies, and commercials. Taken as a whole, these messages encourage boys to be competitive, focus on external success, rely on their intellect, withstand physical pain, and **repress their vulnerable emotions** (emphasis added)."

If you are a male and have been raised in American society, your thoughts and feelings about emotion have been influenced by masculine conditioning and masculine stereotypes.

9. The Women's Liberation Movement:

The women's liberation movement begun in America in the late 1960s was supposed to free women from rigid female stereotypes and allow them to compete with men on an equal footing. Radical feminists declared that there were really no substantial differences between men and women, and they demanded that women be liberated from their confining "feminine" roles.

Unfortunately, when women entered the workforce in large numbers, many merely exchanged the traditional female stereotypes for the traditional male stereotypes: in order to make it in a "man's world," women tried to out-male the males. Women were told that in order to compete with men, they would have to "be tough" and stifle their feelings. Rather than insisting that men learn how to appreciate and nurture their emotional lives, many women hopped on the male bandwagon.

Decades after the women's liberation movement was first initiated, female executives are still being coached to eliminate any obvious signs of their femininity, including overt emotional displays. Female workers and supervisors are often expected to suppress their emotions, just as male workers and leaders have done for hundreds of years. If you are female and have been "liberated" to work outside the home, you have most likely felt the pressure to "act more like a man" in the way you experience and express emotion.

10. Business World Expectations:

Many of us spend 40 hours or more a week on the job, so our work life has a huge influence on the way we process and express our emotions. We leave our homes in the morning and spend the majority of our day in a world of work that is no friend to feeling.

If you are a blue-collar worker, you are expected to "suck it up" and do hard physical labor for several hours with little or no time for emotional expression. You must tune out your feelings and focus on the task at hand. Your bosses or supervisors often have no interest in how you are feeling—they just want you to get the job done. If you are a white-collar worker, you are expected to be "professional" and mask almost any "negative" emotion that you may be feeling, such as anger or fear. It is not "professional" to talk about these feelings or give any indication that you are experiencing them.

Several years ago I served on a hiring committee for one of our college administrative positions. When one of the candidates, a senior administrator at another college, was asked to share his important job qualifications, he told the hiring committee, "No one can ever tell when something gets under my skin." He was quite proud of his ability to act like he never got frustrated, annoyed, or upset!

In businesses with an emphasis on customer service, workers are trained to have smiles on their faces, regardless of how they are actually feeling. Although the "happy face" rule may benefit the company's bottom line, it obviously is not a good way to encourage authentic emotional expression. If you have ever been told that your display of emotion at work was inappropriate or "unprofessional," you have been influenced by the expectations of the business world.

11. Family Training:

Why are people ashamed of their emotions? One reason is that they were trained by their parents or caregivers to feel shame about emotions that truly are not shameworthy. They may have been told, "Big boys don't cry," or "Don't be a scaredy-cat," or "Only dogs get mad." Maybe the people that said these things had good intentions, but their words generated, and continue to generate, shame about ever feeling sadness, fear, or anger. Some people even feel shame about experiencing positive emotions such as joy or happiness because they were told when younger, "Wipe that smile off your face," or "Don't be so giddy!"

Some adults become annoyed or angry with themselves when they become emotional, in part, because the voices that trained them to feel shame about their emotions have been internalized. They no longer need an outside source to create negative feelings about their emotions; instead, their own negative inner voice beats up on them whenever they experience strong emotions. Their inner critic speaks up and chastises the "weakling" who "gave in" to emotion.

I think that if you asked most people to describe my family 12 years ago, they would have used words like "nice" and "loving." Since my wife and I both had had fairly chaotic childhoods, we had worked hard to create a loving, stable home for our two children. However, we were not good at expressing, or allowing our children to express, any "negative" emotions. When my children were younger and started to fight, I would scold them and tell them to be "nice" to each other. Instead of letting them learn to air their differences of opinion and their strong feelings, I would continually intervene and play the part of peacemaker. In addition, whenever my children were unhappy or sad, I felt it was my job to cheer them up and make them feel better. I did not realize that my role of "Mr. Fix It" made it almost impossible for my kids to express or be comfortable with feelings of sadness.

I would like to share another quotation from Allen's book *Angry Men, Passive Men* (found on page 6) which explains how family training contributes to emotional suppression: "In our culture parents tend to discourage so-called 'negative emotions' such as fear, sadness, and anger. We harbor a naïve belief that if we can make our children *act* happy and well behaved, they will become truly happy and well-adjusted adults." If your parents and caregivers acted as emotion "dismissers" instead of emotion coaches, then your family training has influenced you to suppress and repress your emotions.

12. Personal Experience:

In addition to various cultural influences, your past experiences may lead to emotional suppression or repression. If you experienced very strong emotions in the past, you may have felt "out of control." For example, my public speaking students are surprised to discover that their public speaking anxiety can cause their hearts to race, their palms to get sweaty, and their arms and legs to shake. Some feel as if their fear of public speaking had taken over their bodies and turned them into stuttering, stumbling idiots, and they want to avoid ever experiencing such fear again.

The strong emotion that most often makes us feel "out of control," though, is anger or rage. When a rage surge courses through your body, you may start to shake, and you may even "black out" from anger. The comic book character "The Incredible Hulk" taps into our fear of out-of-control anger: whenever mild-mannered Richard Bannister becomes angry, he transforms into the raging green beast, The Hulk.

In addition to the disconcerting involuntary physical effects created by strong emotions, we also fear what we might do while we are under the influence of these emotions. Our legal system, after all, has a category for crimes committed while feeling strong emotions—crimes of passion. If you have ever truly lost control under the influence of a passionate feeling and done something you regretted, then you may fear ever feeling this emotion again. Some people who have experienced emotional trauma shut down the feeling part of their heart in a desperate act of self-preservation. They think that the emotional trauma they endured was so unbearable they can never risk feeling again. Other people remember a time when they opened their heart and honestly expressed their feelings only to have someone they respected or cared about invalidate or even reject these feelings. They may be reluctant to ever share their deep feelings again. Other people have never learned how to appropriately express their emotions. When they are emotional, they may say hurtful or embarrassing things to other people, or they may act inappropriately. If they do not realize that their lack of knowledge is the real problem, they may think that their emotions are the source of their inappropriate comments and actions.

If you carry painful emotional memories that have not been fully processed, you may be suppressing and denying your current feelings. If you have been criticized or shamed for "getting emotional" or expressing strong emotions, you may now hide or camouflage your emotions. If you say and do inappropriate things when you are experiencing emotion, you may be tempted to stifle your feelings instead of taking the time (and making the effort) to learn how to express them effectively.

Self-Assessment

After reading through the "dirty dozen" list of forces undermining your ability to feel good about feeling, you should now understand why you may be tempted to suppress or repress your emotions. From the time we are little children, the process of emotional suppression and repression is begun. We may be teased and shamed about our feelings by our parents, our siblings, and our playmates. As we grow older, some of us are trained to suppress and hide our emotions by our teachers and classmates. When we enter the work force, some of us are encouraged to shut down our feelings by our bosses and co-workers.

When we are at home, we may be encouraged not to feel. When we are at school, we may be encouraged not to feel. When we are at work, we may be encouraged not to feel. When we are at church or in a temple or synagogue, we may be encouraged not to feel. When we are watching a television show or reading a magazine, we may be encouraged not to feel. Have you taken the time to analyze how these many different cultural influences have affected **your** ability to feel and express emotion? If you think I have been exaggerating the effect of these cultural forces, then put my ideas to the test and consider your own life. Which cultural influences have had little or no impact on your ability to emote? Which cultural influences have had some impact? Which cultural influences have definitely made it difficult for you to recognize or share your feelings?

A SELF-ASSESSMENT

Determine whether each cultural influence or life experience has affected your ability to experience or express emotion (1) not at all, (2) very little, (3) somewhat, (4) a lot, or (5) quite a lot.

1.	Greek and Roman Philosophy	1	2	3	4	5
2.	Religious Teaching and Training	1	2	3	4	5
3.	Western Science and Scientism	1	2	3	4	5
4.	The Enlightenment	1	2	3	4	5
5.	Higher Education	1	2	3	4	5
6.	Certain Schools of Psychology	1	2	3	4	5
7.	Ethnic and Cultural Conditioning	1	2	3	4	5
8.	Masculine Stereotypes	1	2	3	4	5
9.	The Women's Liberation Movement	1	2	3	4	5
10.	Business World Expectations	1	2	3	4	5
11.	Family Training	1	2	3	4	5
12.	Personal Experience	1	2	3	4	5

The Benefits of Emotional Expression

This next textbook section is designed to counteract the cultural forces and life experiences that may have influenced you to suppress and repress your emotions. I want to encourage you to fully experience your emotions and to practice a healthy, necessary life skill—emotional expression. Note that this section of your textbook does not contain objective expository writing: since my specific target audience is people who (like myself for many years of my life) are out of touch and uncomfortable with many of their emotions, I will use persuasive prose to convince reluctant emoters that they have much to gain by fully experiencing and expressing their emotions.

Although objective scientific language can deepen our understanding of emotion by employing carefully defined terms, it cannot effectively inspire. For example, are you inspired when I tell you that emotions are the affective aspect of consciousness subjectively experienced as strong feeling usually directed toward a specific object and typically accompanied by physiological and behavioral changes in the body?

The above "scientific" language about emotion may be precise, but it cannot be easily set to music. In order to inspire reluctant emoters, I think it will be more appropriate to use some poetic devices—metaphor, simile, personification, and maybe even some hyperbole. As I wax eloquent about our emotions, I hope you will join in the celebration. It will not harm you if you spend some time focusing on the positive aspects of your emotions: on the contrary, appreciating your emotions and the important part they play in your life may help you to experience personal growth and physical and psychological health.

Obviously, there are pitfalls and problems we must watch out for in our emotional life, just as there are pitfalls and problems in all the other areas of our life. In the final section of this chapter, I will point out some of the negative things that can occur if we do not express our emotions appropriately. For now, though, let us accentuate the positive and not feel guilty about feeling good about our feelings. So, are you ready to celebrate? Let us take time to appreciate a powerful force in our lives—the emotions.

Emotion Is Energy

Over the years, we have learned how to harness various forms of energy to power our technological gadgets—thermal energy, wind energy, solar energy, electro-magnetic energy, and nuclear energy. However, long before we exploited these energy sources, human beings have relied on another energy source to power our psyches—emotion (Figure 6.5).

In his book *The Family* (Health Communications, Inc., 1996), counselor John Bradshaw often places a hyphen in the word "emotion:" he writes that we have e-motions, and then he explains that an e-motion is an energy in motion. Think about it—aren't you energized by your emotions? Although a serious depression will sap our strength, most primary emotions course through our body and give us enormous amounts of energy. The energy of fear lets us run swiftly away from danger. The energy of anger lets us stand our ground and fight for what is ours. The energy of joy sets our feet to dancing and causes us to break out into song.

Figure 6.5 Emotions are an important psychic energy source.

Emotions have the power to stir our hearts and move us to action. People can know with their intellect that they should take some course of action, but still not act. If their hearts are stirred enough, though, they can find the power to do what they know they should do.

The English noun *emotion* is derived from the French verb *emouvoir*, which means "to stir up." The French verb *emouvoir* is derived, in turn, from the Latin verb *emovere*, and the root of this Latin verb means "to move." This same Latin root which means "to move" is found, significantly, in the words *motion*, *emotion*, and *motivation*. Our emotions motivate us to get moving! Even people that don't know a lick of Latin somehow comprehend that emotions are powerful drivers of the psyche. What do people often say after hearing a stirring motivational speech or reading an emotionally powerful essay? They say, "That really moved me," or, "That was very moving."

If you are failing to make progress in a field of study or an occupation, you are probably also failing to feel deeply. If, however, you can find a job or an area of knowledge that you are passionate about, your enthusiasm and zeal will give you all the drive and energy you need to pursue your goals until you succeed.

If you feel that your emotions are "draining" you, then you are probably expending a lot of your psychic and physical energy trying to suppress and mask them. It takes a lot of effort to fight or camouflage your feelings. If, instead, you let your emotional energy flow, you will discover an incredible personal power source.

Modern psychology and modern medicine have teamed up and discovered that many physical ailments actually have psychological causes. Some bodily ailments are not caused by environmental factors outside the body, but by mental and emotional problems in the mind. Our soul (psyche) and our body (soma) are linked together in an intimate psychosomatic relationship. If we do not allow ourselves to experience and express our emotions, we can make ourselves physically ill.

If you are reluctant to accept my assertion that experiencing and expressing your emotions is crucial to your psychological and physical well-being, perhaps you will accept this assertion when it comes from a recognized and respected medical expert. Dr. Norman B. Anderson has been Chief Executive Officer of the American Psychological Association (APA), the largest scientific and professional association in the world. He also served as the first Associate Director of the National Institutes of Health, the federal government's main health-research arm. While working as a professor at Harvard University's School of Public Health, he published a groundbreaking book in 2003 called *Emotional Longevity (What REALLY Determines How Long You Live)* (Viking Penguin).

Dr. Anderson asserts that we need a new definition of "health" that gives an exalted position to our emotions and their ability to increase longevity. According to Dr. Anderson, emotions play a key role in our physical health. His main message is that you need to pay attention to your emotions if you want to live longer: they are more important factors for your overall health than cholesterol, body mass, or blood pressure.

The importance of emotions for human life and health was dramatically illustrated in an article I read in my doctor's office a while ago. The medical intern who wrote the article reported that an elderly man came in to the hospital for treatment. When the intern asked the man what his symptoms were, the man replied, "I am dead." The surprised intern took the man's pulse (yes, he did have a pulse!) and asked again what the man's problem was. The old man looked balefully into the intern's eyes and said again, "I am dead."

As the intern carried out a medical interview, the old man's words started to make sense. Six months before, his wife of many years had passed away. The man had gone into a serious

Figure 6.6 Clinical depression can drain you and rob you of your ability to emote.

depression. His depression had robbed him of his ability to feel, and this inability to emote made the man feel like a walking corpse. Clinical depression is not merely "sadness," it is like a black hole that sucks the life and energy out of a person (Figure 6.6).

Emotions Are Like Colors

Imagine seeing a sunset in black and white. You would have difficulty distinguishing the white of the clouds from the various shades of gray in the evening sky. Now imagine the same sunset in brilliant color. What before was merely blurs of white mixed together with smudges of gray is transformed into a panorama that takes your breath away: brilliant shades of purple, red, and orange are subtly mixed together in an amazing display of beauty.

The colorful sunset represents a life filled with emotions. Emotions "color" our lives and make them enjoyable (Figure 6.7). Although we may sometimes wish that we did not have to deal with our feelings, a life without emotion would be drab and dull.

Comparing emotion to color is not much of a stretch, because we already associate specific emotions with specific colors. When we are angry, we are "seeing red." When we are sad, we are "feeling blue." When we are jealous, we are being attacked by the "green monster." When we are afraid, we are accused of being "yellow."

Note that our strong or "primary" emotions are assigned primary colors. One step you can take to appreciate your emotions more and to express your emotions more effectively is to increase your conscious awareness of the number of emotions on your "emotional palette" (Figure 6.8). Did you know that psychologists have identified and labeled over 150 different human emotions?

Unfortunately, many of us cannot appreciate or verbally express our many emotions because we have not moved very far beyond the basic emotional vocabulary of "mad," "sad," "bad," and "glad." Although the intense primary emotions are important, we should not overlook other softer, subtler emotions. Some emotions are primary, some emotions are neon, and other emotions are pastel.

Figure 6.7 Emotions color our lives and make them more enjoyable.

Figure 6.8 There are many different emotions in your "emotional palette."

Do you appreciate the fact that you can feel … afraid, aggravated, agitated, amazed, ambivalent, amused, angry, annoyed, anxious, apathetic, appreciative, apprehensive, ashamed, awed, bashful, bewildered, bitter, blissful, bored, brave, calm, cantankerous, carefree, cheerful, cocky, concerned, confident, confused, contented, contemptuous, cranky, crushed, curious, cynical, defeated, defensive, dejected, delighted, delirious, depressed, detached, determined, devastated, disappointed, discouraged, disgusted, disheartened, disturbed, ecstatic, edgy, elated, embarrassed, empty, enraged, enthralled, enthusiastic, envious, euphoric, excited, exhausted, exuberant, fearful, fidgety, flabbergasted, flattered, foolish, frazzled, frustrated, fulfilled, furious, gleeful, giddy, glum, grateful, gratified, greedy, grouchy, happy, hateful, helpless, homesick, hopeful, horrible, hostile, humiliated, hurt, hysterical, impatient, impressed, indignant, infatuated, infuriated, inhibited, insecure, irate, irritable, jaded, jealous, joyful, jubilant, lazy, lonely, lukewarm, melancholic, miserable, mortified, nervous, nostalgic, numb, optimistic, outraged, panicky, paranoid, passionate, peaceful, perturbed, petrified, pessimistic, playful, pleased, possessive, protective, proud, puzzled, regretful, relieved, resentful, resigned, resolved, restless, ridiculous, satisfied, scornful, selfish, sentimental, shameful, shocked, shy, somber, sorry, subdued, surprised, suspicious, tender, tense, terrified, thrilled, tired, troubled, uneasy, unhappy, upset, vengeful, vulnerable, weak, wonderful, and worried?

Like colors, emotions can be more or less intense. Some of the terms in the emotion list above refer to the same emotion, but they describe different intensities of that emotion. For example, just as the color green can be dark green, green, and light green, the emotion of anger can be more or less intense.

Since I am not a painter or very artistic, I am unaware of the many shades of green, and I am unable to appreciate and describe all these different shades. Due to my lack of knowledge and sensitivity regarding color, my aesthetic experience when I look at a nature painting will not be as deep or as meaningful as the experience of a person who is well-versed in the many shades and hues of green. They can recognize and appreciate the appearance of emerald green, forest green, lime green, olive green, and so on (Figure 6.9).

Similarly, some people have a limited understanding of and appreciation for their emotions, and they have a limited ability to express their emotions, because they do not have the words to describe different intensities of the same emotion. For example, when some people get angry, they may say that they are "pissed" regardless of the intensity of their anger. They are not able to express different degrees of anger, such as feeling peeved, perturbed, angry, enraged, and livid. To more effectively communicate their emotions, they need to expand their emotional vocabulary so that they do not understate or overstate their emotions.

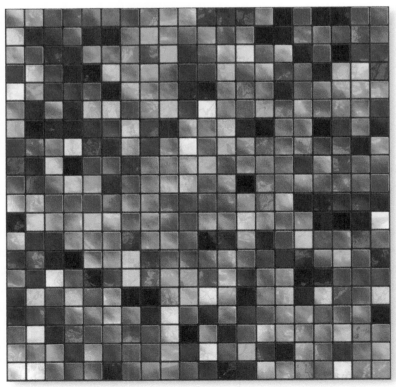

Figure 6.9 Some people can recognize many different shades and hues of green.

Emotions Are Signs

When you turn on the ignition of your car, what do you look at to make sure your car is in good running order? If you are responsible for the upkeep of your vehicle, you pay attention to the gauges on your dashboard. These gauges indicate the amount of fuel in your gas tank, the oil pressure, and the temperature of your engine. It is foolish to ignore the gauges and indicator lights in an automobile. What would you think of people who placed duct tape over the gauges on their dashboard so they wouldn't be distracted by those pesky indicator arrows? They would have no way of knowing when their oil pressure was dropping, their engine was overheating, or their gas tank was almost empty (Figure 6.10).

Likewise, it is just as foolish for us to ignore our emotions and the signals they are sending about our internal psychological state. We need to respect and pay attention to our emotions because they give us important diagnostic information about ourselves.

Because our emotions are usually manifested in our bodies, they are physical indicators of what we are thinking and feeling. For example, when we think something is dangerous, we get afraid and our knees buckle and our throat goes dry. When we think an injustice has occurred, we get angry and our jaw tightens and our fists clench. When we realize that our plans are unfolding, we get calm and our body relaxes.

Instead of *tuning out* or *numbing out* our emotions and their physical symptoms, we need to *tune in* to our emotions and their bodily manifestations in order to discover what is going on inside our mind. One thing modern psychology has revealed to us is that the human psyche is complicated. Not only is it difficult to know what is going on inside someone else's mind or heart; we even have difficulty figuring out what is going on inside our own mind and heart! In the words of Blaise Pascal, "The heart has its reasons which reason knows not of."

Haven't you ever said that you wanted to do one thing, but then found yourself doing something else? Haven't you ever wanted to accomplish something, but then found that for some reason you had a "mental block?" If you are to have any success in learning what makes yourself tick, you are going to have to pay attention to your emotions. Emotions are an important source

Figure 6.10 Like the gauges in a car, your emotions are signals to be respected.

of self-knowledge. And contrary to what you may have been told, you **can** trust your emotions. You are truly feeling whatever you are feeling, so it doesn't make sense to lie to yourself or other people about your emotions.

What you **cannot** trust are all of the *thoughts* which are responsible for generating your feelings. Cognitive psychology has revealed that many of our psychological and behavioral problems come from "stinking thinking." Many harmful, inaccurate, or even totally false thoughts are contained in our unconscious mind. These thoughts can cause us to feel things and do things that we do not really want to feel or do.

For example, someone gives you a sincere compliment, but instead of feeling good about the compliment, you feel embarrassed and uncomfortable and quickly slink away. What has happened? Certainly the sincere compliment is not the cause of your emotion. Rather, what you *thought* while receiving the compliment is the source of your embarrassment. You may have thought, "No one could really think well of me," or, "People who take pleasure in their accomplishments are proud." Whatever the thought you had—this is responsible for the embarrassment you feel.

So how can we root out negative, inaccurate, untrue thoughts? We will never even get close to identifying these thoughts if we ignore our feelings. No matter how uncomfortable a feeling is, we need to acknowledge what we are feeling when we are feeling it, and then we need to ask ourselves why we are feeling that way. When we ask ourselves why an emotion is being experienced, the answer will lead us to an inner thought that we can modify or reject, if appropriate.

Emotions Are Friends, Not Foes

For millennia, people in Western societies have been treating emotions as if they were the enemies of rational thought. At the beginning of the 21st century, modern psychologists and neurologists are helping us to understand that when it comes to rational thinking and decision making, emotions are friends, not foes (Figure 6.11).

In his book *Descartes' Error (Emotion, Reason, and the Human Brain)* (G.P. Putnam's Sons, 1994), Neurologist Antonio R. Damasio destroys long-held beliefs about the necessity of separating reason and emotion. His research demonstrates that emotions are essential to rational thinking, and that the absence of emotion can lead to poor thinking and decision making.

Damasio begins his book with a fascinating account of a man named Phineas P. Gage. In the summer of 1848, Phineas Gage was involved in a terrible accident: a three-foot iron rod entered his left cheek, passed through his skull and the front part of his brain, and exited through

Figure 6.11 Stop fighting your emotions as if they were foes or enemies.

the top of his head. What was so amazing about this accident was that Gage did not *seem* to be seriously effected: he could still walk, talk, calculate, and reason. He was pronounced cured in 2-months' time. However, it soon became apparent that something was drastically wrong: Phineas Gage was no longer able to make good decisions. He hung out with the wrong people, acted erratically, and died a few years later penniless and dissolute.

Damasio spends three chapters of his book on Gage's story because the only part of Gage's brain that had been injured was the part that processed emotions. In his work with dozens of patients with similar neurological problems, Damasio has been able to prove that without the ability to process emotion, human beings cannot make reasonable and rational decisions.

In his book *Emotional Intelligence* (Bantam Books, 1997, p. 28), Daniel Goleman describes Dr. Damasio's patients: "Their decision-making is terribly flawed—and yet they show no deterioration at all in IQ or any cognitive ability. Despite their intact intelligence, they make disastrous choices in business and their personal lives, and can even obsess endlessly over a decision so simple as when to make an appointment."

Goleman goes on to draw the following conclusions: "The emotions, then, matter for rationality. In the dance of feeling and thought the emotional faculty guides our moment-to-moment decisions, working hand-in-hand with the rational mind. . . . This turns the old understanding of the tension between reason and feeling on its head: it is not that we want to do away with emotion and put reason in its place . . . but instead [we must] find the intelligent balance of the two. The old paradigm held an ideal of reason freed of the pull of emotion (Figure 6.12). The new paradigm urges us to harmonize head and heart (Figure 6.13)."

Daniel Goleman's book *Emotional Intelligence* has made a substantial impact on businesses and corporations throughout America. Goleman describes "emotional intelligence" as a number of competencies: recognizing and describing feelings; seeing the links between thoughts, feelings, and reactions; knowing if thoughts or feelings are ruling a decision; learning ways to handle anxieties, anger, and sadness; empathizing with others; and respecting differences in how people feel about things. Goleman goes on to claim that emotional intelligence is more important than IQ in predicting job success. If you want to succeed at work, the latest research indicates you cannot afford to ignore your emotions or treat them as enemies to rational thought.

Figure 6.12 The old dichotomy.

Figure 6.13 The new realization.

The successful employee (and boss) of the future will be expected to express emotions accurately and deal with a variety of emotions effectively.

It is important to realize that all of your emotions are "friends," not just the so-called "positive" emotions. Although some interpersonal communication textbooks, and some psychologists, classify emotions as either "positive" or "negative," I will avoid using this classification system because it may encourage some people to suppress or repress so-called "negative" emotions.

So-called "negative" emotions are sometimes appropriate and necessary. It is appropriate and necessary to experience and express sadness and sorrow during the grieving process. The expression of anger may be perfectly justifiable and appropriate when someone is addressing a serious social or moral injustice. Fear and suspicion are appropriate emotional responses when interacting with a truly dangerous person.

Rather than thinking of your emotions as "positive" or "negative," we encourage you to think of your emotions as "facilitative" or "debilitative," helpful or harmful. When you experience your emotions at the right time and in the right amount, they are facilitative or helpful. If your emotions are experienced at too great an intensity or for too long a duration, they can become debilitative or harmful. Expressing your emotions effectively can help you to process them so that they do not become debilitative.

Emotions Are Relational Bonding Agents

When we acknowledge and share our emotions with other people, and when we allow others to share their feelings with us, we activate a powerful relational "bonding agent" (Figure 6.14). Conversely, if we hold back our emotions from other people, and if we deny people the opportunity to share their feelings, we prevent deep relational intimacy.

Why do shared emotions bond people together? One reason is that people's emotions are uniquely their own. When you share your emotions with another person, you are sharing an intimate part of yourself. Emotions are *personal*, so two people that share their emotions together create an inter*personal* relationship.

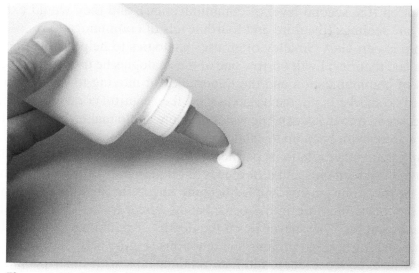

Figure 6.14 Appropriately shared emotions can bind people together.

The wonderful thing about sharing emotions is that almost any shared emotion will create deeper intimacy. If you share silliness and laughter with someone, your relationship will be strengthened. If you share tears and grief with someone, your relationship will be strengthened. Even if you share anger and frustration with someone, your relationship will be strengthened. As long as these emotions are expressed and acknowledged appropriately, the relationship will be strengthened.

Another reason shared emotions bond people together is that revealing feeling demonstrates a willingness to be vulnerable and to trust. If I share with you the fact that I am feeling fearful, then I am making myself vulnerable, and I am trusting that you will not use this information against me. Sharing emotion is risky, but taking this risk demonstrates trust, and trust is a basic building block for any solid relationship (Figure 6.15).

There are five standard "levels of communication" recognized in the field of interpersonal communication: people can share (1) clichés, (2) facts, (3) opinions, (4) emotions, or (5) hopes and dreams. These five levels of communication are hierarchical, going from the shallowest level of communication (clichés) to the deepest level of communication (sharing hopes and dreams).

Cliché communication allows us to initiate conversations with strangers and people we do not know very well. It is a "safe" form of communication because formulaic responses are expected. You say, "Hi, How is it going?" to someone, and you expect them to reply with a phrase like, "Not bad." These safe clichés help us to get through the awkward stage when we are getting to know people, or they allow us to interact with people that we do not really want to get to know.

However, it would be strange and inappropriate if you used only clichés when speaking to your intimate relational partners. They would expect you to communicate on the deeper levels of communication. They would expect you to go beyond just sharing clichés (the first level of communication) and

Five Levels of Communication
1. Clichés
2. Facts
3. Opinions
4. Emotions
5. Hopes and dreams

Figure 6.15 Sharing emotion is a fairly deep and intimate communication act.

factual information (the second level of communication), and they would expect you to share your thoughts and feelings (the third and fourth levels of communication).

Relationship expert Gary Smalley often uses analogies to help people understand interpersonal concepts and theories; I will borrow one of the analogies he uses to help people understand the five levels of communication and the importance of moving to the deeper levels. Imagine that you want to go snorkeling in the ocean to view the beautiful coral reefs that are on the ocean floor. As you descend into the ocean, the water pressure could make you uncomfortable, and you might be tempted to swim back up to shallower water.

When couples and other relational partners reach the third level of communication (the sharing of opinions), disagreements and differences of opinion may occur, and strong emotions may be generated. At this point, many couples become uncomfortable, and (like snorklers uncomfortable with the water pressure in the ocean) they retreat to the shallow "cliché" and "fact" levels of communication. They never reach the depths of relational intimacy because they are not comfortable sharing strong opinions and emotions (Figure 6.16).

If you want to experience deep, intimate relationships with other people, you must learn to share your thoughts and feelings, and you must learn to accept and validate the emotions of others. Shared emotions act as relational bonding agents only when they are expressed and acknowledged appropriately. In the final section of this chapter, we will give you some specific guidelines for appropriate emotional expression. We will end this second section with a poetic summary of the inspirational insights we have offered to emphasize the benefits and positive aspects of emotion:

> **Emotions are forms of energy. Let them flow.**
> **Emotions are like colors. Appreciate them.**
> **Emotions are signs. Respect them.**
> **Emotions are friends, not foes. Accept them.**
> **Emotions are bonding agents. Acknowledge them.**

Figure 6.16 You must dive deep to see the beauty on the ocean floor.

Guidelines for Expressing Emotion

We will wrap up this chapter on emotion by giving you some guidelines and tips for expressing emotion appropriately and effectively:

- Identify and label the emotions that you are feeling. Allow yourself to fully feel your emotions. If you are not sure what emotions you are feeling, pay attention to your body. If you still cannot identify your emotions, ask someone else to observe you as you discuss your feelings. They may be able to identify your emotions by your facial expressions, posture, and your paralanguage (your voice rate, pitch, volume, etc.).

- Analyze your emotions. Emotions are outward signs of inward perceptions and thoughts. Explore the thoughts and perceptions that are creating your emotions. If you are experiencing very strong emotions (such as indignation and outrage), you can determine if they are justified and appropriate by identifying the perceptions and thoughts that are generating these emotions. If your perceptions and thoughts are accurate and true, then your strong emotions may be perfectly appropriate.

- Share your feelings with your close relational partners. Remember that emotional communication is one of the deepest levels of communication that exists. If you want to strengthen and deepen your interpersonal relationships, you need to communicate your emotions. If a "significant other" is not comfortable with (or does not understand the importance of) emotional communication, then explain your desire to have a more intimate relationship with them. Teach them about the five levels of communication.

Do not underestimate the efficacy of taking the basic steps of feeling your emotions, labeling your emotions, analyzing your emotions, and sharing your emotions. Dr. Tian Dayton teaches her patients to take these precise steps in order to heal their emotional traumas and cure their addictions. In the introduction to her book *Trauma and Addiction: Ending the Cycle of Pain Through Emotional Literacy* (Health Communications, Inc., 2000), Dr. Dayton explains how unresolved emotional trauma leads to addiction and how emotional expression can be a huge part of the solution:

"Giving words to trauma begins to heal it. Hiding it or pretending it isn't there creates a cauldron of pain that eventually boils over. That's where addiction comes in: In the absence of sharing and receiving support, pain feels overwhelming. The person in pain reaches not toward people, whom he or she has learned to distrust, but toward a substance that he or she has learned can be counted on to kill the pain, numb the hurt. Such actions are attempts to self-medicate, to manage emotional pain, but the relief is temporary and had at a huge price" (Introduction, p. xvi).

Dr. Dayton's main treatment method for addictive behavior is to teach her patients "emotional literacy." In her clinical practice, trauma victims learn to (1) fully feel their emotions, (2) label them, (3) analyze them, and (4) share them. Once they have learned how to process and discharge their emotions, Dr. Dayton reports, they are freed from the false "relief" of addiction. Dr. Dayton's success treating trauma victims and addicts demonstrates the importance and power of basic emotional literacy.

- In addition to identifying the emotion you are feeling, learn to accurately express the intensity of this emotion. Nurses and other health care workers ask patients to communicate their level of physical pain by placing it on a scale from one to ten. You need to do the same when communicating your emotions to others—develop an emotional vocabulary that will allow you to express various intensities of anger, sadness, fear, happiness, and so on.

- Be aware that emotions are like grapes—they come in clusters. It is not uncommon to experience several emotions at once. To accurately communicate your emotional state to others, you may need to recognize and describe several different emotions that you are feeling at the same time.

- "Own" your emotions. Take responsibility for them, and expect others to do so likewise. Do not blame others for your emotions. Do not express your feelings as a form of "emotional blackmail." Learn to say, "I am angry," and not, "You make me so angry." You have control over your thoughts and feelings. You can choose how you will perceive and respond to the behaviors of others—empower yourself and others to be in charge of their emotions.

- Allow others to be emotional and to express their emotions appropriately. When you acknowledge their emotions, when you respect their right to be emotional, and when you reciprocate and share your feelings, you are forging deeper relationships with them.

- Do not invalidate someone's emotions by telling them that they "should not be feeling that way." Remember, emotions are not right or wrong—they are just signs indicating the psychological state of a person. Do not try to "fix" a person by changing or modifying their emotions. Try, instead, to understand why they are feeling the way they are feeling. Try to empathize with them.

- Do not allow yourself or others to "express" emotions inappropriately. Intense emotions are no excuse for demeaning or abusing other people. Verbal abuse, personal attacks, or violence should not be condoned or tolerated just become someone is very angry or upset.

- Do not apologize for "getting emotional" or for merely displaying or expressing your emotions. An apology implies that you have done something wrong, and that others are doing something wrong, by displaying or expressing emotions. (If, however, you have displayed or expressed your emotions inappropriately, then by all means apologize.)

Earlier in the chapter we mentioned four different conflict management styles. Conflict can generate strong emotions in people, emotions like frustration, anger, fear, and mistrust. You learned that some people and cultures are not comfortable expressing emotion in such a situation. Here are some tips for effective emotional communication during conflict situations:

- When very strong emotions are interfering with your ability to express yourself or listen to others, take a break. You may be experiencing what is called "emotional flooding." You can explain that you need some time to compose yourself and to process your strong emotions.

- Try to develop the ability to use all four conflict management styles. Be aware of the conflict management style that your interpersonal partners are most comfortable using, and adjust your communication accordingly.

- Affirm your respect for, and relational commitment to, a person who communicates or displays strong emotion during a heated discussion, especially if they prefer the discussion style or accommodation style of conflict management. They are likely to experience shame and regret for getting emotional. Assure them that they have done nothing wrong.

- When dealing with people who are uncomfortable with strong emotional expression, "dial it down" and moderate your enthusiasm, especially if you prefer the dynamic style or engagement style of conflict management.

- Realize that when you handle major interpersonal conflicts effectively by expressing your strong emotions appropriately, these major conflicts can actually draw you and your interpersonal partner closer together. If you respect each other's thoughts and feelings during the discussion of the conflict, your relationship can be strengthened even if the conflict is not resolved.

Conclusion

At the end of this chapter, I would like to share my feelings with you. I am hopeful that after reading this chapter many students will be able to identify the major cultural influences and life experiences that have caused them to repress or suppress their emotions. I am glad that I have had the opportunity to explain the benefits and positive aspects of emotional expression. I am excited that the guidelines and tips I offer for appropriate and effective emotional expression may actually be followed and used by the readers of this textbook. To think that their interpersonal relationships and their psychological and physical health may be substantially improved through effective emotional expression brings me great pleasure and satisfaction.

Chapter 7

Listening

By Michael Schulmeister

Let's get personal...

I have been married to my wife Sarah for over 30 years, and I am thankful for a solid, fulfilling marriage relationship. However, there is one element in our marriage that has been a fairly consistent source of frustration for us both—my lack of listening. I want to be a good husband, but I know that I have disappointed Sarah many times by not listening attentively while she is speaking to me. I know that I need to personally apply the listening concepts and principles in this chapter.

— Michael Schulmeister

You need to read this chapter

- To appreciate the importance of listening.
- To understand the six steps of the listening process.
- To identify common listening barriers.
- To learn how to listen deeply.

Chapter 3 of this textbook is devoted to perception and the perception process. Since listening is just one mode of perception, why is another entire chapter of this textbook devoted to the topic of listening? We have devoted an entire chapter to listening because it is the communication skill that human beings use the most. We write, we speak, but most of all, we listen (Figure 7.1).

Ironically, listening is the communication skill used the most but taught the least (Figure 7.2). In the American education system, students get several years of instruction in writing at both the secondary and post-secondary levels, and to get an A.A. degree from a California community college, students must take a required general education course in public speaking. However, over the entire course of a formal American education, only a few minutes (if any!) are devoted to instruction in listening. There are no required courses in listening.

Most people assume that everyone knows how to listen—this is a bad assumption. Listening is a complex communication process that requires knowledge, skill, and focus. Many students

Figure 7.1 Consistent poor listening can become a serious relational transgression.

Writing	Speaking	Listening
Used the least		Used the most
Taught the most		Taught the least

Figure 7.2 This chart demonstrates why people need instruction in listening.

tell me that they *thought* they were good listeners, but after reading a chapter like this on listening, they realize that there is much they can do to improve their listening abilities and practices.

In this chapter, you will learn why listening is an important element of human communication in general, and why listening is a very important element of interpersonal communication in particular. You will learn the six steps of the listening process and how you can improve in all six of these areas. You will learn about a dozen listening barriers that you need to eliminate in order to have clear communication with others. You will also learn how to talk so others will listen to you, and you will learn how to listen deeply to others to strengthen and deepen your interpersonal relationships.

The Importance of Listening

"If you wish to know the mind of a man, listen to his words." (Chinese)
"A loud cat does not catch mice." (Japanese)
"An empty cart rattles loudly." (Korean)

These Asian proverbs demonstrate that people in Eastern cultures often de-emphasize the importance of speaking while emphasizing the importance of listening. If this chapter were being written for an Eastern audience, this section on the importance of listening might be a lot shorter. However, this textbook is written primarily for a Western audience, and we in the West privilege speaking over listening.

In the West, people are encouraged to speak up and share their opinions. The ability to *speak* well is much admired and often rewarded. People who are excellent listeners, on the other hand, are sometimes underappreciated, especially if they are not very verbal. Therefore, we will take some time and space to develop in our Western audience an appreciating for listening.

The Importance of Listening in General

One way to stress the importance of listening is to point out that several elements of the basic transactional communication model directly relate to listening and the listening process. We introduced the basic transactional model of communication in Chapter 1, and you learned there that a communicator must encode a message and send this message through a communication channel. Another communicator must then receive and decode this message and send feedback to the original communicator. Both communicators, the model illustrates, must deal with communication noise.

Four of the basic elements in the transactional model of communication are directly related to listening: (1) communication "noise" is an element that can interfere with the listening process, (2) "receiving" a message is the first stage in the listening process, (3) "decoding" or interpreting a message is the third stage in the listening process, and (4) providing "feedback" is the fourth stage of the listening process. Listening, therefore, is a central activity in almost all forms of human communication (Figure 7.3).

Another general reason listening is important is that it can improve your communication "input." Computer programmers use the acronym "GIGO" to point out the importance of good input. "GIGO" stands for the expression "garbage in, garbage out." As a computer programmer, if you have garbage input, you will get garbage output.

Similarly, as a communicator, if you have "garbage" communication input, you will have garbage communication output. Listening well to others improves the quality of the communication input that you receive. The ancient Greek biographer and historian Plutarch (46 AD–120 AD) said, "Know how to listen, and you will profit even from those who talk badly." Good listening results in the high-quality reception of even a poorly communicated message. Conversely, bad listening can garble even the most clearly communicated message.

Another general reason to listen to others is to learn. If you want to become a lifelong learner, if you want to increase your store of knowledge and practical wisdom, then you need to learn to listen. Other people have much to teach you, but you need to be willing to listen to them. If you will not listen, there is much that you will not learn.

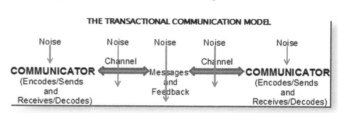

Figure 7.3 Several basic communication elements and activities directly impact listening.

Prestige Testimony about Listening (Found on Brainyquote.Com)

"It's only through listening that you learn, and I never want to stop learning."

(Drew Barrymore)

"I remind myself every morning: Nothing I say this day will teach me anything. So if I am going to learn, I must do it by listening."

(Larry King)

"My parents taught me how to listen to everybody before I made up my own mind. When you listen, you learn. You absorb like a sponge—and your life becomes so much better than when you are just trying to be listened to all the time."

(Steven Spielberg)

Finally, we also have an ethical responsibility and duty to listen to others. We human beings are ethical animals—we care about what is right or wrong, just or unjust. In a nutshell, it is right and just to listen to others, and it is wrong and unjust to ignore the messages of others. The National Communication Association approved a Credo for Ethical Communication in 1999, and this communication credo (posted on the official NCA webpage) asserts that ethical communicators "… strive to understand and respect other communicators before evaluating and responding to their messages."

If we want to be ethical communicators, we must listen to others. We want to be heard and understood. The Golden Rule, an ethical principle enshrined in many world religions and ethical systems, tells us to do unto others as we would have them do unto us. Therefore, if we want to be heard and understood, we must strive to listen to and understand others.

The Importance of Listening For Interpersonal Relationships

Listening is especially important for interpersonal communication interactions because it sends important relational messages (Figure 7.4). Listening shows respect, indicates interest, and demonstrates openness. Speaker and activist Bryant H. McGill says, "One of the most sincere forms of respect is actually listening to what another has to say" (brainyquote.com). Psychologist Joyce Brothers says, "Listening, not imitation, may be the sincerest form of flattery" (quotationspage.com).

If you want to initiate relationships with people, you can signal your interest in them (and in a relationship with them) by paying careful attention to them when they speak. To initiate a

Figure 7.4 Good listening skills help us to create successful interpersonal relationships.

romantic relationship, you do not necessarily need a silver tongue and a killer "pick up" line—good listening skills can send the message (and truly demonstrate) that you are attracted to someone. These same good listening skills can make you an attractive communication partner whom people want to be around.

If you want to maintain loving relationships with friends and family members, you can show your love and concern for them through good listening. In Chapter 9 we introduce to you Dr. Gary Chapman's book *The 5 Love Languages* and we point out that some people have the love language of "quality time." It is especially important that you truly *listen* to these relational partners because gifts and words of affirmation will not communicate your love and care as effectively as your focused time and attention.

Not listening to your interpersonal communication partners may signal to them your disrespect, disinterest, or closed-mindedness. You can *say* that you are open to their ideas, but if you are not willing to listen to them, your mind is obviously closed. You can *say* that you are interested in them, but if you do not listen attentively to them, you may send a very different message. You can *say* that you respect them, but if you ignore them, you have delivered one of the greatest insults possible (Figure 7.5).

In interpersonal relationships, listening or not listening also plays an important part in power displays and power sharing. When there is a power differential in an interpersonal relationship (when one person in a relationship has more power than another person), the less-powerful person is expected to listen, while the more powerful person does not necessarily have to listen. For example, in a parent–child relationship, the child is usually expected to listen. Similarly, in an employer–employee relationship, the employee is usually expected to listen. The parent or employer can display their power and authority by not listening and by demanding that the less-powerful person listen.

On the other hand, parents and employers can share their power with their relational partners by listening attentively to them when they speak. Children and employees can feel especially validated and supported when their "superiors" listen attentively to them. Employers and parents who listen attentively signal that they are willing to share power with their relational partners, and they send the message that they do not think themselves "superior."

Figure 7.5 Not listening to others can signal disinterest and disrespect.

Many interpersonal problems can be solved or avoided through good listening. British actress, author, and screenwriter Emma Thompson says, "Any problem, big or small, within a family, always seems to start with bad communication. Someone isn't listening" (wisdom-quotes.com). On the one hand, pseudoconflicts (apparent incompatibilities between people) are often the result of misunderstandings created by poor listening. On the other hand, actual interpersonal conflicts, even serious ego conflicts, can often be resolved when people carefully listen to one another. Listening is an important skill to practice in conflict resolution. If you want to avoid or effectively resolve conflicts with your friends, family members, and coworkers, then you need to become a good listener.

The Listening Process

THE SIX STEPS OF THE LISTENING PROCESS
1. Receiving: Hearing and seeing auditory and visual communication signals.
2. Recognizing: Focusing on and attending to a message.
3. Rendering: Decoding or interpreting a message.
4. Responding: Providing feedback to a message.
5. Remembering: Committing a message to memory.
6. Relaying: Repeating a message to others.

Figure 7.6 The six "R"s of the listening process.

Listening is a complex process that involves at least six different stages. If you understand what needs to happen in each of these stages for listening to occur, then you can strengthen your abilities and skills in all six of these stages. To help you remember the steps or stages in the listening process, we will use a "mnemonic" or memory device and present to you the 6Rs of listening: (1) receiving, (2) recognizing, (3) rendering, (4) responding, (5) remembering, and (6) relaying (Figure 7.6).

In the next few pages, we will more fully describe each of the six stages of the listening process. We will also point out some of the problems that can arise in each stage, and we will provide some tips about how you can improve your abilities and skills in each stage of the listening process.

Step 1: Receiving

The first step of the listening process is physical and physiological: in order to begin the listening process, we must receive communication signals through the auditory and visual communication channels (Figure 7.7). In other words, we must hear people speak words to us, and we must see and hear the nonverbal cues that they send as these words are spoken.

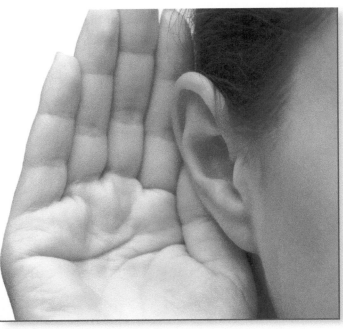

Figure 7.7 Receiving is the first stage of the listening process.

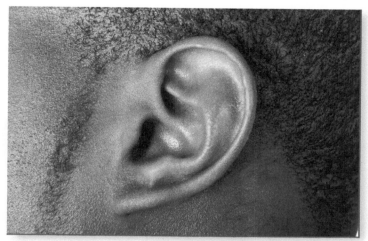

Figure 7.8 He that hath ears to hear, let him hear.

Listening is usually associated with hearing, and hearing is usually associated with the ears. Hearing is a physiological process that involves the processing of physical soundwaves. When human beings speak words, these words are encoded in sound symbols. These sound symbols travel through the air in soundwaves that enter the ear canals of other human beings. Soundwaves entering the ear canal cause the tympanic membrane of the eardrum to vibrate.

Hearing, the first step of the listening process, is basically a passive process. If your ears are uncovered, you are hearing the multitude of sounds being produced in the physical environment around you (Figures 7.8 and 7.9).

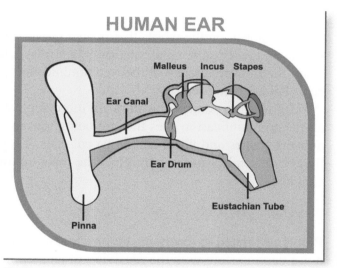

Figure 7.9 Hearing is a physical process.

Although in the West listening is primarily associated with hearing and processing sounds and verbal sound symbols received through the auditory communication channel, effective listening also involves receiving signals and cues received through the visual channel. The Chinese pictogram for the concept of listening, "ting," is made up of four different symbols representing the ear, the eye, the heart, and attention. People in the East think of listening as a process involving both the ears and the eyes.

If you are deaf and use some form of sign language to communicate with others, you have learned to "listen" primarily with your eyes (Figure 7.10). Instead of decoding words encoded in sound symbols, you have learned to decode words encoded in visual symbols. However, even if you are not deaf, you need to train yourself to pay attention to the visual cues that people send to you as they communicate.

If you do not pay attention to the visual and nonverbal cues that people send as they speak verbal messages, you are classified as a "low-context" communicator. Low-context communicators

Figure 7.10 People in deaf culture often "listen" with their eyes.

focus primarily on the words that people speak, and they try to interpret these words accurately. However, low-context communicators can miss a lot in a communication interaction, especially when the nonverbal cues of their communication partners diverge from or contradict the verbal cues that are being sent.

High-context communicators are more sophisticated listeners because they pay attention to all the communication cues that are being sent in a communication interaction, both verbal and nonverbal cues and vocal and nonvocal cues. They understand that the way a sender looks and the way a sender sounds can affect the meaning of a verbal message sent through the auditory channel.

Receiving Problems and Tips

Problems related to receiving are physical noise, phonetic ambiguity, and hearing loss. Physical noise can interfere with the receiving of an audible message. However, even if outside physical noise is not an issue, a sender who does not enunciate clearly can negatively impact the receiving of an audible message. However, even if a speaker enunciates clearly, receiving problems can occur because of hearing loss. Hearing loss can be temporary or permanent. For example, it can be a result of a blockage in the ear canal, exposure to extremely loud noises, or damage to the eardrum. (People may have trouble receiving visual cues because of poor eyesight, lack of light, distracting sights, or too much distance from their communication partners.)

To improve your ability to receive messages through the auditory and visual communication channels, make sure your ears and eyes are in good working order. (For example, make sure you do not have a buildup of earwax in your ear canals.) If appropriate, use optical aids or hearing aids to improve your vision and hearing. Position yourself so you can easily hear and/or see your communication partners. Ask your communication partners to speak and/or sign clearly.

Step 2: Recognizing

Recognizing that a message is intended for you and then focusing on this message is the second step of the listening process (Figure 7.11). Your brain must process thousands of audible

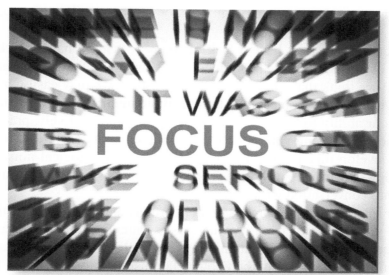

Figure 7.11 Recognizing is the second stage of the listening process.

and visual signals that are continually entering your ears and eyes: most often, this processing occurs at an unconscious level. (You could not function effectively if you were consciously aware of the myriad stimuli bombarding your sense organs.) When you decide that some sounds you hear are important (for example, because they are part of an encoded verbal message), then you can consciously focus on these sounds—this is the *recognizing* stage of the listening process.

Although hearing sounds is a passive process, listening is an active process that takes effort and focus. British stage designer, painter, and photographer David Hockney says, "Listening is a positive act: you have to put yourself out to do it" (quotewave.com). Although hearing is passive, the next five stages of the listening process take effort. In the "recognizing" stage of listening, once you recognize that there is a message coming your way that you could interpret, you must put forth effort to attend to this message.

Recognizing Problems and Tips

People with attention-deficit disorder (ADD) may have problems listening because they have great difficulty focusing on a message or anything else. However, we moderns who have experienced thousands of hours of electronic media have been trained to have short attention spans. We usually receive information in short bursts or small packets, so we may find it difficult to listen to speakers and stay focused on their messages for any extended amount of time. Although an audience before the onset of our modern electronic media culture might have attentively listened to a speaker for an hour or two, we moderns find it difficult to focus on a speaker for even a minute or two.

Physiological noise or psychological noise can also make it difficult for us to focus on a speaker or a spoken message. Physiological "noise" is messages that we receive from our bodies—our stomachs tell us that we are hungry, our muscles tell us that we are tired, our buttox tell us that we have been sitting too long, and so on. Psychological "noise" is distracting thoughts or feelings that we may have as we are attempting to focus on a speaker's message—the message may trigger a memory or create an emotion in us, or we may begin to formulate a response to the message.

Another reason that we may have a lack of focus is that we have a lack of respect for a speaker or a lack of interest in a speaker's message. If we think that a speaker is not worthy of our attention, or if we think that a message is uninteresting, we may easily "zone out" and turn our attention to whatever or whomever we think is more interesting or important.

To improve your ability to focus on a message and listen attentively, practice "living in the moment" and practice focusing your attention for long amounts of time. (Meditation exercises can help you to develop this ability to focus.) Decrease physiological noise by seeing to the needs of your body. Decrease psychological noise by processing your thoughts and feelings before entering into conversation with others.

Increase your interest in your conversational partners and the messages they have to share by realizing that you can learn from anyone. Also, remember that you are sending positive relational messages when you listen attentively. Regardless of the importance of a person's message, you can improve and strengthen your relationship with that person by listening carefully to them.

Step 3: Rendering

In the third stage of the listening process, a communicator decodes the verbal sound symbols that have been received. Some synonyms for "rendering" a message are "decoding," "understanding," "perceiving," and "interpreting" a message. Although hearing (the first stage of the listening process) is primarily physical and physiological, rendering (the third stage of the listening process) is primarily mental.

Rendering or decoding a verbal message, the third stage of the listening process (Figure 7.12), is a mental process that distinguishes human beings from other animals. As far as we know, nonhuman animals do not have the ability to think or communicate using abstract verbal language. The ability to assign meaning (especially multiple meanings) to word symbols is a human ability, so the type of listening that occurs when we process verbal symbols is a uniquely human activity. Although some nonhuman animals can *hear* better than human beings, human beings can *listen* better than any other animal because they have minds capable of assigning meaning to words.

Rendering Problems and Tips

The primary problem that arises when we attempt to render or interpret a message correctly is semantic confusion: the sender of a message may have intended to assign one particular meaning to a word, but the receiver of a message may assign a very different meaning to the same word, or the receiver may not know the meaning of that word.

Semantic misunderstandings can arise if a sender of a verbal message uses vague and ambiguous language,

Figure 7.12 Rendering is the third stage of the listening process.

but semantic ambiguity can also occur when two communicators have very little life experience or very few vocabulary words in common. To speak clearly to one another and to decode the meaning of each other's words accurately, two communicators need a substantial amount of overlap in their mental environments and a shared store of vocabulary words. That is why two people from the same culture will probably have an easier time communicating interpersonally than two people from very different cultures.

One final element that can negatively impact the decoding or interpreting of verbal messages is mental or perceptual filters. Human beings have perceptual filters that cause them to view the world a certain way. These perceptual filters are often a product of the cultures into which people are socialized. We have already noted, for example, that people in Eastern cultures are more prone to value listening, whereas people in Western cultures are more prone to value speaking. Therefore, a very loquacious message may be perceived in the West as well-articulated wisdom, but it may be perceived in the East as shallow, fatuous rhetoric. Perceptual filters can affect our overall impressions and evaluations of communicators and their messages.

To improve your ability to render or interpret verbal messages correctly and accurately, increase your life experience, your knowledge of the world, and your vocabulary. As your life experience and knowledge of the world increases, you will have more in common with the people with whom you communicate. The more words you know, and the more possible meanings you can assign to words, the more accurately and perceptively you can interpret the verbal messages of others.

To increase the objectivity of your perceptions, strive to become aware of the perceptual filters that are usually in operation in your mind. Identify your worldview and the beliefs, values, and attitudes that anchor and are created by this worldview. These dominant beliefs, values, and attitudes color and shape your perceptions of the world and your perceptions of other communicators in the world. Although you have to view the world from some position or vantage point, knowing your personal biases and perceptual filters can help you to adjust your perceptions of others, especially when those others may be operating out of a worldview that differs from your own.

Step 4: Responding

The fourth stage of the listening process, responding (Figure 7.13), can occur before, during, or after a message is sent. As someone is speaking, even before they have finished their message, you can interrupt them and give a response—this premature response is not usually the best type of response to give. Usually, you should listen attentively while you are receiving a message, you should fully process the message to make sure you understand what the sender is saying, and then you should provide a thoughtful response. That is why we have listed responding as the fourth stage of the listening process, after receiving, recognizing, and rendering.

However, be aware that even though you may withhold verbal responses while your conversational partner is speaking, you are sending visual feedback

Figure 7.13 Responding is the fourth stage of the listening process.

messages through your facial expression, your posture, your eye contact, and your body movements. The transactional model of communication was developed by communication theorists because they recognized that communication, especially interpersonal communication, is a two-way transactional process: as two people interact, primary messages and feedback messages are traveling back and forth between them through the auditory and visual communication channels.

Before studying the listening process myself, I thought that I had listened well if I had fully comprehended another person's message. I did not realize that my listening task was only halfway completed, and that there were still three steps to complete — (4) responding, (5) remembering, and (6) relaying.

To verify the importance of the last three listening steps, ask people to name the good listeners that they know, and then ask them to describe what these good listeners do: they will most likely say things like, "He looks me in the eye, nods his head often, and pays complete attention to me," or "She gives such supportive responses and excellent advice." Their comments will reveal that good listeners give good verbal (and nonverbal) responses when they listen to others. French writer Francois de la Rochefoucald (1613–1680) asserted, "To listen closely and reply well is the highest perfection we are able to attain in the art of conversation" (quotes.net).

Responding Problems and Tips

One problem that can arise in the responding stage is that the listener does not give an adequate response, either verbally or nonverbally. Their nonverbal cues may not clearly signal that they have heard and comprehended a verbal message or that they care about this message. Their verbal response may be underdeveloped, or they may not offer any verbal response. When no verbal response is given by a listener, the sender of a message may wonder if their message has even been received, or they may suspect that the listener disagrees with or is displeased with the message.

In interpersonal communication, empathetic responses are appropriate and necessary. The listener needs to acknowledge the emotional state of the speaker. The Chinese pictogram for listening, remember, includes the ears, the eyes, *and* the heart. When you listen to others, you must listen with your heart: you must feel what the other person is feeling, and you must convey that you empathize with their emotions. If you do not acknowledge the experiencing or expression of strong emotion, you can come across as cold, aloof, and uncaring.

Let's get personal. . .

Until I was in my forties, I was very uncomfortable with the expression of strong emotions. If a conversational partner got very emotional, I would often not even acknowledge their emotional state. For example, if a student came to my office and broke down in tears after relating a personal life experience or a difficult situation that they were going through, I might act like nothing had happened, and I would continue our conversation nonchalantly, "Now let's look at page three of your speech outline ...." I was not cruel or cold-hearted: I just didn't know how to respond correctly.

— *Michael Schulmeister*

Another problem that can arise in the responding stage is that the listener can give the wrong type of response. There are several different responses you can give when you provide feedback

TYPES OF LISTENING RESPONSES
1. **Soliciting responses**: Encourage the speaker to clarify or expand a message.
2. **Supporting responses**: Indicate that a listener is interested in and cares about a speaker.
3. **Advising responses**: Instruct a speaker on how to solve a problem or address a situation.
4. **Judging responses**: Pass judgment on the speaker or provide an evaluation of a situation or the people involved in a situation.

Figure 7.14 Good listeners give the right type of response at the right time.

to a communication partner: (1) **soliciting** responses encourage the speaker to clarify or expand their message further; (2) **supporting** responses indicate that a listener is interested in and cares about a speaker, and they may include statements of agreement, praise, or reassurance; (3) **advising** responses instruct the speaker and tell them what they should do to solve a problem or to address a situation, (4) **judging** responses pass judgment on the speaker or provide the listener's evaluation of a situation or the people involved in a situation.

Good listeners develop the ability to give the right type of listening response at the appropriate time (Figure 7.14). Sometimes others need your advice, sometimes others need your unbiased opinion and judgment, and sometimes you need more information before you offer either advice or judgment.

If you want to create successful interpersonal relationships, you need to develop the ability to give authentic supporting responses. Too often we rush to offer advice or pass judgment on others when all they really want is a listening ear and our support. Consultant and speaker Margaret J. Wheatley says, "Listening is such a simple act. It requires us to be present, and that takes practice, but we don't have to do anything else. We don't have to advise, or coach, or sound wise. We just have to be willing to sit there and listen" (brainyquote.com).

I have a colleague at Bakersfield College named Donald Turney. He is a seasoned psychology instructor, he has served as Dean of Students at our institution, and he worked as a prison psychologist for 7 years. Don taught me how to listen effectively to others. He said, "I have studied the seven major schools of psychology, but there is only one thing I have found that really helps people—listen to them and love them." To listen to people and to treat them with unconditional positive regard and acceptance is a powerful communication skill that you can develop. If you develop this skill, you will create solid interpersonal relationships, and you will be able to help others in a deep, significant way.

If you are not sure what type of listening response is required in a particular interpersonal situation, ask your communication partner. Do they want your advice, your judgment, or your support? Give them what they need. As you give your verbal responses, remember that you are also providing nonverbal responses: *look* like you are listening and *act* like you care about them and what they are saying. You need to pay attention to the verbal and nonverbal messages that your communication partners are sending your way, but you also need to be aware of the verbal *and* nonverbal messages you are sending in response.

Step 5: Remembering

In the fifth stage of the listening process, you prove to your conversational partners that you have been listening: you confirm that you have received and processed their message by actually

Figure 7.15 Remembering is the fifth stage of the listening process.

remembering it and repeating it (Figure 7.15). You have failed the listening "test" if you cannot remember what your interpersonal communication partners just told you—they will think that their message "went in one ear and out the other" without ever being received, attended to, and processed.

Remembering Problems and Tips

You have seriously failed as a listener if you cannot remember a communication message at all. If you cannot remember even the gist of a message, there is no evidence that you actually listened to your communication partner. You have also failed as a listener (but not as seriously) if you remember only part of the message or if you remember the message incorrectly.

Communication is complicated. Now you know that a message may not be fully received, or a message may be negatively affected by physiological or psychological noise, or a message may be processed or interpreted incorrectly, *or* a message may be misremembered. You may hear a message clearly and understand a message correctly, but when you try to access the memory of this message at a future time, the message may be unrecoverable or may become garbled in your mind.

To improve your memory ability, practice focusing on and recalling messages that you have received. Remembering (just like recognizing, rendering, and responding) takes effort, so you need to exercise your memory "muscles." To really improve your ability to remember messages and conversations, practice recalling them immediately after they occur, a short time after they occur, and several hours after they occur.

Realize that your mind is like an audio-video tape that has recorded everything that you have seen and heard. With the help of memory recall techniques (such as hypnosis), witnesses to a crime can sometimes recover astonishingly accurate and detailed memories of that crime. You *do* have memories of the messages you have received—you just need to improve your ability to access these memories.

Memory coaches teach people to improve their memory ability by associating ideas together. Your mind operates by creating information "webs," so the more associations you make for an idea or a message, the more paths your mind has for finding and recovering this idea or message. Take time to "file away" a conversation in your mind under several different headings (with several different associations) and you will be able to access the memory of this conversation with greater ease.

If you know that a message from a communication partner is very important, or if you know that your conversational partner expects you to remember this message, record it or write it down. You are not "cheating" when you record or write down a message. Your conversational partner will probably be flattered that you think their message is important enough to write down, and they should be impressed with the effort you are putting forth to record and preserve their message.

Step 6: Relaying

In the sixth stage of the listening process, you relay or repeat a sender's message. If you have listened to a message well, you should be able to relay this message with "high fidelity."

We have all played the game of "telephone" when several people are asked to relay a message multiple times, from one person to the next. When the last person in line finally says the relayed message out loud, it has usually been greatly distorted, and everyone laughs at how poorly the message has been communicated. If the last person repeats the original message accurately, however, a different type of pleasure is created: we appreciate that a message has been communicated clearly several times. Everyone in the line effectively completed all the steps of the listening process, including the sixth step of relaying the message accurately to others.

Although you can relay a message in stage six of the listening process (when you repeat a sender's message to others), you can also relay a message directly back to a sender in stage four of the listening process: another type of response to give as a listener is a **paraphrasing** response. In a paraphrasing response, you repeat what someone else has said in your own words.

The Power of Paraphrasing

Paraphrasing is a powerful communication tool. When you paraphrase the messages of others, you demonstrate your desire and ability to comprehend, you confirm that your understanding is correct, and you allow senders to clarify their messages or to correct your interpretations of their messages.

In some jobs or professions where the unclear communication of a message could result in serious harm or injury, employees are required to verbally clarify and confirm messages through paraphrasing. For example, at a nuclear power plant, when one worker says, "I am preparing to turn the valve knob thirty degrees to the right," the next worker in line is expected to paraphrase this message before anyone proceeds, "You are getting ready to turn the valve thirty degrees clockwise, or to the right."

Although paraphrasing is not a formal requirement in most interpersonal relationships, you should learn this skill, and you should use it often in your interpersonal communication interactions. You may not be *required* to paraphrase your communication partners' messages, but doing so can demonstrate your desire to understand them, and it gives them a chance to clarify or further explain their thoughts and feelings.

Relaying Problems and Tips

If you repeat your conversational partners' messages word for word, they may not be impressed: they may think that you are "parroting" their messages without truly grasping what they are trying to communicate. Paraphrasing messages and putting them in your own words demonstrates that you have truly internalized and comprehended them.

When you paraphrase the messages of others, avoid adding your own judgments, commentary, or advice. You are not paraphrasing well when you place your own thoughts and feelings into a paraphrase. Your job as a paraphraser is to confirm the thoughts and feelings of your conversational partner, not to judge, advise, or even to make your own positive, supportive comments.

In his book *Secrets to Lasting Love* (Simon & Schuster, 2001), relationship expert Gary Smalley describes paraphrasing as "drive-through listening." This is a great analogy to teach people how to paraphrase. When you speak into the drive-through intercom at a fast-food restaurant and place your order, you do not expect the worker taking your order to make comments or give advice: you expect them to repeat your order back to you to make sure you get exactly what you want when you get to the drive-through window. It would be very strange if the voice on the speaker said, "I think you should skip the double cheeseburger and go for something healthier, like the chicken salad."

Similarly, when you are paraphrasing the thoughts and messages of your conversational partners and your significant others, your job is to faithfully repeat back to them your understanding of their thoughts, feelings, and desires. You are not supposed to give them advice, or tell them they shouldn't feel a certain way, or offer your opinion about their wishes or desires. Just repeat back to them your understanding of what they are thinking and feeling.

To be a good interpersonal communicator, you need to develop an understanding of when it is appropriate to paraphrase a message and when a different type of response is needed. Although paraphrasing is powerful and useful, it can also be overused. Add paraphrasing responses to your communication repertoire (along with soliciting responses, supporting responses, advising responses, and judging responses), and paraphrase when necessary and appropriate.

To be a "safe," trustworthy communication partner, think carefully before relaying a sender's message to others. If a sender considers a message to be private and only for the two of you, they may feel betrayed if you relay this message to others, or they may question your ability to distinguish between private messages and public messages.

If you can relay messages appropriately, you are an excellent listener who has mastered all six steps of the listening process: (1) receiving, (2) recognizing, (3) rendering, (4) responding, (5) remembering, and (6) relaying. To improve your listening skills and abilities, keep all six of these stages in mind, remember the problems that can arise in each stage, and make good decisions so you can avoid or minimize these listening problems.

Listening Barriers

In addition to the six steps of the listening process, we want to present to you ten listening barriers that can interfere with your ability to receive and process messages. The first two listening barrier we list may be outside of your control to some extent, but the remaining barriers are actually poor listening behaviors that you can change or correct. When you remove these listening barriers, you will listen more effectively to others (Figure 7.16).

Ten Listening Barriers

1) **Hearing problems:** If you have a conversational partner who sometimes seems to ignore you or consistently misunderstands your messages, perhaps this person has a hearing problem. Hearing deficiencies often go undiagnosed, and sometimes people do not want to reveal that they have a hearing deficiency. If you consistently struggle to comprehend what people are saying, you may also have a hearing problem.

2) **Information overload:** In this "information age" that we live in, a very common listening barrier is information overload. When too much information is shared at once, our mental circuits become overloaded and we are unable to process any messages. You can overwhelm a conversational partner, or be overwhelmed by a conversational partner, when too many thoughts, opinions, and details are shared all at once.

Figure 7.16 Several listening barriers can block effective communication.

3) **Stagehogging:** Stagehogging occurs when we interrupt others or dismiss what they are saying in order to present our own ideas or examples. For example, if someone is sharing a personal experience, a stagehog will interrupt or ignore this personal experience in order to present their own experience (which they evidently think is much more interesting or important).

4) **Pseudolistening:** Pseudolistening occurs when we *act* like we are listening but our minds are far away. Pseudolisteners may nod their heads and scratch their chins to give the appearance of listening, but in reality they may not even be receiving the messages sent by others.

5) **Selective listening:** Selective listening occurs when we only listen to the topics which interest us. Selective listeners "select" or focus only on their favorite ideas or topics. If others are discussing these particular topics, they will pay attention; otherwise, they zone out.

6) **Insulated listening:** Insulated listening is the opposite of selective listening. It occurs when we purposely "tune out" topics or ideas we do not like or find objectionable for some reason. In interpersonal situations, insulated listeners may ignore verbal messages they do not like, or they may ignore any messages sent by particular family members or significant others.

7) **Attack listening:** Attack listening occurs when we listen primarily to gain "ammunition" which we can use against other people. Like a prosecutor cross-examining a hostile witness, an attack listener processes the messages of others primarily because they want to question or undermine what others are saying. Since very few people willingly subject themselves to being cross-examined, attack listeners have difficulty finding conversational partners.

8) **Defensive listening:** Defensive listening occurs when we assume that whatever others say somehow reflects negatively on ourselves. Defensive listeners often have low self-esteem, so they tend to interpret the messages of others as personal attacks. Since they are so focused on these perceived attacks or slights, defensive listeners often miss the point of what others are actually trying to communicate.

9) **Prejudging:** Prejudging occurs when we determine ahead of time that a message will be problematic. Our expectation causes us to overlook the actual content of the message. We may have difficulty engaging in an interpersonal conversation because we assume that a particular person or topic will be boring, offensive, too complicated, or too controversial.

10) **Rehearsing a response:** When we rehearse responses to messages, we stop paying attention to what people are saying. Our desire to craft good responses interferes with our ability to fully receive the messages of others. No matter how well-crafted our responses are, if we do not comprehend what people are actually saying, our responses will miss the mark.

We have taken the negative approach and pointed out ten listening barriers that you need to avoid. We will end this chapter on listening by taking the positive approach and giving you specific, practical suggestions about what to do so that people will listen to you, and so that you can listen deeply to others and strengthen your interpersonal relationships.

Talking So People Will Listen

When I was a boy, I remember a commercial on television advertising the brokerage firm of E.F. Hutton. As I remember it, when someone in the commercial quietly said to their conversational partner, "Well, my broker is E.F. Hutton, and he says …", everyone else in the crowded, noisy room quieted down and turned to listen to that person. The tag line for the commercial was, "When E.F. Hutton talks, people listen."

If you continually find that your interpersonal communication partners are not very good listeners, perhaps you are not a very good talker. You want to manage your communication transactions so that when you talk, people listen. Here are specific things you can do to help your conversational partners listen to you:

- Speak clearly. Do not mumble or run your words together. When you enunciate your words clearly, you make your conversational partner's listening task easier.

- Speak succinctly. Do not drone on, even in your interpersonal conversations. No matter how much your conversational partner is interested in you, they will find it difficult to maintain interest in a prolonged monologue. Singer Dorothy Sarnoff says, "Make sure you have finished speaking before your audience has finished listening" (thinkexist.com).

- Speak commandingly. Do not speak timidly. Speak as if you deserve to be listened to. My wife likes to watch video lessons from a particular female speaker. Every time the preacherlady opens her mouth, she speaks with such intensity (as if she is talking about the most important thing in the world), you feel compelled to listen.

- Speak unambiguously. Do not use very general or very vague language. Do not use unfamiliar idiomatic expressions. Use words and expressions that you think your particular conversational partner can relate to and understand. Make the task of rendering or decoding your message as simple as possible.

- Ask for or demand your conversational partner's attention. Do not speak if they are obviously not listening. Establish the expectation that they will listen when you are speaking.

- Ask for or demand feedback. Do not try to carry a conversation by yourself. After sending a message, pause and wait for a response. Establish the expectation that you will be equal partners in speaking and listening.

Figure 7.17 Great interpersonal communicators talk in a way that makes people listen.

- Provide listening motivators. Do not assume that your partner is aware of the benefits of listening well. Motivate them to listen by reminding them of the importance of listening to what you have to say, or by promising them a reward or payoff for listening well.

- Model good listening behavior by listening well yourself (Figure 7.17). Margaret J. Wheatley, the consultant and speaker I have quoted once already, says, "There are many benefits to this process of listening. The first is that good listeners are created as people feel listened to. Listening is a reciprocal process—we become more attentive to others if they have attended to us" (brainyquotes.com).

Listening Deeply

If you want deep, intimate interpersonal relationships, then you need to learn to listen deeply to your communication partners. Deep listening is very different from shallow listening. Shallow listeners attempt merely to receive and interpret the content messages of their conversational partners; deep listeners attempt to accomplish so much more through their listening.

When you listen deeply to another human being, in addition to understanding their content messages, you also attempt:

- to receive and appreciate their relational messages;
- to understand their unconscious thoughts, feelings, and messages;
- to validate their thoughts and opinions;
- to empathize with their emotions;
- to understand their perspective and their motivations;
- to show interest in, respect for, and openness toward them;
- to demonstrate unconditional positive regard and acceptance; and
- to deepen and strengthen your interpersonal relationship.

Deep listening is not an everyday occurrence. You may have never listened deeply to another human being, and you may have never experienced what it is like to have someone listen, really listen, to you. After reading this chapter, we encourage you to attempt to listen deeply to another human being, especially if you want to strengthen your relationship with them. If they are willing, you can set up a time when you both attempt to listen deeply to one another. Here are some suggestions for deep listening:

- Eliminate physical noise. Get rid of outside distractions. Turn off any blaring radios or televisions. Put away your cell phones. Put aside any books or any other "playthings" you may have. Find a quiet, uncluttered room where you can more easily focus on and communicate with one another.

- Eliminate physiological noise. Get comfortable. Find two decent chairs to sit in. If you are hungry or thirsty, eat a snack or get a drink of water. If you are hot or cold, adjust the heating or air conditioning, or put on or take off a jacket or sweater. Make sure there is good ventilation and plenty of oxygen in the room.

- Eliminate psychological noise. Clear your minds. Put aside time for this deep listening experience so you can focus on your conversation. Put aside distracting thoughts. Process any strong emotions you are experiencing. Avoid prejudging or rehearsing a response. Pledge to stay in the moment and listen deeply to one another.

- Listen first for understanding. Strive to fully understand what your partner is saying. Do not rush to attack your partner or to defend yourself. Do not evaluate the message of your partner until you have made a good faith effort to fully comprehend this message.

- Observe both the verbal *and* nonverbal messages of your communication partner. Listen with your eyes as well as your ears. Seek to reconcile and harmonize the verbal and nonverbal messages that you receive.

- Provide nonverbal and verbal feedback. *Act* like you are listening. Nod your head. Look directly at the person speaking. Provide appropriate verbal responses. You can prompt the speaker to give more information, or you can ask clarifying questions. You can paraphrase a message to make sure you understand it, or you can provide a supportive response to encourage your communication partner.

- Listen with your heart. Be sensitive to emotional and relational messages. If your partner is communicating strong emotions, do not ignore this element of their message. Acknowledge that they are angry, or ecstatic, or sad, and show empathy.

- When you have finished listening deeply to someone, thank them for sharing their thoughts and feelings with you. Give them relational messages that let them know you love and care about them.

Deep Listening Questions

Here are some questions to consider when attempting to listen deeply to someone:

- What are the nonverbal messages being sent? Are these nonverbal messages reinforcing or contradicting the verbal messages?

- In addition to the content messages, what relational messages are being sent?

- What is the emotional state of the person? What are the precise emotions the person seems to be experiencing?

- What are the unconscious thoughts or feelings that the person may be experiencing and revealing unawares?

- What are the values and attitudes of the person? What are the core thoughts or basic beliefs that are creating these values and attitudes?

- What is not being said by the person? What is the person avoiding?

Obviously, this level of thought and analysis is not sustainable for a lengthy amount of time, especially in a live, one-on-one conversation. Deep listening is taxing. However, you can derive a lot of satisfaction and enjoyment from the experience. As the ancient Greeks said, "Fine things are difficult." The effort you take to listen deeply should pay off in greater understanding, greater intimacy and closeness, and greater relational satisfaction.

Conclusion

Figure 7.18 Have you "listened" carefully while reading this chapter? Prove it. What do you remember? What is your response? What do you want to relay to others about listening?

How carefully have you read this chapter on listening? Have you "listened" carefully to what we have written about effective and ineffective listening? Do you understand what you need to do to become a better listener? Will you remember the six steps of the listening process and the ten listening barriers to avoid? Will you relay to your communication partners what you have learned about deep listening? If you understand and apply the information in this chapter, you can develop the skills you need to deepen your interpersonal relationships and to smooth out your interpersonal interactions through effective listening (Figure 7.18).

Chapter 8

Self-Disclosure

By Michael Schulmeister

Let's get personal. . .

For the first four decades of my life, I hid about 80% of myself from other people. I did not consciously choose to hide myself, but, looking back, I see now that I was so afraid of interpersonal conflict, I gave very little opportunity for personal disagreements to arise. As a student and as a teacher, I could and would discuss and debate controversial topics and issues, but I would never actually reveal my personal opinions on these topics.

Since intellection is my strength, I had a rich inner thought life, but I presented very little of my thoughts to other people as *my* thoughts. I also kept my feelings to myself, especially any "negative" emotions such as anger, fear, or sorrow. I was definitely an "under-discloser."

When I learned about self-disclosure and the powerful impact it can have on a person and on others, I learned to open up and share much more of *my* thoughts and feelings. I now feel much more connected to other people, and I am much more at peace with myself.

— Michael Schulmeister

You need to read this chapter

- To understand the benefits and risks of self-disclosure.
- To determine if you are an under-discloser or an over-discloser.
- To learn how to make appropriate self-disclosures.
- To learn how to respond to self-disclosures.

My daughter Julie is an outgoing, friendly person, so she makes friends easily. However, when she was in high school, she had a special "best friend" named Tanya. Julie took great pleasure in her relationship with Tanya. One day, when she was joyfully proclaiming yet again that Tanya was her "best" friend, I asked her what made this friendship so special. She thought for a moment, and then she said, "Dad, we can tell each other anything!"

My daughter had discovered the power and pleasure of **self-disclosure**. Self-disclosure is the willing sharing of personal information that you do not usually share with others, and it is an important element in an intimate relationship. If two people want to create a deeper, more intimate interpersonal relationship, then they must both "open up" and self-disclose.

In this chapter, we will deepen your understanding of self-disclosure by presenting several self-disclosure models and by discussing the factors that affect self-disclosure. We will then discuss the benefits and risks of self-disclosure, and we will help you to determine if you are an under-discloser or an over-discloser. After giving some general advice about making appropriate self-disclosures, we will give some specific advice to both under-disclosers and over-disclosers. Finally, we will give advice about how to receive and respond to the self-disclosures of others.

A Closer Look at Self-Disclosure

To qualify as "self-disclosure," the personal information that you do not usually share with others must be shared *willingly*. If someone else discloses personal information about you to others (against your will), or if a relational partner discovers this personal information on their own (against your will), then this information has not been *self*-disclosed. You yourself did not willingly share this information, so it does not count as self-disclosure.

When you willingly share personal information with your relational partners, you demonstrate that you are willing to make yourself vulnerable, and this voluntary vulnerability can build trust (Figure 8.1). As you entrust your interpersonal communication partner with personal information, they have the opportunity to earn your trust by handling your self-disclosures appropriately.

Self-disclosure involves sharing your "private" self with others. Your "public" self is composed of all the information that you share indiscriminately with others, the information that is widely available to the public. When you share information about yourself that is not normally accessible by, or available to, the public at large, then you are sharing your more intimate, "private" self with others.

Self-disclosures can be made to large groups of people. For example, some people self-disclose personal information to a very large audience on social media or television talk shows. They take their "private" selves public. Such self-disclosure is not necessarily healthy or appropriate, especially if it is motivated by a desire for fame or notoriety. We will not be focusing on these types of self-disclosures, but we will focus instead on self-disclosures in the context of an interpersonal relationship.

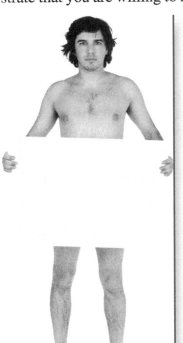

Figure 8.1 Self-disclosure demonstrates that you are willing to make yourself vulnerable.

Social Penetration Theory

Social penetration theory helps us think about the breadth and depth of self-disclosure (Figure 8.2). Imagine the self as a three-dimensional sphere. The surface of the sphere represents the breadth of information that a person shares with others, whereas the core of the sphere represents the depth of a person's self-disclosures. You can deepen your relationships with your interpersonal communication partners by increasing either the breadth or the depth of the information that you share.

For example, casual acquaintances might focus their conversation on a very small area on the surface of the sphere, representing the few things that they normally talk about together. Perhaps they are in a college class together, and so they primarily keep their conversations focused on the class and the homework they must do for that class. As their relationship deepens, however, they will discuss many other topics, and they will self-disclose information about themselves that goes beyond the scope of the class.

Figure 8.2 Social penetration theory focuses on the breadth and depth of self-disclosure.

Other interpersonal relationships are characterized by surface self-disclosures about many different topics, but the depth of self-disclosure is fairly limited. You may have a friend with whom you discuss a wide range of topics and interests, but you do not disclose many personal details of your lives related to these topics. To deepen this type of interpersonal relationship, you and your conversational partner need to be willing to go below the surface of these many different topics and mutual interests. You must disclose your personal thoughts and feelings related to at least some of these different topics and interests.

Some interpersonal relationships can be represented by a narrow "wedge" of the sphere: there are a just a few things you and your conversational partner talk about, but you are willing to go quite deep when discussing these few topics. For example, you and a friend might be "football fanatics," so you can talk passionately for hours about football and your favorite football team. You both enjoy and are committed to sharing your thoughts, feelings, hopes, and dreams about your football team, but your friendship is defined by and limited to football—you are "football" friends, and nothing more.

If you want to create more intimate relationships with your family members and close friends, then you can work on increasing both the breadth and depth of your self-disclosures. As both the breadth and depth of your self-disclosures increase, you will share much more of yourselves with one another.

The Five Levels of Communication

We introduced the five levels of communication to you in Chapter 6, but we will remind you of these five levels of communication in order to clarify how self-disclosures can be "shallow" or "deep." There are five standard "levels of communication" recognized in the field of interpersonal communication: people can share: (1) clichés, (2) facts, (3) opinions, (4) emotions, or (5) hopes and dreams. These five levels of communication are hierarchical, going from the shallowest level of communication (clichés) to the deepest level of communication (sharing hopes and dreams).

The Five Levels Of Communication

Level 1: Clichés

Level 2: Facts

Level 3: Opinions

Level 4: Emotions

Level 5: Hopes and Dreams

In Chapter 6, we pointed out that people use cliché communication when speaking to strangers or people they do not know (or do not want to know) very well. Cliché communication is very useful for initiating conversations because it is "safe:" both conversational partners know the expected responses. However, there is nothing "personal" about this level of communication.

The "fact" level of communication is also fairly impersonal, especially if the facts being shared are very general facts about the world at large, and not about the people involved in a conversation. The fact level of communication can become more personal, however, when people disclose facts about their personal life that other people probably would not know: "I served on a mission in Mexico for two years." "My parents died in a car crash when I was six years old." Some fact-level assertions can be fairly deep self-disclosures: "I have tried to commit suicide twice." "I am having an affair."

The "opinion" level of communication is deeper than the "fact" level if you share your *personal* opinions with others. In the narrative at the beginning of this chapter, I revealed that for years I shared "opinions" about issues while rarely sharing *my* personal opinions. I would talk about religious beliefs, for example, without sharing my religious beliefs. I would talk about politics, but I would not share my personal political positions or opinions. Many of my personal thoughts were withheld from other people.

Sharing personal opinions is a more intimate form of communication than sharing opinions in general, especially when you share your core preferences, values, and beliefs. You are revealing quite a lot of yourself when you share the beliefs and values that anchor your worldview. You are also taking a risk, since other people can criticize your beliefs, trample on your values, and disagree with your most cherished opinions. This risk, however, is what makes sharing your "owned" opinions a deeper act of self-disclosure.

Sharing your emotions is an even more intimate act of communication because your feelings are precisely that—*your* feelings. While other people can adopt your opinions and make them their own, your emotions are uniquely yours. Your anger and your joy and your sorrow and your fear are uniquely *yours*. Someone else may also get angry when you get angry, but you each are experiencing your own anger to different degrees. Someone else may celebrate a special occasion with you, but you each will have a different constellation of emotions attached to this act of celebration.

Expressing your emotions verbally is a fairly intimate act of self-disclosure because you are *willingly* sharing your feelings. Although you may send messages about your emotional state to others through your facial expressions, posture, and tone of voice, these nonverbal emotional cues do not qualify as self-disclosures if they are unconscious and unintentional. When you verbally express your emotions honestly and accurately to your conversational partner, when you put your feelings into words, you are self-disclosing on a fairly deep level.

Figure 8.3 The onion model of self-disclosure emphasizes the depth of disclosure.

Another model of self-disclosure is the "onion" model. As people move from level one communication (clichés) to level two communication (facts) to level three communication (opinions) to level four communication (emotions) to level five communication (hopes and dreams), they are revealing the deeper and deeper layers of themselves. As people self-disclose at deeper and deeper levels, they are "peeling their onion" until they expose to you their core beliefs and values (Figure 8.3).

The Johari Window

One of the most widely used (and most useful) "models of self" related to self-disclosure is the Johari Window. In the 1950s, American psychologists Joseph Luft and Harry Ingham developed the Johari Window to help people understand the different aspects of the self. The name of this model is derived from their first names (Joe + Harry = "Johari").

The Johari Window visually illustrates the parts of yourself that are known and unknown to yourself and to others (Figure 8.4). It is composed of four boxes, and each box represents a different part of the self: the open self, the hidden self, the blind self, and the unknown self. We will describe each of these boxes or quadrants of the self and consider how they relate to the process of self-disclosure.

- The **open self** is the part of yourself that you are consciously aware of and that you share with others through self-disclosure. This self could also be labeled the "public" self or the "presenting" self.

	Known to others	**Not known to others**
Known to self	**Open**	**Hidden**
Not known to self	**Blind**	**Unknown**

Figure 8.4 The Johari Window illustrates four aspects of the self.

- The **hidden self** is the part of yourself that you are consciously aware of but that you hide from others. This self could also be labeled the "private" self.

- The **blind self** is the part of yourself that you are not consciously aware of but that others can see. Both your verbal and nonverbal communication can reveal to others information about yourself that you yourself cannot access on your own.

- The **unknown self** is the part of you that is unknown both to yourself and to others. There are parts of your unconscious mind that are hidden both from your conscious self and from others.

When a person discloses personal information to others, they are increasing the size of their open self, and they are decreasing the size of their hidden self. If we draw personal Johari Windows for different individuals, the size of the four quadrants could vary significantly. A person who self-discloses a significant amount of personal information to others will have a very large box representing the open self and a very small box representing the hidden self. A person who rarely self-discloses will have a very large box representing the hidden self and a very small box representing the open self.

The Johari Window reveals that self-disclosure is most directly related to the parts of ourselves that we are aware of, our open self and our hidden self. However, as you self-disclose to others and they provide you feedback about yourself, you can also decrease the size of your blind self. Furthermore, as you interact with different people and have new experiences, you can decrease the size of your unknown self, and you will then have even more knowledge of yourself that you can self-disclose to others.

If your goal is self-awareness and self-actualization, then you should strive to increase the "open" self as much as possible. In order to fully develop as a person, you need to open yourself up to others so that they can help you eliminate your blind spots and discover your unrealized potential.

Although it takes some effort to open up and share yourself with others, it also takes effort (and creates psychological stress) to hide yourself from others. Hiding takes work. You must keep track of what parts of yourself can and cannot be shared with others. You must guard your

Figure 8.5 You can reveal the authentic self, or you can display a façade.

secrets. In addition, you may also spend a lot of time worrying about what will happen if your private self is accidentally revealed and your secrets are discovered.

We often hide the parts of ourselves that we think others will find shameful or ugly or unacceptable. We keep people in the dark about who we really are and about what we really think or feel because we are afraid of being harshly judged or rejected (Figure 8.5). As John Powell says, "Why am I afraid to tell you who I am? I am afraid to tell you who I am, because, if I tell you who I am, you may not like who I am, and it is all that I have …" (goodreads.com).

However, many people experience great relief when they stop hiding who they are from other people. For example, people who "come out of the closet" about their sexual orientation or sexual preferences often feel like a great psychological load has been lifted, regardless of how this self-disclosure is received by others. Although some people may react negatively to their disclosure, just being truthful about themselves is a positive experience.

Factors That Affect Self-Disclosure

There are several factors that affect the amount and type of self-disclosures that people make, including personality type, family training, individual preferences, cultural expectations, sex and gender, length of relationship, type of relationship, and reciprocity. Let us take a closer look at each of these factors.

Personality type: Some people are classified as "extroverts," and some people are classified as "introverts." Extroverts are outgoing, overtly expressive people who like being with and talking to other people, so they find it easier to self-disclose than introverts. Introverts are more focused on themselves and their inner thoughts, so they may not be as prone to, or as comfortable with, self-disclosure. Although shyness should not be equated with introversion, it is another factor that makes self-disclosure difficult for some people. People who are shy tend to feel awkward or tense during social encounters, so they may have difficulty self-disclosing.

Family training: Some people find it easy to self-disclose, or have difficulty self-disclosing, because of family training. As they interacted with family members in their formative years, they were taught that certain things should not be shared with other people and that other topics were always open for discussion. The types of self-disclosures you think are "natural" and appropriate are very likely the types of self-disclosures that were often made in your family of origin. The types of self-disclosures you think are odd and inappropriate may be the types of self-disclosures prohibited in your family of origin. And if you were brought up in a home where "children are to be seen and not heard," then you may find it difficult to make *any* type of self-disclosure as an adult (Figure 8.6).

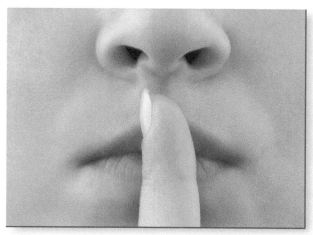

Figure 8.6 Some people are trained by their families to make very few self-disclosures.

Personal preferences: When you enter into an interpersonal relationship with another person, you will have to negotiate certain "dialectical tensions" that may arise. **Dialectical tensions** are conflicts or tensions that arise when relational partners have different personal preferences. One dialectical tension that directly impacts the amount of self-disclosure in an interpersonal relationship is "preference for openness" versus "preference for privacy."

Some people are just "wired" for openness. They want and they expect a large amount of self-disclosure in their relationships. Other people are "wired" for privacy. They want and they expect other people to respect their boundaries. If two relational partners are both wired for openness, their interpersonal communication interactions will often contain a high level of self-disclosure. If two relational partners are both wired for privacy, their interpersonal interactions may contain a fair amount of time intimacy and physical intimacy but very little intellectual intimacy and emotional intimacy. Their preference for privacy will decrease the level of self-disclosures involving personal thoughts and feelings.

What happens when two people with different preferences for openness and privacy are involved in a close relationship? They will have to deal with the dialectical tension that is created by their different preferences. One person may want the other person to "be an open book," but the other person may want to keep their thoughts and feelings "under lock and key" (Figures 8.7 and 8.8). Both relational partners must learn to respect and live with their different preferences.

Figure 8.7 Are you an open book ...?

Figure 8.8 ...Or are you a closed book?

Cultural expectations: In Chapter 6, we pointed out that there are different conversational styles that predominate in different cultures of the world: "discussion style" cultures promote direct and emotionally restrained discourse, "engagement style" cultures promote direct and emotionally expressive discourse, "accommodation style" cultures promote indirect and emotionally restrained discourse, and "dynamic style" cultures promote indirect and emotionally expressive discourse.

On the one hand, people enculturated into "discussion style" cultures (people in England, Germany, and the United States, for example) may find it easy to directly disclose conflicts they are having with other people, but they may find it much more difficult to disclose their feelings about these conflicts. On the other hand, people from "dynamic style" cultures (people from Saudi Arabia and other Arab countries) may find it easy to self-disclose their strong emotions, but they may find it much more difficult to directly disclose what conflicts are generating these emotions.

People from "accommodation style" cultures (like Japan and other Asian countries), however, may have difficulty directly self-disclosing either the conflicts they are having with other people or their emotions related to these conflicts. Clearly, general cultural expectations influence the amount and type of self-disclosures that people make.

In addition, each culture has specific "conversational taboos" that you should be aware of when interacting with people from other cultures. You may think it is no big deal to ask your conversational partners about their political affiliations or their religious beliefs, but your communication partners may have difficulty self-disclosing because you are asking them to violate one of their culture's "conversational taboos." Many visitors to America, for example, assume that capitalistic Americans love talking about money, but they do not realize it is "taboo" to ask Americans to share their yearly income in a casual conversation.

Sex and gender: The amount and type of self-disclosures can be affected by the sex and gender of the people involved in an interpersonal communication transaction. First, whether you are a man or a woman and whether you are masculine or feminine (or an "androgynous" mixture of masculine and feminine) has an effect on your self-disclosures. Whereas biological sex is primarily a matter of nature, gender is primarily a matter of nurture. Males and females are enculturated into traditional gender roles, so they are taught what is appropriate and inappropriate to discuss as "masculine" men and "feminine" women. In order to fit these gender roles, people may limit their self-disclosures in certain areas. For example, traditionally "masculine" men may limit their emotional self-disclosures, whereas traditionally "feminine" women may self-disclose about their relationships a lot.

Second, whether you are speaking to a man or woman has an effect on your self-disclosures. There are cultural rules and expectations about what can or cannot be discussed among members of the opposite sex. If you are a male talking to a male or a female talking to a female, the types of self-disclosures you make in an interpersonal exchange will be somewhat (or even very) different than the self-disclosures you would make when talking to a person of the opposite sex (Figure 8.9).

Length of relationship: A crucial factor affecting the amount of self-disclosures in an interpersonal relationship is the length of that relationship. When an interpersonal relationship is first initiated, both partners usually self-disclose fairly safe, fairly limited, "shallow" information until they get to know one another. If trust is established, and if they decide to enter into a more intimate relationship, then they often self-disclose deeply in short bursts. Once their relationship has been firmly established, deep self-disclosures often

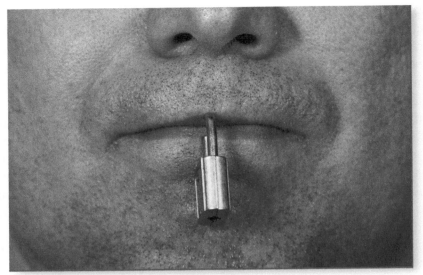

Figure 8.9 A man may find it very difficult to self-disclose certain things to a woman.

taper off. It is not uncommon for long-term relational partners to self-disclose very little even though they are in a close relationship.

The self-disclosure pattern described above is one of the most common patterns for an interpersonal relationship, but there are other, more unique, self-disclosure patterns that may take shape. For example, sometimes two people just "click," and they share substantial self-disclosures immediately. After just a few minutes or hours, they may describe themselves as "soul mates," and their relationship is characterized by a high level of trust and self-disclosure.

Type of relationship: In addition to the length of a relationship, the exact type of relationship you are in will affect your self-disclosures. Your self-disclosures in a professional relationship will differ from your self-disclosures in a romantic relationship, or they should. Your self-disclosures to a casual acquaintance will differ from your self-disclosures to a therapist or spiritual advisor, or they should. Different types of relationships require different types of self-disclosures.

If you are a parent in a parent–child relationship, you probably would not make the same kinds of self-disclosures about your sex life to your young child as you would to your best adult friend. The "pragmatic" rules of language demand that you consider the context of your interpersonal communication: who is speaking to whom and in what communication situation? What may be a perfectly acceptable and appropriate self-disclosure in one interpersonal relationship may be a very unacceptable and inappropriate self-disclosure in another interpersonal relationship.

Reciprocity: The primary factor determining whether you continue to self-disclose in a relationship is **reciprocity.** When you self-disclose to a conversational partner, you expect that partner to reciprocate and self-disclose personal information to you in return. If your self-disclosures are reciprocated, you will continue to self-disclose, and you may even decide to deepen the level of your self-disclosures. If your conversational partner then reciprocates and also shares deeper self-disclosures with you, you may deepen your self-disclosures further, and so on (Figure 8.10).

Salespersons understand and exploit the human desire for, and expectation of, conversational reciprocity. In order to quickly establish a relationship with potential customers, salespersons will often self-disclose personal information about themselves in the first few minutes of a conversation in the hopes that the customers will reciprocate. Most people, even those who know about this sales strategy, find themselves responding to the salespersons with their own self-disclosures. The salespersons have used the principle of reciprocity to initiate and establish a "personal" (rather than an "impersonal") relationship that is more likely to result in a successful sales transaction.

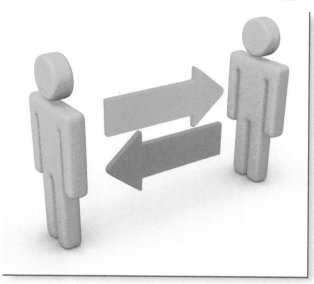

Figure 8.10 To continue, self-disclosures usually need to be reciprocated.

Police interrogators also exploit the principle of reciprocity in order to coax confessions out of criminal suspects. Instead of attempting to demand or force a confession out of a suspect, interogators will often self-disclose something "bad" they have done and then ask the suspect to do likewise. Even though most criminal suspects know that a confession will lead to severe legal penalties, some cannot resist the impulse to reciprocate: they confess of their own free will because of the powerful pull of reciprocity!

The Benefits of Self-Disclosure

We want to encourage you to engage in appropriate self-disclosure by listing and positively describing the benefits of opening up and sharing your thoughts, feelings, and life experiences with other people, especially your significant others.

1. Reciprocal self-disclosures:

Although some people (like salespeople and police interrogators) use self-disclosures to manipulate others, you can look forward to the fact that when you find the courage to open up and share your inner thoughts and feelings with others, they will probably return the favor. When you self-disclose personal, sensitive information about yourself to others, you are taking a risk, but this risk has a definite payoff: there is a good chance that they will reciprocate and let you see more of who they really are.

2. Enhanced, more meaningful relationships:

At the beginning of this chapter, we claimed that if two people want to create a deeper, more intimate interpersonal relationship, then they must both "open up" and self-disclose. Now that you have a better understanding of self-disclosure and its effect on self and others, we hope you can see the validity of this claim.

You may have satisfactory long-term relationships that do not involve much self-disclosure, and this is fine. We are not suggesting that your close relationships are in danger of dissolving if you

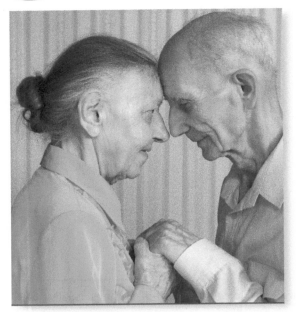

Figure 8.11 Reciprocal self-disclosure can make a satisfactory relationship extraordinary.

do not increase your self-disclosures. Many people have relationships that last 20, 30, even 40 years with fairly low levels of self-disclosure. We are suggesting, however, that with more self-disclosure many of these "satisfactory" relationships can be enhanced and become more meaningful. Deep, reciprocal self-disclosure might even make a satisfactory relationship extraordinary (Figure 8.11).

3. Increased communication effectiveness:

Chapter 1 introduced the transactional model of communication, and one of the basic concepts in this model was the **context** of communication: "The inner communication context is the mental environment that exists in a communicator's mind. The more the mental environments of two communicators overlap, the easier it is for them to communicate. Conversely, the less two communicators have in common in their mental life and experience, the harder it will be for them to connect and communicate."

The more two interpersonal communicators engage in reciprocal self-disclosure, the more their mental environments overlap, and the easier it is for them to communicate. If you and your conversational partner have a good understanding of each other's thoughts and feelings, core beliefs and values, memories, and life experiences, then you will decode each other's verbal and nonverbal messages more easily and more accurately.

4. Improved psychological and physical health:

In Chapter 1, you learned that adults (just like infants) can "fail to thrive" if they do not fulfill their love and belonging needs, and we suggested that if you want to live a long, full life, you need to pay attention to the quantity and quality of your interpersonal interactions and your social relationships. Since deep self-disclosure is one important key to creating high-quality relationships, the link between self-disclosure and your physical and psychological health should be obvious.

In Chapter 6, you learned that suppressed and repressed emotions can lead to both psychological problems and physical illness. You also learned that (according to Dr. Norman B. Anderson) emotional expression (one of the deepest forms of interpersonal self-disclosure) was a more important factor in your overall health than your cholesterol level, body mass, or blood pressure.

Earlier in this chapter, we pointed out that it creates psychological stress when you hide yourself from others. It also creates psychological stress when you continually worry about what will happen if your private self is accidentally revealed and your secrets are discovered. Leaders of addiction recovery programs often assert, "You are only as sick as your secrets."

For your physical and mental health, you need to practice appropriate self-disclosures that will help you to (1) fulfill your love and belonging needs, (2) effectively process your emotions, and (3) eliminate unnecessary psychological stress and anxiety.

5. Increased self-awareness and self-esteem:

When you self-disclose to significant others, not only do they get to know you better, but they can help you to know yourself better. The private, "perceived" self that you share with others may not accurately reflect who you really are. In other words, your self-perceptions of who you are may be warped and inaccurate. You may think less of yourself than you should, especially if you have negative self-talk.

When you self-disclose your self-perceptions to people who know you well, they can help you to correct any self-perceptions that are warped, inaccurate, or false. If you accept their feedback, you can do some "cognitive restructuring" and revise your inaccurate, negative self-concepts in order to improve your self-image and your self-esteem.

6. Help and support from others:

Often people are afraid to self-disclose things they have done (or are doing) that they think people will judge as shameful or unacceptable. They do not want to be harshly judged or criticized or rejected. Their fear of criticism and rejection keeps them in hiding. However, when they find the courage to self-disclose their problem or flaw or bad behavior, they often receive help and support and encouragement from others (Figure 8.12).

7. Help and support for others:

Sometimes people self-disclose not for their own benefit, but for the benefit of others. When you self-disclose even very negative, traumatic experiences, you can help other people. Abuse victims can help other abuse victims by self-disclosing. Negligent drunk drivers can help prevent future drunk driving accidents by self-disclosing. Through courageous, appropriate self-disclosures, people can use the memories of horrific occurrences and experiences to help heal trauma survivors and to help prevent future tragedies.

Figure 8.12 Self-disclosures are often made in recovery programs and support groups.

8. Experiencing unconditional love and acceptance:

Perhaps the greatest personal benefit of self-disclosure is that it creates the opportunity for you to experience unconditional love and acceptance. You may have people in your life that love you and accept you unconditionally, but if you are hiding any part of yourself from them, you might be tempted to think that they wouldn't *really* love and accept you if they knew who you really were.

Unconditional love and acceptance is a gift that human beings can give to one another, but not a gift that everyone is capable of giving or receiving. Some people only offer *conditional* love and acceptance: they do not love and accept you unless you meet certain conditions. Some parents, for example, reject their own children if their children do not meet their expectations or fulfill certain conditions. Some people will reject their romantic partners if conditions change (sickness, loss of income, disfigurement, etc.)—their love and acceptance is only "conditional."

Over the years, I have asked my college students if they believe that human beings are capable of giving and receiving unconditional love and acceptance—so far, my informal poll (involving several hundred students) stands at about 50%: about half of my students say they have experienced giving and receiving unconditional love, and about half of my students say they do not think unconditional love and acceptance is possible.

The students who believe in unconditional love and acceptance often provide as evidence their personal experience of having a parent or spouse or sibling or friend who knew the absolute worst about them, and yet still loved and accepted them without reservation. No matter what dark deed they confessed, no matter what serious character flaw they admitted, their parent or spouse or sibling or friend loved and accepted them anyway. This love and acceptance, they assert, was unconditional.

Note that these students were certain that they were loved and accepted unconditionally because they had self-disclosed (or their significant other had discovered in some way) the absolute worst about themselves. Self-disclosure of your true, authentic self, warts and all, is a requirement for really *receiving* unconditional love and acceptance (Figure 8.13). You may *hope* that your significant others love and accept you unconditionally, you may *suspect* that your

Figure 8.13 Full self-disclosure allows you to receive unconditional love and acceptance.

significant others love and accept you unconditionally, but until you self-disclose what you think is the worst of yourself, you will not *know* that your significant others love you unconditionally.

The Risks of Self-Disclosure

Although self-disclosure has many benefits, it is not without risk. Those readers who determine that they are under-disclosers should focus on the proceeding section which champions the benefits of self-disclosure. However, those students who determine they are over-disclosers should carefully consider the following risks that come with self-disclosures.

1) **Relational risks:** Self-disclosures can strengthen and deepen a relationship, but they can also negatively affect or even lead to the termination of a relationship. If you attempt to deepen your self-disclosures in an interpersonal relationship, there is a chance that your conversational partner may not reciprocate and may not appreciate your self-disclosures. They may de-escalate the relationship, or if they are very uncomfortable or upset with your self-disclosures, they may even end the relationship. And if you search for unconditional love and acceptance in your closest relationships, your full self-disclosure of self may reveal that a significant other is only capable of conditional love and acceptance.

2) **Professional risks:** Certain jobs and professions have certain behavioral expectations and standards, and if it is discovered that you have not met these expectations or have violated these standards, you may lose your job, or you may be barred from your profession. Disclosing sensitive personal information to your boss, co-workers, customers, or employees may negatively impact your job or your chance of job advancement.

3) **Legal risks:** Self-disclosing criminal behavior or past crimes can put you at risk of prosecution, and it may also put the receiver of your self-disclosure at legal risk if they do not report your disclosure or your criminal behavior to the appropriate authorities.

Under-Discloser or Over-Discloser?

I began this chapter by confessing that I was a serious under-discloser for the first 40 years of my life. My bias in this chapter, therefore, should be fairly obvious. I want to help under-disclosers who (like myself) have shut themselves off from intimate relationships and deep human connections. I want to help them open up and begin self-disclosing and sharing themselves with the world much more often.

I hope I have not over-sold the benefits of self-disclosure. Since I rationalized my own under-disclosing for so many years of my life, I have had to work hard to convince myself that self-disclosure is primarily beneficial and necessary. I now want to work hard to convince other under-disclosers that their excuses for hiding from others are just excuses.

However, I do not want to encourage over-disclosers to continue with their copious and inappropriate self-disclosures. There really is a thing such a thing as T.M.I.—Too Much Information. Therefore, I ask my readers to complete the Chapter 8 Activity Sheet that will help them determine if they are under-disclosers or over-disclosers.

We will end this chapter with advice on appropriate self-disclosure: advice about self-disclosure in general, advice for under-disclosers, advice for over-disclosers, and advice for people receiving self-disclosures.

General Advice About Self-Disclosure

- Consider your motivation for self-disclosing. You should self-disclose in order to help yourself, to help others, or to improve your relationship. You should not self-disclose to hurt others or to punish yourself.
- Consider whether you have an ethical duty to self-disclose.
- Consider the communication context. You should pick the right time and place for self-disclosure. You should not self-disclose when your conversational partner will not have time to reciprocate or process your self-disclosure. You should not self-disclose in a place where other parties may overhear your self-disclosure.
- Consider whether your conversational partner is wired for openness or privacy. You should respect their personal preference.
- Consider the benefits and risks of your self-disclosure. You should weigh the pros and cons of self-disclosing, and then make a wise decision.
- Consider the amount and type of your self-disclosure. You should make the type of self-disclosures that are appropriate for the type of relationship you have with your conversational partner. You should usually not make deep self-disclosures in a casual relationship.
- Consider the amount of reciprocal self-disclosures given by your conversational partner. You probably should not continue to self-disclose if your conversational partner is not self-disclosing in return.

Advice for Under-Disclosers

- Do not let past bad experiences with self-disclosure prevent you from self-disclosing in the present.
- Do not rationalize your desire to keep from self-disclosing.
- Rehearse the benefits of self-disclosure until you have internalized them.
- Practice self-disclosure with a "safe" person.
- Be willing to trust people. If you self-disclose to someone and they betray your trust, who really has the problem? You did nothing wrong by trusting them. You gave them the benefit of the doubt and tried to benefit your relationship.

Advice for Over-Disclosers

- Avoid deep self-disclosures with casual or new acquaintances.
- Pay attention to your conversational partner's verbal and nonverbal feedback.
- If you think someone may be uncomfortable with your self-disclosure, perform a "perception check." Ask them.
- Discontinue self-disclosing if your self-disclosures are not reciprocated.

- Make sure your reciprocal self-disclosures match the self-disclosures of your conversational partner. Do not be a "stage hog" and try to top their self-disclosures.
- Do not rationalize your desire to self-disclose if the risks really outweigh the benefits.

Advice for Receivers of Self-Disclosures

- Listen carefully and empathetically.
- If appropriate, reciprocate with a self-disclosure of your own.
- Do not judge or evaluate the self-disclosure.
- Provide a supportive response.
- Thank your partner for self-disclosing.
- If requested, keep the self-disclosure confidential.

Figure 8.14 Self-disclosure can open you up to the world and open the world up to you.

Conclusion

After reading this chapter, you hopefully now have a deeper understanding of, and a stronger motive for, self-disclosure. You know the factors that affect self-disclosure. You know the benefits and risks of self-disclosure. With this knowledge, you should be able to make wise decisions about self-disclosure that will strengthen and deepen your interpersonal relationships and create a more "open" you.

Chapter 9

Close Relationships

By A. Todd Jones

After reading this chapter you will

- Understand different types of relationships
- Learn to express closeness and trust
- Understand the different ways people express closeness

Figure 9.1 Family vacations are often spent with those we are closest to

I'm excited to talk to you about close relationships. Close relationships are often our principal reason for being happy, and feeling joy and contentment. As many of us think back on our lives, we realize that so much of our happiness has come from our relationships and been experienced with those we are closest to. Happy moments such as the birth of a child, winning a baseball game with team members, or going on a family vacation are often experienced within the context of our most intimate relationships. Some of our saddest moments also happen within our closest relationships. Difficult times such as a breakup or the death of a loved one are particularly painful. These relationships are of utmost importance to us because of their potential to influence our general well-being.

Defining Closeness and Intimacy

The first thing we naturally think about when close relationships or intimacy are mentioned are romantic relationships. We often think of the word "intimacy" to describe our romantic relationships or a relationship where we are sexually active with another person. When in reality, a romantic or sexual relationship is just one type of intimacy. It's important to note that intimacy does not always involve sexual activity. In fact, most of the people we have intimate relationships with are not of a sexual or romantic nature. Although we will talk about romantic relationships at length, it's important to understand other close relationships such as friendships, family, and even professional relationships. Before we discuss the details and types of close relationships, let's talk about what a close relationship is. As we proceed in this chapter, keep in mind your current or ideal romantic partner, your closest platonic friend, and a family member you are close to. Although there are obvious differences in these types of relationships, there are a few general similarities. Close relationships have three things in common. They require maintenance, dedication, and an atmosphere where partners can rely on each other.

Figure 9.2 Romantic relationships are just one type of relationship where we experience intimacy.

© Akhenaton Images/Shutterstock.com

Figure 9.3 Close relationships can occur in professional settings as well.

© Pressmaster/Shutterstock.com

Maintaining a Relationship

It's not uncommon for a movie or a children's book to end with the statement that everyone goes on to live happily ever after. That may sound great at the end of a story or a movie, but it doesn't take into consideration the reality of day-to-day living, that is, that *any* close relationship will require maintenance. Let's first define relational maintenance and then address maintenance strategies. Dindia and Canary (1993) suggest four standard definitions. First, relational maintenance means *keeping the relationship in existence*. Consider all of the Facebook friends many of you have. Do you personally communicate with all of them on a regular basis? Not likely. But the fact that they are your "friends" online allows you a convenient and low-maintenance connection. The relationship remains in existence as long as you have this connection.

Figure 9.4 Facebook and other form of social media have made it easier to maintain relationships.

Figure 9.5 Married and committed couples should continue to date each other after the honeymoon period has ended.

Second, relational maintenance *involves keeping the relationship in a specific state or condition, or a stable level of intimacy, so that the status quo is maintained* (Ayers 1983). For example, coworkers may work to keep their relationship professional, or best friends may seek to keep their relationship close even though they are now attending different colleges.

Third, relational maintenance *means keeping the relationship in satisfactory condition*. Just like an athlete must continue to work out and train to stay fit and prepared for his or her sport, a married or a committed couple should continue to date each other and maintain the relationship once the wedding or the commitment has taken place. Obviously, we don't work hard to create a great relationship and then not put forth the effort to maintain it. Although not as demanding, a friendship will need to be maintained as well. This can become more difficult as time goes on because of natural life changes, such as graduation, moving away, or a change of jobs. The true test of friendship is time and inconvenience.

Fourth, *relational maintenance requires keeping the relationship in repair*. Ideally partners or friends will work to prevent problems and difficulties from happening. However, no relationship is perfect. When conflict or misunderstandings occur, it is important to talk about the issue, apologize, and work together to correct the problem.

Keeping a relationship or a friendship healthy and intact takes a lot of work. This is especially true after years and years of knowing this person. You may ask yourself what kind of communication and interaction will best serve this relationship, and how will you know what is appropriate? Your maintenance strategy will obviously depend on the type of relationship. Maintaining a marriage or a committed romantic relationship is very much different from maintaining a friendship or a family relationship. A conscious awareness of maintenance strategies

Figure 9.6 Open communication is essential in maintaining a healthy relationship.

and how they might work in your various relationships is key. Guerrero et al (2013) suggests several strategies:

- Openness in communication: listening, self-disclosure, routine talk.
- Positivity: communicating in a positive manner, giving compliments, and acting cheerful.
- Giving support: encouragement, comforting each other, and making sacrifices for each other.
- Joint activities: spending time together, playing sports, shopping, travel, etc.
- Romance and affection: Saying "I love you," communicating caring feelings for each other, touch, and spending time alone together.

© Monkey Business Images/Shutterstock.com

Figure 9.7 Romance, saying "I love you," and affection are just a few ways that a romantic relationship can be maintained long term.

- Humor: Not taking yourselves too seriously, laughing at each other's jokes, inside jokes, laughing together.
- Balance: Keeping the relationship fair and equal. Putting forth an equal effort in the relationship.

© Valery Sidelnykov/Shutterstock.com

Figure 9.8 Picking your battles carefully and being respectful during conflict are important strategies in maintaining a relationship.

Another important maintenance strategy that warrants extra discussion here is the ability to handle conflict in a respectful manner. I know I am not the first person to tell you to pick your battles carefully. In other words, not all disagreement is worth an argument or a fight. Ask yourself, "Is winning this fight more important than keeping the peace in the relationship?" Not likely. That isn't to say that these issues should be avoided—on the contrary! A healthy discussion in which each side of an issue is politely considered will often be resolved where both are satisfied with the outcome. I have found that one of the simplest ways to gauge your partners' wants, or position on an issue, is to rate things on a scale from 1 to 10. For example, I might ask, "On a scale from 1 to 10, how much would you like to go out to eat tonight?" The other person might be an eight, while you are at a ten. Chances are you'll be eating out. But if one of you is at a two, and the other is at a seven, the end result may be different. This method lets the other person know more specifically where you stand on an issue. When you consider your partners' wants and preferences, often before your own, it communicates respect and a level of importance. This is particularly helpful when you are romantic partners.

Dedication and Commitment

When we discuss dedication and commitment in a relationship, again, we most often think of a romantic relationship. However, let's first consider commitment in family relationships and friendships. Commitment in a family relationship manifests itself in several ways. Obviously, parents are committed to raising their children in the best environment possible. A newborn baby requires complete commitment and relies on its parents for everything. Those of you who have had children know that this commitment is life encompassing, sometimes difficult, demanding, and very rewarding.

Figure 9.9 Commitment in a friendship or a family relationship is important as well.

© Phovoir/Shutterstock.com

As children grow they become more independent, but the commitment in a family setting remains. It may feel or look different as we get older. Once siblings reach adulthood and move out of the house, the type of commitment may change depending on factors such as physical distance between them, how often they see each other, their marital status, and how the relationship has evolved. Being committed to another person, regardless of the type of relationship, isn't always easy or convenient.

Are you quirky, unique, or maybe a little different? A challenge in almost any relationship is putting up with the other persons' quirks. This can take commitment and dedication. For several years, I have asked my students if anyone wanted to claim that they weren't quirky. So far, I haven't had anyone raise their hand. Some of these quirks can be annoying or just weird. It can be anything from your partner not cleaning up oneself to wanting to have the dishwasher loaded a specific way. I remind myself and my classes that people are a package deal and that everyone has good, bad, and weird in them. The reality is that being in a committed relationship, whether romantic, friendship, or a family relationship, means being patient and looking the other way from time to time when the other doesn't do things or see things exactly as you do.

Figure 9.10 Marriage is a statement to family, friends, and society that you are committed to this relationship.

One of our greatest joys in life is finding that special person to spend the rest of our lives with. What makes this relationship so special is the process of coming together, including romance, touch, and commitment. Many romantic couples feel as if they have the most unique and special relationship ever and wonder if anyone else has ever felt this way before. I assure you that we have, but you should enjoy it as if it were the only relationship of its kind ever! We feel a sense of security as we blend our lives together. This commitment often takes on the form of marriage, living together, or holding the title of boyfriend, girlfriend, or partner. Being engaged, for example, makes a public statement to family and friends that you are committed to this relationship. In American culture, an engagement is often accompanied by rings—a symbol of commitment.

Interdependence and Relying on the Other

Finally, close relationships often carry with them a sense of interdependence and reliance on the other person. This can vary widely depending on the type of relationship. A friendship, even a best friendship, isn't likely to have the level of long-term interdependence that a marriage will have. Interdependence in a marriage can manifest itself in an almost endless list of ways. Partners may rely on each other financially, for transportation, emotional support, conversation, sex, accomplishment of a task, or a feeling of acceptance—just to name a few. Interdependence in close or best friendships is different in that there isn't an element of romance in the relationship. However, many of the same indicators of interdependence still exist. Think of your best friend and how you rely on him or her. It is also likely that the level you rely on your friend is quite different from your reliance on the person sitting next to you in class. Interdependence in its many forms varies depending on the dynamics of the relationship and from person to person.

Relational Culture

Figure 9.11 Inside jokes are just one of the things that make your relationship unique and add to your relational culture.

As we have discussed earlier, each relationship is unique. Just like there are differences from one culture to another, there are differences in each relationship. In fact, researchers Turner and West (2006), Wilmont (2006), and Galvin and Wilkinson (2006) suggest that each relationship has its own relational culture. Think of your best friend, your sister, or your romantic partner. What inside jokes do you share in your relationships? How do you communicate differently in one relationship compared to another? Are there some relationships where you seem to be more funny or more serious than others?

The experiences you have had with the other, how you met, your similarities, and the conversations you have had will shape the way you interact with them. Some relationships are defined by their history, while others are shaped by things that you have in common. What is the relational culture like in your relationships? The reality is that no two relationships are exactly alike. The chemistry will always be different. When I was in high school, two of my best friends were identical twins. Very few people could tell them apart. Once I got to know them, it became easy to know who was who based on their expressions, communication patterns, and their nonverbal communication patterns. The relational culture that I shared with each of them was different. Relationships are like fingerprints—no two are alike. If one of your relationships ended, it would be impossible to replace it because the chemistry and the relational culture will always be different.

Figure 9.12 Each relationship we have will have different chemistry. No two relationships are alike.

Relational Scripts

Societies and cultures of all sizes have expectations and norms for different types of relationships. These are called relational scripts (Holmberg & MacKenzie 2002). A relational script is a set of norms and expectations that are socially constructed by a group. Consider the relational script or the expectations of a marriage in your culture. Think of each step from first date to the wedding and even after. How different is it from the relational script in a culture where marriages are arranged? These scripts help us to understand the norms of a particular kind of a relationship quickly. This understanding helps us to know how to act in different relational contexts. These scripts can be general in nature, such as how a dating relationship should develop. Or they can be specific, such as expectations for taking someone to their senior prom. Often, we consider these relational scripts to be "normal" and "just the way things are" when in reality the scripts have been socially constructed and are usually different, sometimes very different, in other cultures (West and Turner 2012, IPC, p. 201).

Figure 9.13 Culture has a strong influence on the relational scripts that we have.

According to Wilmont (1995), as relationships develop, partners create communication patterns and interactional norms. As the relationship grows, things happen in a specific order. First, as we spend more time with another person we are able to predict how the other will act or what he or she will say in a certain situation. For example, if your friend were to hear an inappropriate joke, you will have a good guess as to how he or she will react. Your guess will be based on past experiences with this person. If your friend had reacted negatively to a racist comment in the past, you can assume with a fair amount of accuracy that this friend will be offended again. Second, we become aware of a past, present, and future together. We generalize our expectations of the other based on past interactions, reactions, and events. If this person is typically on time, and has made comments about others being late, you can bet that he or she will be on time the next time you plan to get together. Third, the other person gains a title. This title could be "friend," "best friend," "girlfriend," or "partner" to name a few. Giving the relationship a title signifies closeness and commitment and announces to others the nature of your relationship.

Figure 9.14 Our relational scripts may determine dating rituals as well.

Social Penetration Theory

Altman and Taylor (1973) stated that humans, like onions, have several layers. Over the years this theoretical perspective has gained popularity because of the simple way it describes different types of relationships. This model suggests that each relationship can be described or measured by looking at the depth and breadth of communication in the relationship. The layers of an onion symbolize the depth, or the how intimate the relationship is. The outer layers represent general information about you, such as your name, your job, and how you physically present yourself.

These outer layers aren't typically private information and are often among the first things that are discussed or gets noticed when we meet someone for the first time. Middle layers may include your age, your relationship status, your income, your politics, or your level of education. Examples of the inner layers may consist of our religion, our feelings about our bodies, the positive and negative aspects of our romantic relationship, or our sex life. As we get to know someone, there are opportunities, through conversation, to disclose information about ourselves to others. Sometimes the disclosure is shallow and superficial, while other times, typically after several interactions, the conversation deepens along with the relationship. Close relationships often touch on all layers. There is nothing wrong or offensive with keeping a relationship superficial. In fact, most of the people we meet or interact with are superficial relationships.

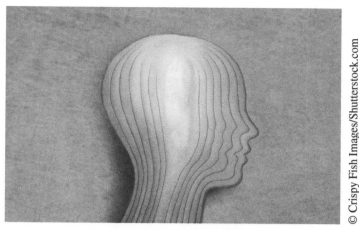

Figure 9.15 Social Penetration Theory suggests that each relationship has layers of closeness and self-disclosure.

© Crispy Fish Images/Shutterstock.com

© HappyPictures/Shutterstock.com

Figure 9.16 When we refer to the breadth of the relationship, we are referring to the number of different topics, activities, and common interests that it is based on.

Figure 9.17

Figure 9.18 Some relationships have little breadth and focus on one topic or activity.

In addition to understanding the depth of a relationship, it's important to understand breadth. When we refer to the breadth of the relationship, we are referring to the number of different topics, activities, and common interests that it is based on. If you have a buddy that you play basketball with once a week, the relationship isn't likely to have much breadth. It will simply be based on the activity of playing basketball. However, another friend might be someone that you grew up with or someone you share a lot in common with. These relationships will likely have a lot more breadth.

I have a friend who is a Raiders fan. (I know, me either). When there is a game, his Raiders friends come over, barbeque, and watch the game. They discuss nothing but the Raiders, and maybe a little about how to grill a good steak. When Raiders season is over, their communication stops until the following fall. Their relationship has little breadth in that it is based on these two things. There's nothing wrong with this. In fact, relationships that are based on only one or two topics or activities are common.

Some relationships have little breadth, while others are based on several different activities and interests. Typically a friendship that is based on very few things will fade over time. However, if a romantic relationship, especially a marriage is to last, the breadth of this partnership needs to be significant. Simply put, your marriage needs to be based on several activities, interests, beliefs, and topics. The more you have in common, the more interests and opinions you share, the more likely your marriage is to succeed.

Romantic Relationships

It may surprise you to know that about a third of us under the age of 25 has never had a boyfriend or girlfriend! That's right; you may not be as different as you thought you were. I have had so many students either write about this in papers or confess this to me—most of them embarrassed. Please! You are normal; give yourself a break. It will be that much more enjoyable when

Figure 9.19

Figure 9.20 Moving from first date to committed relationship is an exciting process.

it happens. There are so many factors that contribute to being ready for, available, and wanting a relationship, such as age, culture, gender, religion, sexuality, and family rules. When the time is right it will happen for you.

When I first started teaching interpersonal communication at Bakersfield College, I would ask if anyone wanted to self-disclose their relationship status to the class. Some were married, others were dating, and some were "talking." Talking? I was confused. Did this mean they were communicating? No, "talking." Hmmm, what does that mean? I later found out that "talking" was the stage between first date and committed relationship. While this term may be local, this stage is an important one. It's how you get to know the person and find out if you are a match. What is that person's personality like? What are his or her likes, dislikes, hobbies, education, goals, family relationships, and so on? This is a time to proceed with caution and to keep your eyes wide open. Remind yourself that the purpose of your relationship, for the time being, is to enjoy each other's company and to get to know one another better.

After you have spent some time with this person, and have started to like him or her, the next natural step is to have the DTR talk—define the relationship. This conversation can be welcomed, or it can be feared. When you have this defining conversation, you should discuss what each of you wants, what each of you expects in the relationship, how you feel, and what titles you should use in the relationship. Be specific—it is not uncommon for one to ask the other, "What are we?" Most of us like to have a title such as "boyfriend," "girlfriend," or "partner" when committing to a relationship. Having a title helps to define the partnership to each other; it also informs others of your relational status.

The outcome of this talk could move the relationship toward committed relationship, could end the relationship, or you may decide to keep it as it is and give it more time. Regardless, you will have a better idea where the

Figure 9.21 Defining the relationship is necessary for it to progress.

other person stands. This talk is required if you are going to ever move a relationship forward to dating, commitment, or marriage.

Now that you have gone through the "talking" stage and things have gone well, your relationship will likely advance to the dating stage. This can mean a lot of different things to a lot of different people. By its very nature, the word "dating" suggests some kind of relationship. To some, dating is just simply going on dates or spending time with the other person. This may even mean playing the field—dating, or going on dates with more than one person. However, in most cases, this is the ideal stage to define the relationship.

So you meet someone, you are impressed and you are attracted to him or her. You'd like to get to know the person better; you want more information about the person. You want to know if there is any relational potential there. How do you move the relationship from your first introduction to romance? According to Tolhuizen (1989), the most common method of relational progression is increased contact or spending more time together. This often comes in the form of a date. Volumes have been written about dating—far too much to cover here. However, let's discuss a few pointers about early dating. First, when you ask someone out it's ideal to do it in person. A phone call would suffice as well. You should not ask someone out via text or social media. Second, if you are not interested or not available to spend time with this person, politely tell him or her. Don't make excuses, and don't lead someone on if you have no intention of ever going out with him or her. It is better that the person knows the truth and has a temporarily bruised ego than to have hope in a possible relationship with you that will never exist.

Figure 9.22 If you are asked to go on a date with someone you are not interested in, politely tell him or her. Don't make excuses.

Figure 9.23 The honeymoon period of a relationship is a time of discovery and a can be very exciting.

Your first love isn't likely to be the only person you will ever have romantic feelings for or a relationship with. Most often this will be nothing more than a simple crush when you are younger. For some of you it may not happen until you are in your twenties, or even later. However and whenever it happens or has happened for you, your first relationship will be like no other. It is a time of discovery and learning what it is like to be romantically connected to another human being. It is often quite emotional. We find out what we like and what we don't like in a relationship. We also become accustomed to what it is like to be a couple and to have a shared identity.

The beginning of most relationships is what we often call the honeymoon period. This stage can be as short as a few weeks or as long as a few years. Most of us, especially if we are young, experience a euphoric feeling of being completely engulfed in the other person. This may not happen when you first start spending time together, but once the relationship becomes more real, usually through conversation and touch, our emotions and the connection we feel become stronger. During the honeymoon stage, the other person seems to be perfect and it is as if they can do no wrong. We often don't notice their faults or weaknesses, and it seems like the sun always shines, the birds always sing, and that you are walking about a foot off of the ground. Don't worry; you'll come back to Earth eventually. However, in the meantime, enjoy it and learn as much as you can. Reality will return soon enough.

The next stage can vary from couple to couple. Once you are in a committed relationship, and (in my opinion) you have spent at least 2 years (yes, 2 years) together, depending on your stage of life, most couples want to take the relationship to the next level. This can either mean living together or getting engaged. Many believe that living together will allow you to try out the relationship at a more intimate level. My students have told me that living together can be very revealing. Does he put the toilet seat down? Does she spend too much time on the Internet? What does your partner look and act like in the morning? Is he or she financially responsible? Living together can answer a lot of questions. However, those who live together before marriage are statistically twice as likely to eventually end up divorced. Make these decisions wisely.

Figure 9.24

Getting engaged to be married can also have different meaning to different people. It can simply mean that someday you will get married, or it can mean that you have set a date, have a ring, and are making arrangements for a wedding ceremony and festivities. I have had several engaged students and couples in my classes over the years. I'm always a little surprised when I hear of an engagement that is 2 years, 3 years, or even longer. I grew up in a conservative culture where if you didn't have a ring and a date, you weren't engaged. I suppose that may seem a little harsh to some of you, how-

Figure 9.25 Engaged couples should consider what they are committing to and what level of commitment they are making.

ever, consider what you are committing to and what level of commitment you are making. You may also want to consider your priorities. **Are you planning a wedding or a marriage?** When you get engaged there are so many things to consider. Where will the wedding be? How

Figure 9.26 Are you planning a wedding or a marriage?

© Africa Studio/Shutterstock.com

much will it cost? Where will you live? What is your financial situation? What other commitments such as school, work, bills, and family do you have? I realize that this is one of the happiest times of your life, but it can also be one of the most stressful. When getting engaged, do so with your eyes wide open and an awareness of the realities of both of your lives. Be aware of how much you are committing to spend on your wedding and how that will have an effect on your finances for the first year or two of your marriage. We have all heard of couples that spend $20,000 to $30,000 or more on their wedding and find themselves at an unnecessary level of debt as they begin their marriage. You would be wise to be financially responsible and reality based when planning a wedding.

Figure 9.27

© huahinpanda/Shutterstock.com

The wedding is over. It was beautiful! All of your thank-you notes have been mailed, you are setting up a new home together, and you are so in love. Volumes and volumes have been written about marriage. Obviously, there is too much to write about it in one paragraph here. However, realize that much of what we discuss in this chapter and book will apply to marriage. Marriage is an official agreement that not only makes your union legal; it communicates to everyone the permanent nature of your relationship. Often, marriage creates a joint identity. You may be known by your last name (e.g., "the Hudsons"), and others will often see and refer to you as a couple. Also, marriage can be difficult and require educating yourself to be better equipped to understand your spouse and his or her needs. Later in this chapter, we will discuss the five love languages which have helped thousands of individuals and couples understand each other better.

Family

Throughout the ages families have typically been defined as a group who are related either through marriage or by birth. These families have often consisted of father and mother figures along with children. Although that scenario is still common, the percentage of families in the United States consisting of heterosexual couples who are married with biological children has dropped from about 40 percent in 1970 to 20 percent in 2010 (Tavernise 2011). These days "family" is broadly defined to include childless couples, gay or lesbian couples, unmarried couples, empty-nest

Figure 9.28

Figure 9.29

Figure 9.30

Figure 9.31

couples, couples with adopted children, step parents or siblings, intergenerational families, and, as some argue, even a close group of friends. We should also remember that the makeup of a family will often change. Of course there is the traditional scenario of children growing up and moving out of the house, thus changing the living arrangements. But there are also several other changes that may take place altering what we may call the immediate family. Although not as common as it was 10 years ago, divorce is still a reality for about 40 percent of marriages. Once divorced, there is always a possibility of getting remarried, forming a blended family with step children and siblings. The reality is that family is now defined in a variety of ways. The definition we each have of family may vary from one person to the other based on our memories, our past experiences, the environment, and interactions with the members of our own family.

My earliest memories of close relationships were with my parents and my siblings. I was my parents' first child, and although I was the guinea pig, I knew I was loved. I remember the nightly bedtime ritual of my parents of reading story books to my siblings and me. We would all sit in a row on the couch—the smallest two got to sit next to the parent that was reading. Although my siblings and I would sometimes argue about what book to read and anything else we could think of, I remember feeling close to my family.

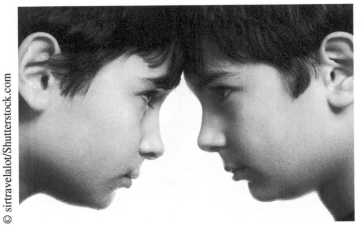

Figure 9.32 Sibling rivalries.

Figure 9.33 Holding your own child for the first time is an instant bonding experience.

Some of our close relationships happen as a result of the birth of a sibling, cousin, and others. However, it is not uncommon for siblings to have rivalries or to be very different from one another. I have four younger brothers and two younger sisters. I was three and a half years old when my brother—my first sibling—was born. Although I don't remember feeling this way, I was told that I was jealous of this new baby in our home. I was no longer the center of attention. As he grew up I teased him unmercifully and he didn't like it at all. This particular brother and I were close enough in age when we were younger to have some of the same friends. However, once I started junior high school, that arrangement changed. Like many siblings, we developed different interests and talents, and grew apart. As adults we now live in different states and communicate from time to time at family reunions, on the phone, and through social media.

As time went on our family grew, and as the oldest of seven children, I was expected to help around the house and to take care of myself. Other than my large family (which was very common back then), my adolescent and teen years were typical. I was more interested in my relationships with my friends than I was with anyone in my family. Many of my students have noticed the same thing. I have also had many students comment on the evolution of their relationships with their parents as they get older. The transition of aging in a family setting may be complicated, especially if these children live with their parents a few years past high school graduation. Letting go of parenting responsibilities and negotiating a new adult relationship with their children can be difficult for some families. However, once this new way of interacting has been established, it can be one of our most rewarding relationships.

Many of you have been told that you won't understand the love and feelings parents have for their child until you are parents yourselves. I can't express to you how true this is. I was lucky enough to have two kids—a girl and a boy. The first time I held each of them, my heart was instantly fused to theirs. I had no idea where this strong love for this new, tiny baby came from, but it was undeniable. When my first child, my daughter, was born her mother was exhausted after giving birth so I got to hold her for the first 2 hours of her life. She was awake, quiet, and her eyes were open. I talked to her about all of the fun we were going to have and how much I already loved her. I just couldn't stop looking at her.

My second and final child was my son. Like most fathers, I was ecstatic to have a boy. My reaction to him was similar to my reaction to his sister. I just couldn't believe that this tiny human was mine and relied on me and his mother completely. I wanted to be there for every second of their lives. I didn't want to miss anything. However, babies, especially newborn babies, can be very high maintenance. As you may know, newborn babies need to eat every few hours. My son wanted to eat at midnight and 5 a.m.—not the best schedule to get a good night sleep. After he ate he wanted to be held and we wanted to sleep. I ended up taking him downstairs to sleep on the couch with me so his mom could get some rest. I loved having this baby boy sleep in my arms. For several months that was our routine. I believe that because of this, he still loves dad hugs, and we continue to share a special bond. There is nothing quite like the love that a parent has for his or her child.

Closeness in family relationships manifests in different ways. Some families are more verbal and say, "I love you," and give compliments. Some are physical with hugs, back rubs, and kisses—even on the lips! (I know, my family either.) Other families are more reserved and choose to express their closeness by spending time together. Regardless how closeness is communicated in your family, our relationships with our parents, siblings, and extended family are unique in that we didn't choose them—these relationships were handed to us through our birth, or the birth of a sibling, cousin, and so on. This can be a good or a bad thing. It is not uncommon for siblings to have rivalries or to be very different from one another. Regardless of the relationship you have with your siblings now, most of us will be connected to our siblings, parents, and extended family for the rest of our lives.

As we talk about families it is important to note that not all families have good relationships; in fact, some of you may not be in touch with some or any of your family members. For whatever reason, this can be emotionally difficult and damaging. If this is the case for you, you may want to consider counseling and/or support from friends or others in your life. Understanding yourself and your place in a dysfunctional family can be very healing and can allow you to move your life forward in a healthy

Figure 9.34 Closeness can be expressed in a variety of ways.

© polya_olya/Shutterstock.com

direction. It can also help you to form your own healthy family relationships with your children. As I stated earlier, we typically don't pick our families. However, sometimes, when things don't work out as we had hoped, we meet friends and/or extended family members who become our family. Friends can often fulfill the needs for family bonding that our family has not.

Friendship

Our families aren't the only people we may be close to in our lives. I was lucky enough to live in a neighborhood with majority of kids my age. If we weren't at school, we spent every waking minute together. We played sports, board games, and night games and went ice skating and sledding just to mention a few of our activities. Thanks to Facebook and other social media, I have been

Figure 9.35 How have you benefitted from the friendships you have?

able to connect or reconnect with many of these old friends. As I think back on these memories, I realize that experiences and the early relationships I had were central to the forming of my personality, disposition, humor, opinions, politics, religious views, values, and social skills. My guess is that many of you have these same memories and have had some of these same realizations. If not, take a few minutes to reflect on your earliest close relationships. What are your early memories of those you were close to? What made them so important to you? How did these friends influence your views and expectations for your close relationships now? Have those influences been good, bad, or mixed? What influence do you want to have on your children and grandchildren?

Before we go any further, let's define friendship. Friendships are relationships in which we voluntarily interact, bringing happiness, satisfaction, and rewarding feelings about ourselves to each other. Although there is often an element of friendship in romantic relationships, when we discuss friendships we are talking about relationships where there are no romantic desires or feelings. A friend is someone who is easy to be around, who likes and accepts you as you are, and someone you can trust. You feel the same about that person. Much of our happiness in life, especially in our childhood and early adult years, comes from friendships.

Reciprocal Friendship

There are a few different types of friendships we should discuss. As we do so, take an inventory of your friendships. What kind of friendships do you have? What kind of a friend are you to others? An ideal friendship is a reciprocal friendship. This is the type of relationship where each of you contributes equally. These are the friendships that are close, loyal, generous, self-sacrificing, and where the value and importance of the relationship is similar to the other. Have you had friends like this? These are often the most rewarding and satisfying of friendships.

Figure 9.36 Friendships that are equal are the most rewarding and satisfying form of friendships.

Receptive Friendship

Receptive friendships are where one person is typically the giver and the other person is typically the taker. This is the type of friendship where the one taking has more power than the one receiving. If you find yourself in this type of friendship, it may be wise to ask yourself what is in it for you. There was a girl I went to high school with who was probably the most popular girl in our class. Unfortunately, she wasn't very nice to people and she used her social power to get what she wanted. She was a "mean girl" long

Figure 9.37 Beware of friendships where one person has more power than the other.

before the movie! It seemed that several of her friends maintained their relationship with her because it made them look popular by association. Finally, one of her friends called her on the way she treated others. It was a typical high school drama, but it seemed to have made her more aware of the inappropriate way she was treating others.

Associative Friendships

Not everyone we meet will become our close friend. Associative friends are those relationships where giving and receiving is minimal and the association is surface level rather than deep. These are those you may meet in a class, at work, a social gathering or through other friends. There is no special loyalty, trust, or connection. Typically, for example, these associative friends you meet in a class will not become long-term friends after the class is over. Reasons may be as simple as lack of connection or similarity or as simple as not enough available time to

Figure 9.38

pursue a closer friendship. Is it bad to have this kind of friendship? Not at all. If you think about it, we all have several of these kinds of acquaintances.

Specialty Friendships

Sometimes we meet friends who fulfill a specific need or with whom we have just one or two things in common. These are specialty friends. A specialty friend is someone we have a specific common interest with, such as movies, video games, or sports. Our interaction with this person is centered on this particular interest or activity only—there is little breadth. This friend may be

Figure 9.39

someone we play on a sports team with or someone with whom we share the same hobby. When we discussed this concept in class, one of my students asked if "friends with benefits" was a specialty friend. We all laughed, but agreed that, indeed, friends with benefits fit the description of a specialty friend.

Best Friendships

A discussion about friendship wouldn't be complete without discussing the concept of best friends. While there are many who consider their spouse or romantic partner to be their best friend, when we discuss best friendships from an academic perspective it refers to your closest nonromantic, platonic relationship. That's what we will briefly discuss here. Many of us have a best friend as we grow up. He or she is typically the closest person to you. A best friend accepts you as you are. He or she is altruistic, committed, dependable, fun to be around, and someone who is similar to you. This friendship can be fulfilling and give a great learning experience to help us in our adult relationships. It may enhance our self-esteem, combat loneliness, and help us to feel more secure in social situations. Your best friend is the person you count on to be there in times of need and times of fun. I'm sure many of you have stories you could tell about the fun, crazy, and bonding times you have had with your best friend.

Figure 9.40 Your best friend is the person you can count on during the good and the bad times.

Aging, Gender, and Friendship

In our younger years, we tend to become friends with our siblings, neighbors, and those we go to school with. We tend to bond with those who we are able to see often and spend time with. As we get older and friends move away or go to different schools, it becomes more difficult and less convenient to maintain these friendships. We simply aren't around these friends anymore and don't have as much opportunity to interact. This same scenario often applies to adults as well. Think of fellow students you may have gone to high school with or taken a college class

Figure 9.41 The true test of friendship is time and inconvenience.

© Diego Cervo/Shutterstock.com

with. While you were in class with them, it was convenient to interact. But when school or the class ended, you no longer saw them and the relationship faded away. Although social media has made it easier to maintain contact with these friends, we rarely spend as much time together face-to-face as we used to. When a friendship is important it should be maintained or it will cease to exist. Time and inconvenience is the true test of friendship. If a friend exerts the effort to maintain contact over time and the inconveniences of distance and schedule, then it is worth keeping.

A cautionary note while we are discussing friendships. Over the years I have noticed that as we get older, men and women typically do not experience friendship the same way. Often women are more focused on their friendships and relationships than men. After women marry and have a family, they are still in touch with best friends, sisters, family members, college friends, cousins, and others. They often invest time and effort to maintain these relationships. In comparison, men, especially straight married men, have very few, if any, friends that they regularly spend time with. Although there are exceptions, men don't typically put forth the effort to acquire and maintain new friendships. I have also noticed that this seems to be specific to American culture. Men, I believe that we would be wise to acquire and maintain friendships with other men. These relationships meet needs that no one else can meet. In my opinion, maintaining and spending time in these friendships will often make us better fathers and better husbands.

Expressing Closeness

Now that we have discussed specific types of relationships, let's explore closeness in general. Closeness is often manifested with those who hold a title such as spouse, partner, sibling, best friend, friend, acquaintance, coworker, and so on. While there are obvious differences between a romantic relationship and a friendship or other types of relationships, closeness is often communicated or experienced in similar ways. What does closeness look like between you and your romantic partner, parent, best friend, brother, and others? What makes you close? Activities? Words? Trustworthiness? Think about it.

Open Communication

My research (Jones 2001) has shown that there are several ways closeness in relationships is apparent. Out of all the ways to communicate closeness, the most common is open communication. Close relationships typically have comfortable, easy, positive, open communication. Obviously, to be close to someone, you have to talk to them. Open communication is the ability to honestly and freely communicate what you think, feel, or want without the fear of a negative reaction from the other person. Don't you love that the people you are closest to seem to always know exactly what to say in any situation? Direct discussions about the relationship or overt expressions of love and closeness are among the most important building blocks of a close relationship.

Figure 9.42 One of the most effective ways to build closeness in a relationship is open communication.

In addition to romantic relationships, many friendships define their relationship verbally. If you introduce someone as your best friend, that communicates to the other person as well as your friend that he or she is, indeed, your best friend. Having the title of best friend, boyfriend, girlfriend, husband, wife, spouse, partner, and so on communicates to that person as well as to everyone else that you consider this person to be close to you.

A surprising amount of people have a hard time accepting compliments—even from a best friend or a romantic partner. Their response is either of these: a denial of the truthfulness of the compliment, a downplay of the compliment, an assumed obligation to compliment the person back, or acceptance of the compliment. The final option is by far the best. If taking a compliment is difficult for you, simply say, "Thank you."

Direct communication about the relationship is a necessity in a romantic relationship. Even if you are just "talking," you will sooner or later need to further define this relationship. In addition to defining the relationship, which can be very bonding, directly communicating your feelings to the other person is important. This can be as easy as saying, "I love you," or "I'm so happy to be with you." Or as detailed and intimate as discussing the needs, desires, and future plans of a relationship. Direct communication in a friendship may not be as frequent or intimate as a romance, especially for men, but it is nevertheless important and beneficial to both.

Open communication can also cause anxiety or stress. Many people are uncomfortable with such open communication because of shyness, being overly private, a fear of being vulnerable, homophobia, or a lack of communication skills necessary to communicate or to get into close relationships. Close relationships don't just happen; they take effort and open, honest communication. Earlier in this chapter we discussed the fearful phrase "We need to talk?" Metacommunication, or communicating about the relationship, is common in most close relationships and a necessity in a long-term romantic relationship. Those who have learned to communicate directly, openly, and honestly often find themselves in happier, more satisfying relationships than those who lack these skills or who lack the confidence to take the risks necessary.

It's not uncommon for straight men to be close to one another without ever verbally expressing that closeness to the other(s). Gentlemen, while this might work for a time with your buddies, it's not going to fly with your partner, girlfriend, wife, or kids. The danger in any of these communication barriers listed above is underdeveloped skills when they are most important and needed for happiness in life. Imagine the unwillingness or the inability to express to your future spouse how you truly feel about him or her, or not knowing how to communicate love, acceptance, pride, or closeness to your children. Imagine your partner or future spouse unable to openly and completely express his or her feelings to you. As humans, especially adults, good communication skills are a necessity for successful relationships and for overall happiness in life. Unfortunately, there are far too many people out there that lack communication skills or are simply unwilling to communicate frankly and openly. I believe that this is most often the reason relationships are difficult or dysfunctional or fail. Improving our communication skills in general and in a specific relationship will take time and effort. Talking about your relationship(s) may not be your cup of tea, but to maintain and enjoy these relationships, you will have to do so. No one person is an island. We all have to learn to communicate in relationships. Some of us may

Figure 9.43 Closeness needs to be expressed in marriages and to your family members.

Figure 9.44 Open communication is not optional in close relationships.

have been taught or had a good example to follow—such as parents—but effort and education in relational communication are necessary to form, maintain, and keep successful relationships.

Self-disclosure is one of the most common methods of bonding with another person. Sharing personal feelings, experiences, beliefs, and opinions is one of the most common ways to bond with someone. What makes us tell someone else our secrets or private information? Why is it that the more intimate and private the information we share, the closer we feel to that person, and the greater the likelihood that he or she will in turn share similar private information with us. We bond and feel closer to another by trusting that person through self-disclosure. As we continue to communicate openly, we build more trust in the relationship, and this brings us to our next indicator of closeness: trust.

Trust

Few things can bring two people together more than trust. Trust is an expected necessity in a close relationship such as a best friend, family member, or romantic partner. Violation of trust can damage or end a relationship. It can be as simple as relying on the other person to tell you when the clothes you are try-ing on don't look good to something as monumental as finances or faithful-ness in a romantic relationship. Defin-ing trust is difficult because it is such a universally understood construct. Trust includes sharing and keeping secrets, being dependable, doing what they say they will do, not breaking promises, and being honest and loyal. Someone you trust may also defend you in front of others. This person would not talk behind your back or betray you. Trust is also a necessity in maintaining a relationship.

Figure 9.45 Few things can bring two people together more than trust.

Respect

Similar to trust, respect is also a com-monly understood idea, but is still dif-ficult to define. What does it feel like when you are respected? Have you ever been disrespected? Maybe a rude or insensitive comment from someone has caused you to feel this way. Is it possible to respect someone whom you disagree with? What if you question the morals of their actions or opinions? On the other hand, is respect the same as being impressed with or approving of another person's opinions or actions?

Figure 9.46 Respect is a necessity in close relationships of all kinds.

Think about these ideas as you interact with those you are close to.

Trust and respect may exist in relationships that are not close. Perhaps you respect a boss or supervisor that you are not close to. You may not particularly like them, yet you respect them for their position, knowledge, and authority. While trust and respect are more associated with close relationships, these constructs can exist in almost any relationship.

Physical Touch

Along with open communication, physical touch can be one of the most direct forms of com-municating closeness. Of course, touch in romantic relationships is often different from how it is in a friendship. Touch in straight male friendships may be limited to different versions of a handshake, while female friends may be more open to hugs or other types of physical affection. Of course, romantic relationships, especially those who are married, will have a sexual compo-nent to their interaction as well. How two people touch may also be influenced by our culture, age, and the relationship itself.

Figure 9.47 Human touch can be very bonding.

Helping Someone Complete a Task

Have you ever had a friend or loved one do something nice for you? Maybe they helped you out with a task that you had to accomplish or surprised you with cleaning the house. Helping someone complete a task can communicate love and closeness in any relationship. We will discuss a similar concept when we address the five love languages.

History

When we look at relationships from a long-term perspective, we tend to hold on to those relationships that have positive outcomes. As these relationships continue to be fulfilling, we tend to stick with them. A long relational history may not be the first thing that comes to mind as a way to communicate closeness, but think about it this way: Would you stick with a relationship of any kind that wasn't meeting your needs in some way? The simple fact that you have been friends or romantic partners for so long—that you have history—indicates that there is value in the relationship.

Figure 9.48

Figure 9.49 Simply maintaining a friendship over a long period of time communicates that the relationship is valued, and is one of closeness.

Time and Interpersonal Enjoyment

Do you have inside jokes in your close relationships? Can you look at the other person or say a word or a phrase and laugh? As we spend time together in these relationships, it is common to develop an idiosyncratic way of communicating. Close relational partners seek each other's companionship because of the comfort level. When we feel at ease around another person, we seek them out. For many, spending time together is a much more comfortable way of expressing closeness than verbally doing so.

Figure 9.50 Laughing and having inside jokes make us feel more at ease with others.

Enhancing Attractiveness

Years ago, I had a friend who came from a family of eleven kids. She was one of the youngest, so she grew up in a household that was established and organized with schedules and chores. Her mother was quite progressive and often asserted a woman's equality to men. So, you'll imagine my surprise when I learned that she changed her clothes and put on makeup every day just before her husband came home from work. I asked my friend about that and she told me that it was her mother's way of being attractive to her dad because that was important to him.

Figure 9.51 An attractive self-presentation may be one way to communicate closeness and interest in a relationship.

Making ourselves attractive to others is just another way of communicating closeness. Although this is more likely to happen in romantic relationships, I have been told that when women go out on the town, they dress up to impress (and compete with?) each other. Guys? I suppose that guys often make efforts to improve their looks for those they date. However, somewhere between the ages of 25 and 35 men care less and less about their outward appearance—it becomes far less of a priority. Guys, we would be wise to be aware of our visual presentation and to shape up and groom a little more. Your girlfriend, wife, or partner will appreciate it.

Gifts

Every time I would return from a trip when my kids were younger, they would ask me, "What did you get us?" I'm sure they missed me, but my little gift of a story book or a toy communicated to them that I was thinking of them and that I loved them. Gifts can symbolize your

Figure 9.52

thoughts and feelings toward another person. Consider giving flowers. I may never understand why this might mean so much to another person—flowers die! But, I have learned, that is not the point. The point is that flowers signify that the one person was thinking of the other, and that the relationship is important to both.

Relationship Progression

Getting to know someone and moving from being an acquaintance to being a friend or a potential romantic partner can be an interesting journey. If you think about it, how many people do you meet in a year? That number can vary widely depending on your job, schedule, and lifestyle. Ask yourself, "Of these hundreds of people that you meet each year, how many of them become friends, or intimates?" Very few. Other than the reality that there just simply isn't enough time to bond and become friends with that many people, there are

Figure 9.53 Out of the potentially hundreds of people we meet each year, very few of them become our friends.

several other factors that filter others out as well. These filters may include lack of similarity, gender, age, location, interests, religion, etc. As we meet people we often get to know them to determine if there is a potential to become friends or more. Along the way our filters eliminate most of these people. This isn't a bad thing; it is one of the realities of being a social human being.

Once we have filtered out those who we are less likely to bond with, we enter into relationships of different kinds. We also maintain them, and sometimes we terminate them. Again, when we talk about relationships we most often think of romantic relationships. However, much of the information about relationships also applies to friendships, family, and professional associations as well. Communication scholars Knapp and Vangelisti (2006) studied this progression of relationships and came up with a ten-step model that relationships often go through. This ten-step process doesn't always go exactly in this order, but generally speaking, it is accurate.

Coming Together

There are three steps of coming together in a relationship. The first step is **initiating**, in which we meet the other person and indicate to them that we are friendly and worth getting to know. This is often accomplished by a simple handshake, a greeting, or an introduction of our self to the other. For those of you who are shy, this may be one of the most difficult steps. Many have found the anonymous and relatively safe route of social media and online dating to be the preferred method of initiating contact with another person. The second step is **experimenting**, where we determine whether or not this relationship is worth pursuing. Small talk and getting to know the person on a surface level dominate this phase. At this point it is not uncommon for dyads to either move forward with their relationship or terminate it. This termination may be nothing more than seeing each other less and less until contact has been eliminated. Third, is the **intensifying** stage. This is when dating couples or friends start to spend more time together. This can also be the beginning of the honeymoon period of the relationship. Couples will start to define the relationship, while some friendships will take on the title of friend or best friend.

Figure 9.54 Meeting someone and getting to know them is a process.

© Hans Kim/Shutterstock.com

Maintaining the Relationship

The next four steps describe relational maintenance. If you think about it, we spend relatively little time getting into and falling out of relationships in comparison to the amount of time we spend in them. Understanding the importance and stages of maintaining a relationship can save us all a lot of heartache and drama.

The first stage is **integrating**. This early stage of maintenance assumes that the relationship is now clearly established. Others begin to view the dyad with a shared identity. Couples start to jointly own items, share resources, and attend each other's events. They will also start to develop an idiosyncratic way of communicating and interacting with inside jokes and subtle nuances, which may include touching, nonverbal communication such as facial expressions, a daily routine, and traditions. Second is the **bonding** step. This is the stage in which couples make a public announcement of their relationship by getting engaged and married. Friendships may also reach this stage although less formally. Friends may become roommates, start a business together, or may take on the title of best friend.

Third is **differentiation**. This is the stage where couples begin to reassert their individual identity again. Independence and the need for autonomy are not necessarily an indication that the relationship is in trouble. The need to be ourselves and explore our own interests can sometimes be put on hold during the integrating and bonding phases of a relationship. This is the stage when the honeymoon period is over. It is a natural part of the progression of a relationship. Our fourth and final stage of maintenance is **circumscribing**. Communication in the relationship will decrease, making our conversations shorter and of lower quality. This is a common stage for those who have been together

Figure 9.55

© Yurchenko Yulia/Shutterstock.com

for a long time—perhaps an older couple that has been married for forty or fifty years. Conversations may not happen as regularly because they already know what their spouse or partner will say. However, if couples who haven't been together for long enter this stage, they may want to take inventory of their relationship, work on their communication, and even consider counseling.

Coming Apart

Finally, let's take a look at relationships coming apart and terminating. These last three stages may seem like a downer to talk about, but if you think about it, most adults have been in a relationship at one point in their lives that have ended. It is important to understand how this happens so that once it is over we can learn from the experience and move on with our lives. It should also be noted that not all relationships that enter the first two stages of coming apart are doomed to end. Sometimes couples will have a change of heart, will educate themselves on how to more effectively communicate, or will seek counseling to work things out.

The first stage of coming apart is **stagnating**. Those couples who continue in the circumscribing stage for too long often enter into this stage. The attraction and excitement that brought the relationship together no longer exists. Interaction and conversation happen less and less, and the relationship is a hollow frame of what it used to be. The second stage is **avoiding**. Like stagnation, the name of this stage speaks for itself. The individuals may sleep in different rooms and take separate vacations. Conversation and interaction are avoided. One of the reasons a couple may enter these stages is the lack of communication and a lack of willingness to work things out when issues come up or when the relationship starts to deteriorate. Things may not look good, but all may not be lost.

Terminating and Moving On

However, when counseling or a change of heart does not occur, the relationship will most likely **terminate**. It is over. Terminating the relationship can happen in several different ways. Most couples break up face-to-face, some over the phone, and some are wimps and break up with the use of technology—don't do that. Those who were friends before they started dating are more likely to remain friends after the breakup. Those of us who were married with children will be connected to our former spouse for life, like it or not. Once the breakup has happened we often create a narrative to explain it to our family and friends. The

Figure 9.56 Ending a relationship can be one of life's most difficult events.

level of negativity and blame associated with this narrative will often influence how well you will each get along afterward.

On a more positive note, once you are ready to enter another relationship of this nature, you will have a better idea of what kind of person you are looking for and what you are trying to avoid. Your list of deal breakers may grow a bit, but more importantly it will become more specific. You'll know what works and what doesn't work for you in the future. If your partner was quiet, shy, and didn't like to socialize as much as you do, then you may seek after potential partners who enjoy socializing as much as you do. Obviously, it should be noted that not all relationships terminate. About 50 to 60 percent of marriages, many business partnerships, and friendships will last a lifetime, and many believe, longer.

Turning Points

Another theoretical perspective that seems to align with the above research is that of turning points. A turning point is "any event or occurrence that is associated with change in a relationship" (Baxter and Bullis 1986). For example, James and Jennifer met in their chemistry class. James asked Jennifer if she'd like to study for their first exam. As they studied and got to know each other, the conversation drifted from chemistry to their personal lives. The more they talked, the more they realized that they had a lot in common. When the library closed James walked Jennifer to her car. As he was saying good night, Jennifer asked him if he'd like to get together for lunch the next day. As they ate lunch, James asked Jennifer to go

Figure 9.57 Although we are rarely aware of it at the time, a turning point in a relationship can affect the rest of your life.

out with him that weekend. They went out to dinner and to a party and had a great time. When James walked Jennifer to her door, they kissed for the first time. The turning points so far in this story are meeting to study, going on dates, and the first kiss. Anyone of us could finish this story with the typical turning points of having the "define the relationship" talk, meeting the parents, getting engaged, getting married, having children, and so on. Turning points are simply any occurrence that marks a progression of the relationship in one direction or another. These are the re-

Figure 9.58 Even something as simple as a kiss can be a life-altering turning point!

lationship-defining moments that stand out in our minds. Of course, not all turning points move the relationship forward. Sometimes there are turning points that cause harm to the relationship, such as being unfaithful, a health crisis, or getting caught in a lie.

Social Exchange Theory

Social exchange theory (Molm 2001) is based on the simple economics of costs, rewards, profits, and losses. Costs are the investments you make to gain a reward. A business owner invests time, money, effort to sell his or her product or service—these are the costs. This business owner also brings in money from customers as payment for their product—these are the rewards. When the rewards outweigh the cost there is a profit; when the costs outweigh the rewards there is a loss. Simple economics.

Figure 9.59

Let's apply this simple concept to relationships. We tend to get into and stay in relationships when there are profits; and we tend to leave when there are losses. The difference between an economic model and a relational model is that economics are based on a spreadsheet that declares a monetary profit or loss. It is objective; it is black and white. While the relational application of this economic model, social exchange theory, requires personal application, is subjective, and is based on our own perception, it is different for everyone. For example, have you ever known someone to be in a relationship where they are treated poorly, disrespected, or even abused? Why do they stay in the relationship when there are so many negatives? The answer is simple; in their mind, the rewards still outweigh the costs. This person may be financially supporting them, they may have nowhere else to go, or there may be children involved. From an outside perspective, it may look like your friend is suffering a loss in the relationship, and that may be true, but remember profits and losses are calculated in the mind of your friend—it is all in their perception.

Ultimately, if the costs of doing business outweigh the returns, you as the owner may decide to close the business to avoid further losses. This same concept applies to relationships. If the investments you have in the relationship such as time, money, effort, emotion, and so on aren't producing perceived rewards such as companionship, contentment, or a good relationship, you may decide that staying with this person isn't worth it.

Relationship Lessons I have Learned

Since we are writing this textbook in first person, I'd like to share a life-changing experience I had that may be another cautionary tale to many of you. I have learned a lot from my marriage and divorce. I have also learned a lot from students in class discussions. These lessons are a result of my experience as well as classroom conversations. I hope that by sharing this and discussing these issues you will be able to learn from the mistakes made by my students and me.

Figure 9.60

© pikselstock/Shutterstock.com

I met the woman who was to become my wife at a church function. We started dating about a week before Halloween and fell in love quickly. By Thanksgiving we were engaged to be married—yes, about 5 weeks after we started dating. Because of the nature of the religious culture that we both came from, we had a short engagement and were married in March. I know, I know, many of you are shaking your heads and rolling your eyes—and rightly so.

Our first years together were good. We had two kids, I finished graduate school, and I was hired to be a professor in California. It seemed that everything was going great. We had a nice house, a small family, and great friends. What could possibly go wrong? As time went on we realized more and more that we had nothing in common; in fact, we had nothing to talk about except about our kids and people we knew. We also both liked to travel so we took many vacations as a family. However, when we arrived at our destination, we had very different ideas of what a vacation should consist of. I wanted to see things, experience the culture through art and performance, visit museums, hike, and shop. She wanted to spend all day at the beach and attend local sporting events. Our last attempt to save our marriage—travel—didn't work either. We soon started taking separate vacations. It had become apparent that our relationship was over.

We discussed options for our future and the future of our kids and came to the conclusion that divorce was the best option for us. For those of you who have never been through a divorce or the divorce of parents or a close family member, let me tell you that it is not something that you want to go through. It was the worst experience of my life. I have heard that some divorces end amicably, but that is the exception and not the rule. It is stressful, emotional, and expensive.

I hope that the following ideas and "lessons" that my students and I have learned will help you to be aware and to make wise decisions. Some of these lessons are obvious, while others are more subtle. Let us educate and advise—please learn from my mistakes and from the mistakes of a few of my students.

Lesson One

Don't make any long-term decisions or commitments during the honeymoon period of a relationship. You can commit not to date anyone else and to call each other boyfriend, girlfriend, or partner, but that is all. My former wife and I dated for a month and got engaged to be married. Don't do that. Most of us are not completely in our right minds during this phase. We think that the other person is perfect in every way. Like I said before, we float about a foot off of the ground and we simply cannot be bothered with reality. Awesome! Enjoy it! Falling in love is one of the most exciting of human experiences. The honeymoon period is a time to be enjoyed and a time to get to know this person, to understand his or her world, opinions, morals, values, interests, beliefs, personality, likes, and dislikes. It is a time to meet the person's friends and family, explore his or her plans and goals for life, and to see how well they match yours. It is a time, for lack of a better way to say it, to try them out. Dating during the honeymoon period is a trial to see if this is the one for you. It is not a time to get engaged, married, or move in together. Even if you are completely convinced

Figure 9.61 Take the time you need to find out if this is the one for you.

that he or she is "the one." The honeymoon trial period is different for everyone. Some are as short as 9 months; others take 2 years. In my opinion, if you are under 35 you shouldn't make any of these decisions or commitments in the first 2 years of your relationship. If you are over 35 you should wait at least a year. Remember, even though you are head over heels in love, it is still a trial period.

Lesson Two

Love is not enough. As a freshman in college I had a psychology professor who explained that in a marriage, love is not enough. He explained that while the physical attraction is often one of the strongest forces that can bring a couple together, couples that base their relationship on what he called "huggy body kissy face" or physical attraction were often in for a rude awakening once the newness and excitement of the honeymoon phase had faded. The reality is that there is a lot more to a committed relationship or a marriage than being in love and physical affection. In 1989, Madonna released a song entitled "Express Yourself!" One of the lines in this song makes the statement and asks the question, "Satin sheets are very romantic, but what happens when you're not in bed?" In other words, what about the rest of the relationship? What happens when you aren't being romantic or "in love"?

Figure 9.62 There is a lot more to marriage than being in love.

The reality of a marriage is that someone has to clean the house, cook, and do the laundry. A household is a lot of work and so is a marriage. Is your partner willing to be an equal partner? What kind of an agreement for division of housework and support of the family do you have? Do you want children? How many? Will one of you stay home with the children while the other one works? What about finances, yard work, common interests, religion, your partner's family and friends, and his or her ability to communicate? You should also consider your hobbies and interests as well as your partner's. If your boyfriend or future husband watches 15 to 20 hours a week of football from August to February, are you going to be ok with that? What if he has an expensive truck or car that he spends a lot of time and money on? If your girlfriend or wife-to-be collects porcelain dolls, are you going to be ok with that? What kind of time and money commitments are there involved with these interests? Are you going to be ok giving up some of your football time, your big expensive truck, or your hobby?

Another question that you should ask yourself is, What kind of a relationship does this person have with his or her family? How do your partner treat his or her parents and family members? Disrespect, yelling, fights, or simply not having a close appropriate relationship with family members may be a red flag. On the other hand, sometimes the apron strings haven't been

Figure 9.63

Figure 9.64

© Rob Wilson/Shutterstock.com

Figure 9.65

cut yet. We have all heard stories of men still being referred to as a "mamma's boy" after he is married. We have also heard of women (or men) who needs to visit or talk to their family members every day. If you are married or in a committed long-term relationship, your partner should be your most important and intimate relation—not your best friend, your mother, your father, or one of your siblings. While it is ideal for these family relationships to remain close, there is a healthy balance that should be maintained. Your spouse should be number one. The bottom line here is that although it may not sound very romantic, all of the practical considerations need to be considered before committing to marriage. Again, love alone is not enough.

Lesson Three

We tend to attract romantic partners who will confirm our identity and level of self-esteem. In other words, if you have a healthy or unhealthy self-concept you will attract those who will validate that self-concept. Be aware of what kind of person you are attracting. We have all heard someone comment that they are unlucky in love. "Why do I always attract jerks?" Or, "Why do I always end up with women who use me?" What do you think causes them to go through one romantic partner after another? The answer is their expectations. In negative cases, these expectations may have emerged from a lifetime of negative relational experiences. Often starting with a parent or a sibling when young, to friends and those they date when they get a little older. Unfortunately, many of these people end up in several unsuccessful marriages or relationships. So, how do you correct this problem? It all goes back to your identity and awareness of your expectations in a relationship. You must come to terms with your expectations and this is often done in counseling. Be aware that this

Figure 9.66 Those who have a positive identity and who expect to be in a successful relationship will often attract those who will confirm that positive identity.

© sirtravelalot/Shutterstock.com

concept can also work for you. Those who have a positive identity and who expect to be in a successful relationship will often attract those who will confirm that positive identity.

Lesson Four

To love someone romantically is a decision. No one falls in love against their will or without their knowledge. We have all heard about love at first sight. Although that is a nice romantic notion, it isn't reality. We can be physically attracted to a person, impressed by him or her, enjoy the person's company, or even get butterflies in the stomach when in his or her presence, but the desire to be in a committed romantic relationship with someone is a choice.

Lesson Five

The ability to communicate in a relationship will not improve without effort and education. Although communicating is a natural human desire and experience, we are not born with the ability to communicate effectively. It is a learned skill. Some of us are blessed to have parents who teach us appropriate and positive communication skills, while others have to learn for themselves—often the hard way. Our ability to communicate in a relationship, especially at the beginning, is independent of that relationship unless effort is made to understand the other person and their point of view.

Figure 9.67 Our communication skills don't automatically improve with age. Educating ourselves and putting forth the effort to become better communicators will serve us well.

© Monkey Business Images/Shutterstock.com

None of us is born good communicators; we have to be taught and we should seek communication education. This education can be acquired by taking this class, by counseling, or by reading relationship and self-help books. Logically one would think that if a particular communication strategy caused a negative reaction from their partner or others, they would attempt to change that strategy. Unfortunately not everyone learns from their mistakes. We would all be wise to be aware of our communication patterns and strategies and improve where needed.

Lesson Six

Actions do not always speak louder than words. In previous chapters we have asserted that meaning is in people not in words. The same is true for our actions—not all actions will mean the same things to everyone. As I will discuss in the next section in this chapter, we all love in different ways. Have you ever tried to do something nice for someone, compliment him or her, or given a gift and not gotten the response that you wanted? This may be because these actions don't have the same meaning to them as they do to you. Now let's address this topic in more detail as we discuss the five love languages.

The Five Love Languages

In 1993, Dr. Gary Chapman, a family therapist, wrote a book entitled *The Five Love Languages*. In this popular self-help book, he explains how people love each other in romantic relationships. As it turns out, we all have different expectations in committed romantic relationships. Love, loving another person, and being loved by the other can mean very different things to different people. This is especially important to be aware of after the honeymoon period of the relationship is over. Of course, you still love each other, but the realities of daily life have returned and this relationship isn't the only thing on your mind—you now have your feet firmly planted on the ground again. Dr. Chapman examines why so many couples seem to disconnect after the initial excitement of the relationship is over. He explains that there are five love languages "spoken" and that unless we are aware of the love language of our partner and vice versa, we may have difficulties in our relationship. Let's further explore this simple, yet groundbreaking idea.

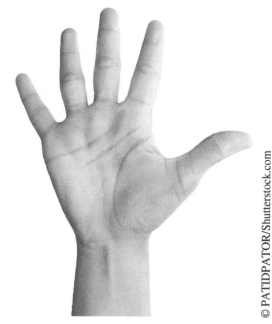

Figure 9.68

Basic to the understanding of this theory is the concept of the "love tank." Dr. Chapman explains that the *love tank is an analogy for how loved someone feels.* Your love tank is full when you feel that your partner truly loves you and you are satisfied with the amount of love you are getting. If your love tank is less than full, then the need you have to feel loved is not being met. The trick to loving your partner is to "speak" the love language that they best understand. In other words, to love them the way they prefer to be loved and on their terms. For some, the difficult part is that loving the other on their terms, or in their language, may be uncomfortable or unnatural.

Figure 9.69

The five love languages are words of affirmation, quality time, receiving gifts, acts of service, and physical touch. While many of us like all five of these languages spoken to us, we will usually have one primary language, and often a secondary language that we prefer. The metaphor of language is used to help us understand the ways your partner loves you and the way you prefer to be loved. Your love language may be foreign to him or her. A simple

© PATIDPATOR/Shutterstock.com

© Jelena Aloskina/Shutterstock.com

awareness that these languages exist can be the beginning of healing issues that may exist in the relationship. Actually loving your partner the way he or she wants to be loved will speak volumes to him or her.

Jake and Tina had been married for just over a year. Jake was busy with his new law practice, while Tina worked part time out of the home. Tina's love language was quality time, and because of their schedule, this need wasn't being met. When Jake finally came home from work, often late, he wanted to eat, watch TV and snuggle or have sex, and go to bed. Because of the rejection she felt due to lack of quality time spent together, she became less willing to be physical with him. His love language was physical touch. Obviously, this caused negativity and a lack of closeness in their relationship.

After several months of this stagnation, Tina went to lunch with an old college roommate who was visiting their area. She told her friend about the difficulties that she had been having in their relationship. Her friend told her about the five love languages and suggested that Tina and her husband read this book. Tina was excited to finally have a basic understanding of what was happening in her marriage. She bought the book, read it, and asked that Jake make an effort to do the same. He did, they discussed it at length, and they agreed to go to counseling. With this new understanding, their relationship began to heal.

These love languages can also apply to family relationships. As a parent, I learned to apply these to my kids. My daughter is now 15 and entering an exciting time in her life. She loves to talk about boys, art, books, and which tween celebrities she thinks are hot. My job is to listen and ask questions. Her love language is quality time. Since I have given her my undivided attention, our relationship has greatly improved. As I mentioned earlier in this chapter, my son, who is 13, is a snuggle bug. He still loves to sit close as we watch TV or to have a quick snuggle after he climbs into bed. His love language is physical touch.

Figure 9.70 Understanding your partner's love language can literally save the relationship.

Figure 9.71 Spending quality time with my daughter has improved our relationship.

Take a few minutes to think about your romantic and family relationships. How do these love languages work in your family? Can you see where an understanding of this simple concept can save you and your loved ones a lot of drama and grief? What is your love language? Are your needs being met? Are you meeting the needs of others you are close to? I encourage you to take the time to understand your needs and the needs of your loved ones.

Conclusion

Having close relationships is the backbone of happiness in life. When we share our lives with others, it increases our joy and quality of life exponentially. When we are old and we look back on our lives, what do you think we will think about most? It will be our relationships with our family members and our romantic partners. Keep this idea in mind as you interact with those closest to you. Love and treasure these relationships as if they were more important than anything—because they are. You'll be glad that you did.

Figure 9.72

Figure 9.73

Figure 9.74

Figure 9.75

Key Terms

Associative Friends: Relationships where giving and receiving is minimal and the association is surface level rather than deep.

Best Friend: Closest, nonromantic, platonic relationship.

Breadth: The number of topics, activities, and common interests that relationship is based on.

DTR: The conversation where couples define their relationship.

Family: A group of people who are related either through marriage or by birth. May also include childless couples, gay or lesbian couples, unmarried couples, empty-nest couples, couples with adopted children, step parents or siblings, intergenerational families, and, as some argue, even a close group of friends.

Friendships: Relationships in which we voluntarily interact bringing happiness, satisfaction, and rewarding feelings about ourselves to each other.

Honeymoon Period: The beginning of most relationships where couples experience a euphoric feeling of being completely engulfed in the other person.

Love Tank: An analogy for how loved someone feels (Chapman 2010).

Metacommunication: Communicating about the relationship.

Open Communication: The ability to honestly and freely communicate what you think, feel, or want without the fear of a negative reaction from the other person.

Receptive Friendship: A relationship where one person is typically the giver and the other person is typically the taker.

Reciprocal Friendship: Each person contributes equally to a relationship.

Relational Culture: Unique communication patterns in a relationship, experiences and conversations you have had with the other.

Relational Maintenance: Keeping the relationship in existence, in a specific state or condition, in satisfactory condition, and requires keeping the relationship in repair.

Relational Scripts: Societies and cultures of all sizes have expectations and norms for different types of relationships.

Self-Disclosure: Sharing personal feelings, experiences, beliefs, and opinions normally not known to others.

Social Exchange Theory: Based on the simple economics of costs, rewards, profits, and losses in a relationship.

Social Penetration Theory: Relationship can be described or measured by looking at the depth and breadth of communication in the relationship

Specialty Friend: Someone we has a specific common interest with such as movies, video games, or sports.

Talking: The stage between first date and committed relationship.

Turning Point: Any event or occurrence that is associated with change in a relationship.

Class Discussion Questions

1. What does relational maintenance mean to you? What maintenance strategies do you use to keep your different relationships where you would like them?

2. What does commitment in a relationship mean to you? Is there commitment in a friendship? How is that different from a romantic relationship?

3. What types of inside jokes do you have with your romantic partners, your friends, or your family members? How do these bring you closer together?

4. What types of relational scripts do we have in this country? How do they differ from relational scripts in other countries? Do you believe it is possible for relational scripts to vary from one relationship to another?

5. Typically, how long should a romantic couple be in the "talking" stage?

6. In your opinion, what is the difference between planning a wedding and planning a marriage?

7. How do you define family?

8. Is it possible to have more than one best friend?

9. Why do you think it is common for men in some cultures to have fewer friends as they grow older?

10. What caused your breakup? What did you learn from this relationship and the breakup? How has it affected your expectations in the future?

11. What turning points have you had? How did they change the trajectory of your life?

Surveys and Web sites

1. The five love languages are beneficial for us to utilize when trying to determine how we communicate with our loved ones. This website covers marriage, family, social issues, and so on.

   http://www.focusonthefamily.com/

2. This site has a quiz to determine your love language.

   http://www.5lovelanguages.com/

3. This site has the transactional model of communication from a business aspect as well as additional links to other communication models.

   https://www.businesstopia.net/communication/transactional-model-communication

4. This website covers nonverbal communication and ways to improve it. It discusses cues and types of nonverbal communication.

   https://www.helpguide.org/articles/relationships/nonverbal-communication.htm

5. This site discusses the importance of nonverbal communication and nonverbal abilities.

   https://www.ethos3.com/speaking-tips/the-importance-of-non-verbal-communication/

6. This site discusses the benefits of human touch.

   https://www.psychologytoday.com/blog/wired-success/201503/8-reasons-why-we-need-human-touch-more-ever

Movies and TV shows

Grace and Frankie (Netflix TV Series) 2016

For as long as they can recall, Grace and Frankie have been rivals. Their one-upmanship comes crashing to a halt, however, when they learn that their husbands have fallen in love with each other and want to get married. As everything around the ladies is coming apart, the only thing

they can really rely on is each other. The movie stars Jane Fonda, Lily Tomlin, Martin Sheen, Sam Waterston.

https://bepl.ent.sirsi.net/client/en_US/default/search/detailnonmodal/ent:$002f$002fSD_ILS$002f0$002fSD_ILS:1996682/ada

Moonstruck (Movie) 1988

Loretta Castorini, a book keeper from Brooklyn, New York, finds herself in a difficult situation when she falls for the brother of the man she has agreed to marry.

http://www.imdb.com/title/tt0093565/

Long Term Relationship (Movie) 2007

Out of all the gay men in Los Angeles, Glenn has finally found his soul mate. From the moment they met, it was instant attraction. Now, Glenn is in love for the first time, and it feels great. But naturally, there are problems. Are they big enough to be deal breakers, or can Glenn and Adam work through their differences?

http://www.imdb.com/title/tt0494253/?ref_=nv_sr_1

Joy (Movie) 2015

Joy is the wild story of a family across four generations centered on the girl who becomes the woman who founds a business dynasty and becomes a matriarch in her own right. Betrayal, treachery, the loss of innocence, and the scars of love pave the road in this intense emotional and human comedy about becoming a true boss of the family and enterprise facing a world of unforgiving commerce. Allies become adversaries and adversaries become allies, both inside and outside the family, as Joy's inner life and fierce imagination carry her through the storm she faces. Jennifer Lawrence stars, with Robert De Niro

http://www.foxmovies.com/movies/joy.

First Wives Club (Movie) 1996

Reunited by the death of a college friend, three divorced women seek revenge on their husbands who left them for younger women. The movie stars Goldie Hawn, Bette Midler, and Diane Keaton

http://www.imdb.com/title/tt0116313/?ref_=nv_sr_1.

Mrs. Doubtfire (Movie) 1993

Daniel Hillard likes to entertain children. His job is providing voices for cartoons, but when he disagrees with the image that the studio wants to convey to children, he's fired. It is also his son's birthday. Feeling down and wanting to do something special for him, he throws a wild children's party. His wife, Miranda, comes home and finds the house in shambles. After everything settles, she tells him that they are on different paths and thinks that they should get divorced. Because he's unemployed the judge feels that it's best if he gets his life in order first, so he allows him to see his children just one day a week. But he can't bear to be away from them for so long, so when Miranda decides to hire a nanny, he alters the ad, answers it himself, and pretends to be Mrs. Doubtfire. Donning a disguise, he becomes the new nanny.

Twilight (Movie) 2008

Bella Swan is a clumsy, kind-hearted teenager with a knack for getting into trouble. Edward Cullen is an intelligent, good-looking vampire who is trying to hide his secret. Against all odds, the two fall in love but will a pack of bloodthirsty trackers and the disapproval of their family and friends separate them?

http://www.imdb.com/title/tt1099212/plotsummary?ref_=tt_ql_stry_2

References

Altman, I. and D. Taylor. 1973. *Social Penetration: The Development of Interpersonal Relationships.* New York, NY: Holt.

Ayers, J. 1983. "Strategies to Maintain Relationships: Their Identification and Perceived Usage." *Communication Quarterly* 31: 62–67.

Baxter, L. A., and C. Bullis, C. 1986. Turning Points in Developing Romantic Relationships. *Human Communication Research* 12: 469–93.

Chapman, G. 2010. *The Five Love Languages: The Secret to Love That Lasts.* Chicago: Northfield Publishing.

Dindia, K., and D. J. Canary. 1993. "Definitions and Theoretical Perspectives on Relational Maintenance." *Journal of Social and Personal Relationships* 10: 163–173.

Floyd, K. 2009. *Interpersonal Communication: The Whole Story.* Boston: McGraw Hill, p. 333.

Galvin, K. M., and C, A. Wilkinson. 2006. "The Communication Process: Impersonal and Interpersonal." In *Making Connections: Readings in Relational Communication*, edited by K. M. Galvin and P. J. Cooper, 4–10. Los Angeles, CA: Roxbury.

Guerrero, L., P. A. Andersen, and W. W. Afifi. 2013. *Close Encounters: Communication in Relationships*, 2nd ed., p. 191. Los Angeles, CA: Sage Publications.

Holmberg, D., and S. MacKenzie. 2002. "So Far, so Good: Scripts for Romantic Relational Development as Predictors of Relational Well-being." *Journal of Social and Personal Relationships* 19: 777–96.

Jones, A. T. 2001. *No Ordinary Friendship: A Narrative Analysis of the Communication of Relational Value in Male Best Friendships.* Thesis, Arizona State University.

Molm, L. D. 2001. "Theories of Social Exchange and Exchange Networks." In G. Ritzer & B. Smart (Eds.), Handbook of social theory (pp. 260–72). London: Sage.

Knapp, M. L., and A. L. Vangelisti. 2006. *Interpersonal Communication and Human Relationships*, 6th ed. Boston: Allyn & Bacon.

Tavernise, S. 2011, May 26. Married Couples are no Longer a Majority, Census Finds. *The New York Times.* Retrieved from http://www.nytimes.com

Tolhuizen, J. H. 1989. "Communication Strategies for Intensifying Dating Relationships: Identification, Use, and Structure." *Journal of Social and Personal Relationships* 6: 413–434.

Turner, L. H., and R. West. 2006. *Perspectives on Family Communication.* New York: Mcgraw-Hill.

West, R., and L. H. Turner. 2012. *IPC* (pp. 201). Boston, MA: Wadsworth Cengage.

Wilmont, W. W. 1995. *Relational Communication.* New York, NY: McGraw Hill.

Wilmont, W. 2006. "*The Relational Perspective.*" In *Making Connections: Readings in Relational Communication* edited by K. M. Galvin & P. J. Cooper, 11–19. Los Angeles, CA: Roxbury.

Scholarly Journal Articles

Early adulthood has been viewed as a time of significant transition. Regardless of the particular theory of development, early adulthood is viewed as a life stage associated with a variety of changes on many levels. Early adults are changing socially and are beginning to ponder what lies ahead of them in the future. Identity is formed as individuals experience the consequences of their choices and decisions. Identity is shaped as young adults balance attachment to and separation from parents. The experience of a safe and secure parent–child attachment bond early in life that continues into adulthood is seen as promoting the exploration of self and of the world (Blustein, 1997). The nature of the attachment bond is linked to the development of social competencies (Coble, Gantt, & Mallinckrodt, 1996). The defining aspects of the parent–young adulthood relationship that seem particularly important during identity development include the amount of encouragement received concerning autonomy and independence, the degree of control desired by parents, and parents' expectations set forth during childhood and adolescence.

http://search.proquest.com/openview/2651bd82304cabb58a9f7597d6a61f5f/1?pq-origsite= gscholar&cbl=18750&diss=y

The majority of young married Americans lived with their spouses before the wedding, and many cohabited with partners they did not wed. Yet little is known about how cohabitating relationships progress or the role gender norms play in this process. This article explores how cohabiting partners negotiate relationship progression, focusing on several stages where couples enact gender. Data are from in-depth interviews with 30 working-class couples ($n = 60$). The women in this sample often challenged conventional gender norms by suggesting that couples move in together or raising the issue of marriage. Men played dominant roles in initiating whether couples became romantically involved and progressed to a more formal status. Although women and men contest how gender is performed, cohabiting men remain privileged in the arena of relationship progression. The findings suggest that adherence to conventional gender practices even among those residing in informal unions perpetuates women's secondary position in intimate relationships.

http://journals.sagepub.com/doi/abs/10.1177/0192513X10391045

Utilizing equity theory, this study extends previous research on maintenance strategies. The manner in which relational maintenance strategies are reported and perceived is examined.

It was hypothesized that maintenance strategies are used more in equitable relationships than in relationships characterized by underbenefitedness. Further, the use of maintenance efforts by individuals in overbenefited relationships was explored. In addition, this study examined the relative contribution of self-reported maintenance strategies, perception of partners' maintenance strategies, and equity in predicting the relational characteristics. Overall, the level of felt equity was found to be related to individuals' use of, and perceptions of partners' use of, maintenance strategies in a pattern consistent with equity theory. However, the findings varied somewhat when relying on wives' versus husbands' equity judgments. Moreover, self-reported maintenance strategies as well as perceptions of partners' maintenance strategies predicted the relational characteristics of control mutuality, liking, and commitment.

http://nca.tandfonline.com/doi/abs/10.1080/03637759209376268

Identity Management and Relational Culture in Interfaith Marital Communication in a United States Context: A Qualitative Study

Laura V. Martinez, Stella Ting-Toomey & Tenzin Dorjee
Journal of Intercultural Communication Research
Volume 45, 2016 - Issue 6

This study explored the identity management processes in interfaith marital communication in a U.S. setting. Sixteen marital partners participated in this interview study. Interviews were transcribed verbatim, interpreted, and analyzed. Guided by identity management theory, the interview data analysis revealed three general themes: development of the interfaith relational identity via the co-creation of a superordinate spiritual and value system; implementation of relational boundaries to prioritize the relational identity; and identification of key milestone decisions (i.e., wedding plans and children socialization coordination) interfaith partners face in their intimate relationships. Contributions, limitations, and directions for future studies on interfaith marital communication are addressed.

http://www.tandfonline.com/doi/abs/10.1080/17475759.2016.1237984

Social Penetration Theory

Amanda Carpenter & Kathryn Greene

The International Encyclopedia of Interpersonal Communication (2015). Social penetration theory describes the role of disclosure in relationship development, focusing specifically on how self-disclosure functions in developing relationships. The onion model serves as a framework for describing the process of social penetration. In developing relationships, people use self-disclosure to increase intimacy including through breadth, depth, and the norm of reciprocity. Social penetration progresses through several stages to develop relationships. The theory also incorporates rewards and costs in relation to social penetration and has influenced the development of a number of theories in relationship development and information management.

http://onlinelibrary.wiley.com/doi/10.1002/9781118540190.wbeic160/abstract?userIsAuthenticated=false&deniedAccessCustomisedMessage=

Romantic Relationship Stages and Social Networking Sites: Uncertainty Reduction Strategies and Perceived Relational Norms on Facebook

Fox Jesse & Anderegg Courtney

Cyberpsychology, Behavior, and Social Networking. November 2014, 17(11): 685-691. https://doi.org/10.1089/cyber.2014.0232

Due to their pervasiveness and unique affordances, social media play a distinct role in the development of modern romantic relationships. This study examines how a social networking site is used for information seeking about a potential or current romantic partner. In a survey, Facebook users (*n*=517) were presented with Facebook behaviors categorized as passive (e.g., reading a partner's profile), active (e.g., "friending" a common third party), or interactive (e.g., commenting on the partner's wall) uncertainty reduction strategies. Participants reported how normative they perceived these behaviors to be during four possible stages of relationship development (before meeting face-to-face, after meeting face-to-face, casual dating, and exclusive dating). Results indicated that as relationships progress, perceived norms for these behaviors change. Sex differences were also observed, as women perceived passive and interactive strategies as more normative than men during certain relationship stages.

Grandparents Raising Grandchildren in the United States: Changing Family Forms, Stagnant Social Policies

Lindsey A. Baker, Merril Silverstein & Norella M. Putney
J Soc Soc Policy. 2008; 7: 53–69.

As a consequence of increased divorce rates, the proliferation of single-parent families, and patterns of economic stagnation, parents are increasingly relying on extended family to care for children. In the past few decades, a substantial increase in the number of grandparents raising grandchildren has been observed within the United States. Grandparents who raise their grandchildren are particularly vulnerable, as are the grandchildren in their care; however, U.S. policy currently presents many barriers, gaps, and unintended consequences for grandparent caregivers. In this paper, we use two theoretical paradigms: (1) structural lag and (2) the political economy of aging perspective to argue that U.S. policy has not kept pace with the reality of the family and—as a result—those families that are most vulnerable often receive the least support. We propose that as family forms become more diverse a redefinition of the family to one that is less bound by residence and biology, to one based more on function, will be required.

https://www.ncbi.nlm.nih.gov/pmc/articles/PMC2888319/

Best Friends Forever?: High School Best Friendships and the Transition to College

Debra L. Oswald & Eddie M. Clark
Journal of Personal Relationships

The transition from high school to college is an important phase for adolescents in social as well as academic aspects. This study examined the changes that occur in high school best friendships during the first year of college. Results revealed that during the first year in college high school best friendships declined in satisfaction, commitment, rewards, and investments. During this period there was also an increase in costs and alternatives to best friend relationships. Proximity did not influence the friendships; however, level of communication did moderate friendship deterioration. Furthermore, individuals who continued their best friendship reported engaging in more maintenance behaviors of positivity, supportiveness, self-disclosure, and interaction than individuals who reported a change in the relationship to close or casual friendship. Maintaining the best friendship also appeared to buffer adolescents from social loneliness. The results are discussed in terms of the implications of transitions on adolescent friendships.

http://onlinelibrary.wiley.com/doi/10.1111/1475-6811.00045/full

Attachment Styles and Patterns of Self-Disclosure.

Mario Mikulincer & Orna Nachshon
Journal of Personality and Social Psychology, Vol 61(2), Aug 1991, 321-331.

In three studies, 352 undergraduate Israeli students were classified into secure, avoidant, and ambivalent attachment groups, and their differences in trait like measures of self-disclosure willingness and flexibility and in disclosure reciprocity and liking of hypothetical or real partners were assessed. Findings indicated that both secure and ambivalent people disclosed more information to, felt better interacting with, and were more attracted to a high discloser partner than a low discloser partner. In contrast, avoidant people's self-disclosure and liking were not affected by the partner's disclosure. Secure people showed more disclosure flexibility and topical reciprocity than ambivalent and avoidant people. Findings are discussed in terms of the interaction goals of attachment groups (PsycINFO Database Record (c) 2016 APA, all rights reserved).

The Process of Relationship Development and Deterioration: Turning Points in Friendships That Have Terminated

Amy Janan Johnson, Elaine Wittenberg, Michel Haigh, Shelley Wigley, Jennifer Becker, Ken Brown & Elizabeth Craig
Communication Quarterly Volume 52, 2004 - Issue 1

This study examines friendships that have ended. Five recalled trajectories for dissolved friendships were found. Certain turning points were generally associated with increases in friendship closeness, while others were associated with decreases in closeness. In addition, gender differences were found for several of the turning points reported. Implications are discussed for interpersonal communication research based on a traditional linear conceptualization of relational development and deterioration.

http://www.tandfonline.com/doi/abs/10.1080/01463370409370178

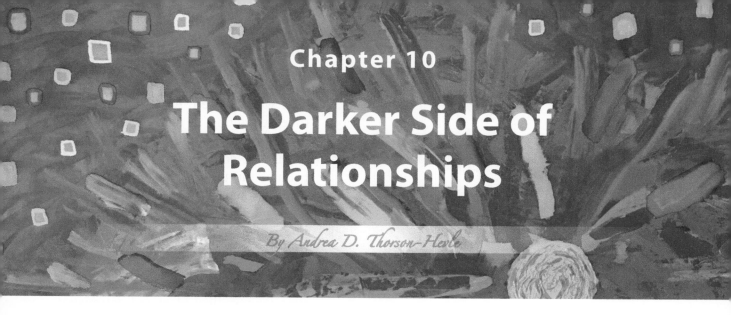

Chapter 10

The Darker Side of Relationships

By Andrea D. Thorson-Hevle

Let's get personal. . .

A good friend of mine has been in what I would call an unhealthy relationship for a long time. It has been difficult for me to stand by and watch her be treated poorly. It wasn't always bad, of course, it was wonderful at times, but when she would call me crying or upset I would so badly want to yell "Just leave! You deserve better. You are smart and beautiful, funny and kind! You give her everything and she gives you nothing in return." One day I finally decided to be totally honest with her. I told her why I didn't think the relationship was good and why I wanted better for her. I was worried my friend would be angry and hang up the phone. But she didn't, thankfully. She accepted my opinion and understood it came from a place of love. This could have been a very different ending, but it wasn't and perhaps in part because we are both professors of Communication in California who understand the power of speaking and listening honestly, plainly, kindly, and with love.

— Andrea D. Thorson-Hevle

You need to read this chapter

- To understand interpersonal conflict.
- To learn and understand attachment styles.
- To diminish your chances of hurting others.

Figure 10.1 Conflict can be helpful, it's not always bad even if it feels that way at the time.

Conflict is often thought of as a bad word. It makes me sad to hear couples avoid conflict because they believe it will worsen their relationship. Often times engaging in conflict helps relationships, but people have to actually engage in conflict, not fight, and not become hurtful. So, what exactly is interpersonal conflict? Interpersonal **conflict** can be perceived as incompatible goals between two individuals and that is exactly where we need to start this chapter. The idea that two people can have the same set of goals all the time is more than ideal and optimistic; it's just not possible. Therefore, we will inevitably have conflict. Some of the more common ways have conflict include, but are not limited to, intimacy issues, social issues, trust issues and proximity issues, such as:

Lack of affection
Lack of sexual contact
Lack of physical touching
Lack of emotional connection
Jealousy
Possessiveness
Neediness
Inability to trust because of previous experiences
Lying
Infidelity
Habits
Grooming
Occupation Status
Money
Appearance
Political affiliations
Social roles
Driving skills
Punctuality
Time spent with person/people
In-laws

But, there are ways to have productive conflict and there are ways to ensure we minimize the likelihood that our behaviors and words will cause others pain.

In this chapter I would like to begin by discussing the basics of conflict with you and then work our way to attachment theory and hurtful events in relationships. **Attachment Theory** explains why we attach to our romantic partners the way we do and provides us information about how we communicate and perceive based on our experiences as children. **Hurtful events** are the relational transgressions that take place in our relationships that cause others pain. These three ideas are interrelated and this chapter will hopefully make their relationships and interactions more clear. Let's begin with attachment styles and hurtful events and end our conversation with a discussion of conflict and ways to handle it better in the future.

"Aren't you glad we had this meeting to resolve our conflict?"

Figure 10.2 Getting our emotions out can be very helpful, even if done in controversial ways at times.

Attachment Theory

Attachment theory asserts that the ways our primary caregivers interacted with us as children fundamentally affects the ways we attach to romantic partners in the future.[1]

[1] Ainsworth, Blehar, Waters, & Wall (1978).

Significant research has established that our adult behavioral patterns are constructed by our early childhood experiences with attachment and intimacy.[2] Attachment Theory postulates that attachment relationships continue to persist throughout our entire lifespan.[3] Attachment theory is important for you to understand, because it will help you understand how you process hurtful events and how you form attachments to your romantic partners. This information will help you approach your communication with your intimate partners differently, and it might even be information you share with your partners to help them understand how you communicate and why you communicate the way you do, and thus why you get hurt the way you do.

Adults' general orientations toward romantic relationships, which is what we call *attachment style*, reflects expectations and beliefs about the worthiness of the self in the eyes

of significant others. This idea of self-worth is formed in the first 5 years of life and constructed from the interactions of the persons the child considered their caregiver. Research suggests this interaction with our caregiver and subsequent effect on our self-worth influence our daily interactions, our relationships with significant others, and our ability to cope when dealing with stressful events, including the experience of symptoms or health-related threats.[4] Infants and children ages 0–5 construct inner working models of their interactions with primary caregivers in the attachment process. Bowlby (1973) identifies two key features of these internal representations of attachment:

1) whether or not the attachment figure is judged to be the sort of person who in general responds to calls for support and protection, [and]

[2] Bowlby (1973)
[3] Ricks (1985)
[4] Wearden, Cook, & Vaughan-Jones (2003).

2) whether or not the self is judged to be the sort of person toward whom anyone, and the attachment figure in particular, is likely to respond in a helpful way." Representations also include impressions about the availability and responsiveness of attachment figures.[5]

Figure 10.3 The ways in which caregivers interact with their kids from 0 to 5 has a long-term effect on their ability to form and maintain relationships.

Over the years, different ways of assessing and classifying adult attachment styles have emerged using both questionnaire, one most commonly used was constructed by Bartholomew and Horowitz in 1991[6] and another that was based on interview techniques, which was crafted by Bifulco, Moran, Ball, and Bernazzani in 2002.[7] Bartholomew and Horowitz developed a model based on Bowlby's attachment theory to explain individual differences in adulthood attachment styles. Based on the positive and negative views of the self and others in relationships, four distinct attachment styles emerge: *secure, dismissive, fearful avoidant*, and *preoccupied*. Using this model composed of views of one's self and others, scores on the measure produce one of the four possible attachment prototypes. It is helpful to know what kind of attachment style you are because it affects how you communicate, how you perceive hurt, and how you think about hurtful events in romantic relationships. Take a look at the categories and description. See which one most closely resembles you.

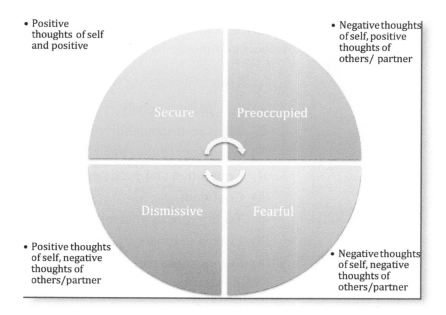

- Positive thoughts of self and positive

- Negative thoughts of self, positive thoughts of others/ partner

Secure

Preoccupied

Dismissive

Fearful

- Positive thoughts of self, negative thoughts of others/partner

- Negative thoughts of self, negative thoughts of others/partner

[5] Bowlby (1973).
[6] Bartholemew & Horowitz (1991).
[7] Bifulco, Moran, Ball, & Bernazzani (2002).

Secure Attachment Style

Individuals who are characterized as having a **secure attachment style** see themselves and others in relationships positively. These individuals tend to trust their partners initially and maintain

Figure 10.4 Secure attachment styles tend to have good coping strategies and view others and themselves in a positive way.

trust easily.[8] Secures are comfortable with intimacy and autonomy in relationships, they would not be categorized by others as overly needy or obsessive, nor would you find them often defined as avoiding. In studies, *secures* are less likely to exhibit anger than the other styles.[9] A *secure attachment style* is also associated with better motivation, coping strategies, and psychological well-being.

People who are characterized as having a *secure attachment style* tend to perceive others as well-intentioned, trustworthy, and reliable. Children who are classified as "*secure*" are reported to be friendly, empathetic, and less hostile than other children,[10] while also being confident enough to ask for help, receive help, and provide help to others.[11]

Research has shown that *secure attachment styles* contribute to subjective well-being, high self-esteem, high self-efficacy, self-control, and well-adjusted interpersonal behavior. High self-esteem traits are traits that *secure* individuals commonly have high-self-esteem traits.

Figure 10.5 Children who are classified as "secure" are friendly, empathetic, and less aggressive than other children"

Indicators of High Self-Esteem

1) Sets personal goals
2) Takes re-responsibility
3) Forgiving
4) Committed and persistent
5) Confident
6) Taking care of yourself emotionally/physically
7) Listens to others well
8) Demonstrate self-respect

[8] Mikulincer & Florian (2001).
[9] Mikulincer (1998).
[10] Casidy & Berlin (1994).
[11] Lieberman, Doyle, & Markiewitz (1999).

Figure 10.6 *Secure* individuals tend to be able to communicate more effectively than the other types.

9) Show love to oneself

10) Receives love well and easily

11) Is okay with oneself

12) Being balanced

13) Being able to say sorry

14) Ability to trust intuition

15) Recognizing our strengths and weaknesses and being okay with it

16) Strives to improve

17) Takes criticism well

18) Feeling that others with support and love you

19) Feeling that if you make a mistake it will be okay

20) Able to accept the past

Dismissive Attachment Style

Individuals who are classified as *dismissive* are seen as having a positive view of themselves and a negative view of others. These individuals have high self-esteem (see the list of traits above). But, unfortunately, these individuals also try to control their relationships because they view others negatively. If you don't trust others, you wouldn't want them to have control. *Dismissives* have been found to have the shortest relationship duration of all the types of attachment styles,[12] most likely because of the constant need to push people away when they get close.

Dismissive attachment styles are characterized as having had caregivers who were generally unresponsive and made the child feel ignored or unimportant. *Dismissives* are also known

---

[12] Feeney & Noller (1991).

Figure 10.7 *Fearful avoidant* styles want to have significant relationship, but have a deep fear of others.

to actively resist intimacy, suppress emotions, and be compulsively self-reliant.[13] It is theorized that adults classified as *dismissive* are this way because they have an internal need to protect themselves against the inevitable disappointment of close relationships. In their past experience, those closest to them disappointed and ignored them, if they avoid close relationships, or at least the closeness of these relationships, they maintain a sense of security.

Fearful Avoidant Attachment Style

Fearful avoidant attachment style individuals view themselves and others negatively. Because of this, they have the least amount of opportunity to practice their communication skills and intimate communication specifically. *Fearful avoidants* are characterized as having low self-esteem (refresh the list offered previously) and being socially avoidant due to their own insecurities about relationships. *Fearful avoidants* generally do want to have close relationships, unlike dismissives, but they have a deep fear of others that keeps them from relationships. Although *fearful avoidants* would like to have close relationships with others, they often avoid relational intimacy because they worry about being hurt.[14] Sadly because being in a constant state of fear or anxiety is stressful on the body, *fearful avoidant attachment* individuals are the most commonly depressed of the attachment styles.

Preoccupied Attachment Style

Preoccupied attachment style individuals tend to view themselves negatively and others positively. These adults seek closeness to others, worry that others do not love or want to be with them, and sometimes scare others away with their intense need for closeness. These are the individuals you have encountered that you may have described as "clingy" or "needy." These individuals are also the most sensitive. In a study I conducted in graduate school, *preoccupieds* were far more likely to perceive being hurt by others and that they were hurt to a greater degree

---

[13] Bippus & Rollin (2003).
[14] Guerrero & Jones (2005).

Figure 10.8 Individuals characterized as "preoccupied" tend to be the least able to handle hurtful events and conflict in relationships.

than any other attachment type. This may be due in part to the fact that *preoccupieds* have a high level of interpersonal dependency on others, so when they feel hurt by others it is felt deeply.

Unfortunately, once this hurt has occurred, preoccupied individuals also appear to be the least equipped to handle the conflict and relational maintenance that is required in interpersonal relationships. Additionally, research conducted by Collins and Feeney (2000) found *preoccupied* individuals reported the least satisfaction with support they receive from their partners during disclosures of a problem.[15] Perhaps the most telling sign of a preoccupied individual will be their constant need to obtain praise, attention, or adoration from others.

Now that you have the foundation of how you attach to romantic partners, we can discuss how your romantic partners have harmed you and how you hurt others. Your attachment style may affect the ways in which you perceive hurt, as you may have noticed. As you read this section, reflect on your own experiences.

Hurtful Events

Hurtful events are dark intruders in romantic relationships. Individuals feel their romantic partner has harmed them when transgressions are committed against them or hurtful messages are expressed toward them.[16] Infidelity, betrayal, vengefulness, unfair accusations, and deception are only a few hurtful events assaulting romantic relationships. Research suggests that no matter how committed or in love romantic partners are, events causing feelings of hurtfulness to occur.[17] Relational transgressions have played a sizeable role in challenging and often ending romantic relationships.[18] **Relational transgressions** violate relationship expectations and

[15] Collins & Feeney (2000).
[16] Folkes (1982); Mongeau & Schultz (1997); Mongeau & Hale (1994); Young (2005).
[17] Bachman & Guerrero (2006); Reynolds (2006); Vangelisti & Crumley (1998).
[18] Spitzberg & Tafoya (2005).

standards resulting usually hurting the feelings of one partner.[19] **Hurtful messages** have also played a significant role in damaging relationships,[20] which is why I find it essential to discuss them here. *Hurtful messages* have been defined as verbal communication that results in hurt feelings.[21] This definition admittedly leaves room for a great number of things to be deemed hurtful events, and that is okay.

Relational transgressions and *hurtful messages* are all *hurtful events*. *Hurtful events* in ongoing romantic relationships are common to relationships and will likely continue to occur. However hurtful an event may be, *hurtful events* are nonetheless important aspects of romantic relationships, and as such, understanding these events may provide valuable insight. Do you know what your partner defines as a *hurtful event* or relational transgression? Perhaps you should ask.

Attachment Theory asserts that humans have a physiological tendency to seek closeness to another person. It is theorized that this initial attachment occurs toward one's caregiver (from the time of birth) creating or diminishing one's sense of security.[22] Based on a child's interpersonal interactions and experiences with their caregiver, one of four types of *attachment styles* will develop (secure, anxious preoccupied, dismissive avoidant, and fearful avoidant). This *attachment style* is then carried through into the child's adult years. The ways in which each child bonds to their caregiver affects their social development and relationships.

Figure 10.9 When a person has low self-esteem, it seems to make hurtful events seem even more hurtful.

Attachment Theory is "one of the best established frameworks regarding individuals' approaches to interpersonal communication" (Pietromonaco & Barrett, 1997). Investigating the relationship between hurtful events and attachment styles may yield significant findings because individual differences in adult attachment behavior reflect expectations and beliefs people have formed about themselves and others, which subsequently effect ones likelihood to engage in certain harmful behavior in close relationships. These *attachment styles* may influence how frequently individuals participate in *hurtful events* toward a partner, as well as influence what events they deem hurtful, and the level of hurtfulness they experience. Given this, I have examined both *hurtful events* and Attachment Theory in this section for you.

Romantic relationships are some of the most important and influential relationships in our lives. While these relationships provide many positive experiences, examining the darker experiences may tell us the most about who we are and aid us significantly in future relationships. Negative

[19] Bachman & Guerrero (2006); Metts (1994).

[20] Bachman & Guerrero (2006); Bachman & Guerrero (2003); Reynolds (2006); Miller (2005); Waite (2003).

[21] Bachman et al. (2006); Metts (1994); Vangelisti & Crumley (1998); Waite & Roloff (2003).

[22] Bachman & Guerrero (2006); Bachman & Guerrero (2003).

communication experiences (hurtful events) are unavoidable in close relationships. Studies show that we are most likely to hurt those we are closest with.[23] We are also most deeply hurt by those we love.[24] People tend to overlook the stranger who insults them, but when it is a loved one, a trusted partner who insults them, it is a far more complicated and painful endeavor.[25] We often call this the **defense of unfamiliarity**. If someone one knows the victim well and hurts them, the victim cannot rationalize the event by saying "If that person knew the real me that person would like me and wouldn't hurt me." This cannot be rationalized when the person who hurts the victim knows the victim well especially if the person is a romantic partner.[26]

Hurtful events are usually identified though interaction with others resulting in feelings of hurtfulness. *Hurtful events*, common to romantic relationships, can be intense (i.e., deception, sexual infidelity, unfair criticism).[27] *Leary* (1998) and colleagues found that "Other *hurtful events*—such as forgotten birthdays, unreturned phone calls, and ingratitude—involve less weighty consequences, but nonetheless may create considerable distress and strain relationships as well" (p. 1225). Leary et al. (1998) claimed researchers considering only the instances in which people were hurt by something someone else said (hurtful messages) failed to address other "types of hurtful behavior" or "situations in which people were hurt by things that others did not say or do" (p. 1226). In this study, both hurtful messages and relational transgressions (infidelity, avoidance, jealousy, etc.) are taken into account (i.e., hurtful messages).

Vangelisti et al. (2005) found relational satisfaction and self-esteem are key reasons people feel another person has hurt them. Because *attachment styles* are defined by both relational satisfaction and self-esteem and people claim these relational satisfaction and self-esteem contribute to their feelings of hurtfulness, it makes sense that certain *attachment style* types will perceive hurt differently.

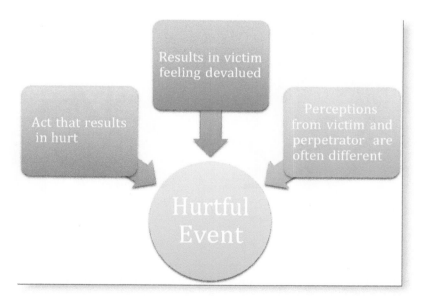

---

[23] Leary et al. (1998); Young (2005).

[24] Bachman et al. (2006); Young et al. (2006).

[25] Taylor (1989); Leary (1998); Vangelisti (1994).

[26] Stausser (1997).

[27] Leary et al. (1998).

Hurt

Individuals deem an event to be "hurtful" when someone does or says something that hurts their feelings, therefore, people tend to define a *hurtful event* based on interactions with others and how an interaction affects them emotionally.[28] "Subjectively, **hurt feelings** appear to involve feelings of general distress or upset in which common distinctions among emotional states" (Leary et al., 1998, p. 1225). In response to *hurtful events*, people often describe feeling "crushed," "stung," "burned,"… (Leary et. al., 1998, p. 1226). Because "hurt" is a complex emotion meaning different things to different people, as previous research has found,[29] defining the feeling of "hurt" from other feelings such as anger, upset, and anxiety is a difficult task.

Each person will likely explain their feelings regarding a *hurtful event* in different ways. Vangelisti's research (1994) claimed that *hurt feelings* are different from other emotions because of the attributions associated with the *hurtful event*. Vangelisti and Crumley (1998) found "that relational satisfaction was positively associated with active verbal responses and negatively correlated both with the degree of experienced hurt and the perceived impact of the hurtful message on the relationship" (p. 173). While many researchers may disagree on how to best examine a hurtful message, event, or transgression, most agree that the victim of the *hurtful event* feels the perpetrator does not value the relationship.[30] This is very important. In the end, all that really matters in terms of you and your relationship is that "hurt" was felt by someone and caused by another. We must try our best to avoid hurting our partners and one way to do that is understand how they feel "hurt", what is hurtful to them and why, and knowing how to say we are sorry.

Figure 10.10 "Hurt" means something different to different people.

---

[28] Vangelisti (1994); Vangelisti & Young (2005); Vangelisti & Crumley (1998); Young (2005)
[29] Leary et al, (1998).
[30] Vangelisti (1994); Leary et al. (1998); Miller (2005); Waite (2003).

When a hurtful event occurs, it has been suggested that negative effect plays a role. Because the person, during a hurtful event, sees the event as threatening, certain feelings will be created.[31] The damage incurred as a result of a hurtful event can damage a person for years. Although research is scarce concerning hurtful events, many researchers have examined hurtful messages and relational transgressions.

From this previous research several main themes surface. The first is the idea that any act or communication that results in *hurt feelings* can be deemed a hurtful event. Second, hurtful events usually result in the victim feeling devalued. Third, perceptions from both the victim and the perpetrator regarding the hurtful event are often different.

And finally, although initially, men and women were thought to have different views on perceived levels of hurtfulness and *hurtful events*,[32] recent research has shown there is no sex/gender differences in the types of events that caused hurt feelings, attributions, or perceptions of consequences resultant from the *hurtful event*.[33]

Relational Devaluation

It has been noted that hurt feelings are a response to *relational devaluation*. **Relational devaluation** is classified as a *hurtful event*. Leary and colleagues found that the "hurtful events identified in this study all appeared to involve real, implied, or imagined social disassociation" (1998). This is an important component of *hurtful events* and a very important concern when evaluating a *hurtful event* from an attachment style standpoint. The notion that hurt can be imagined is significant; this means we must examine the variables that influence perceptions in order to achieve greater understanding of hurt feelings and thus hurtful events. Leary (1998) found that relational devaluation was often present in hurtful events, such as betrayals and negative interpersonal evaluations.

Figure 10.11 Relational devaluation is a type of hurtful event that occurs in most relationships. How hurtful is a relationship devaluation to you?

[31] Leary et al. (1998).
[32] Miller & Roloff (2005).
[33] Leary et al. (1998).

Harsh criticism, for example, often suggests to the victim that the perpetrator is acting to hurt the victim intentionally or unintentionally and regardless of which the victim feels the perpetrator does not value their relationship or victim in general. Teasing was also found to be a type of criticism that results in hurt feelings; therefore teasing could also be deemed a hurtful event by a given individual."[34] Teasing may be interpreted as veiled criticism" (Leary et al., 1998, p. 1237).

Often researchers have identified relational devaluation as occurring in the mode of communicative hurtful messages;[35] however, relational transgressions can also reflect a perpetrators decreased respect for the relationship.[36] Among the most common *hurtful events* mentioned in previous research are the events of deception,[37] rejection,[38,39] criticism,[40] jealousy,[41] and disassociation.[42]

[34] Leary et al. (1998).

[35] Waite et al. (2003); Reynolds (2006); Bachman & Guerrero (2003).

[36] Feeney (2005); Metts (1994); Roloff, Soule, & Coarey (2001).

[37] Bachman et al. (2003); Jang & Levine (2002); Metts (1994); Waldron & Kelley (2005).

[38] Leary (1998), Leary (2001); Waite (2003).

[39] Infidelity Leary (1998); Metts (2003); Metts (1994); Mongeau & Schulz (1997); Spitzberg et al. (2005); Waldron et al. (2005); Roloff & Cloven (1994).

[40] Bachman et al. (2003); Bachman et al. (2005); avoidance/denial (Vangelisti et al., 1998); Tucker, Chavez-Appel, & Rex (2005); Young et al. (2005).

[41] Webb & Warford (2005); Cayanus & Both-Butterfield (2004); Yoshimura (2004); Bevan (2004); Dainton (2001); Carson et al. (2000); Guerrero & Eloy (1992).

[42] Feeney (2005); Tucker, Chavez-Appel & Rex (2005), Leary et al. (1998).

Deception

Deception has several sub-variables. In general, people tend to feel they have been deceived when they have been lied to too, misled, tricked, or manipulated. Deception is second only to infidelity as the least forgivable offense.[43]

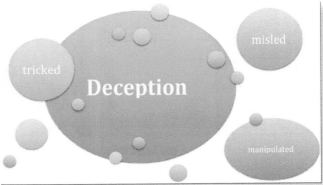

Rejection

Research shows that a significant portion of emotion revolves around "real, anticipated, perceived, and potential rejection" (Leary et al., 2001, p. 1237). Interpersonal **rejection** often results in hurt feelings, especially when the rejection comes from a romantic partner.[44] The younger a person is when they experience rejection the more painful it can be. Depression, suicide, anxiety disorders, and aggressive behavior are all found to be outcomes of ongoing rejection in a persons life. Again, the younger the person is the more the more hurtful the rejection is

Figure 10.12 Relational rejection is a painful experience.

felt. It is especially important that children feel like their needs have been met by their caregivers. Children who experience early rejection learn to expect rejection as a part of normal life. This expectation will continue into adulthood and alters the ways in which that person responds to rejection in romantic relationships.

Infidelity

Infidelity is defined as cheating or adultery, which means the person went outside their relationship to find sexual, intimate, or emotional closeness with another person. Sexual infidelity is

---

[43] Bachman et al. (2003).
[44] Leary, Koch, & Hechenbleikener (2001); Carson & Cupach (2000).

Figure 10.13 Infidelity is the least forgivable hurtful event for couples in the U.S.A.

among the least forgivable hurtful events.[45] Infidelity has been found to not only be a relational transgression but also an intentional communicative act; meaning sometimes romantic partners participate in extradyadic affairs as a means of sending their partner a message.[46] Research shows that more than half of people in relationships are unfaithful. It has been found that people under the age of 30 are far more likely to cheat than other age groups. The use of social networking, "hook-up" Aps, and time away from each other seem to contribute to this number. Infidelity often involves several hurtful behaviors: lying, misleading, and potentially spreading sexually transmitted diseases and infections, and unintentional pregnancy.

It is important that you have a conversation with your partner that specifically defines what "cheating" is to each of you. For some people an "emotional affair" is not a real affair, a real affair is only one in which sexual intercourse occurred. To others, any sexual act is a form of infidelity while to some, engaging in sexual acts with certain people or a certain sex is acceptable. For some a kiss is acceptable and for others a dream about sex with another is still cheating.

Researchers have distinguished a few types of infidelity: sex-only, emotion-only, and combined sexual and emotional infidelity. These three are usually evident in one or more of these **four types of infidelity:**

1) one-night stands
2) long term affairs
3) emotional affairs
4) philandering

Do not make the mistake of assuming your definition of infidelity is the same as your partners. Have the conversation early rather than later.

Signs of cheating may include:

1) Your partner is putting more effort into their appearance, especially when they are not with you.
2) Your partner has new skills in the bedroom without discussing them with you.
3) Your partner doesn't want to have sex at the same times and frequency as before.
4) Your partner lacks patience with you

[45] Bachman et al. (2006).
[46] Spitzberg et al. (2005).

5) Your partner increases "alone" activities; they say they want to be on their own more often.

6) Your partner texts and hides the content so you can't see it.

7) Your partner avoids telling you who they were talking to or texting.

8) They start grooming differently (especially in their private areas).

9) You notice they are deleting text messages quickly.

10) You notice your partner has erased some calls or texts from the "history." (Tip: Check the cell phone bill and compare it with their history in the phone. If there are missing calls you know know what number your parter is communicating with and hiding from you- what you do is up to you).

11) Your partner has to work late or is suddenly rarely available during their work breaks.

12) Your partner clears the browsing history consistently when they never used to do that.

Ryan's Story

Recently (september 2013) I had an incident. One day, out of the blue, a person sent me a message on facebook. She said that she had a dream about me. The person that sent me this message was a close friend of my wife's. she had also worked with me for some time at Hall Ambulance. I read the message and then went on with my day. However, I later asked her about her dream. She told me about it and we began to have a conversation on Facebook. That conversation moved to my phone,on the facebook app. It quickly became very explicated. I posted songs and other very personal details. Long story sort, my wife found out and rightfully was very up set. The person and I never made any contact, but the contact we made on line was very graphic. Since then, I have deleted her as a contact and blocked her. I have worked every day to since then to improve my marriage. I have gone to counseling, and I have begun going to a 12 step program. over the course of the last 9 months, I have recommitted my self to my wife and family. I am not proud about what I have done. My sons both know about it, and they have worked through some or their issues. Jennifer and I deal with this incident on a daily basis. I have not shared this story with many people, and I am reluctant to share it with you. This has made me feel like less of a person. Could I have said NO? should I have said something to my wife? Should I have not replied to her message? These and many other questions haunt me. A friend put it this way, am I a bad person who does good things or am I a good person who does bad things. Both are true.

Avoidance/Denial

People with disinterest in their partners tend to hurt their partners by avoiding them or denying there is a problem within the relationship. If you "avoidant" you may be hurting your partner much more deeply than you think. Because "avoidant" people are able to shut down their emotions quickly and not react to emotional situations they tend to make their partners feel like they don't care about the relationship or their feelings. "**Avoidant/denial**" people will often avoid physical closeness with their partner and that can be harmful to a relationship. These individuals may not want to have sex, avoid sleeping in the same bed, refuse to walk side-by-side, avoid conversations, fail to return calls, fail to verbally say they will not attend events and/or craft excuses for not attending important events. People who use active distancing (avoidance-denial tactics) are also more likely to have lower degrees of relational satisfaction (Young et al., 2005).[47] Avoidance/denial is the only response to hurtful events that is always linked to low relational satisfaction.[48]

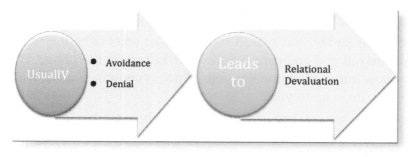

Figure 10.14 Individuals who tend to avoid their partners and communication with their partners have the highest rates of relational dissatisfaction.

Criticism

Regardless of whether the communication is helpful constructive criticism or vengeful intentional criticism, interpersonal **criticism** is commonly noted as a hurtful event in romantic relationships. Criticism occurs when the "perpetrator" communicates a judgment, opinion, or begins a discussion regarding what is potentially wrong, faulty, or lacking about somebody. Jokes and teasing have also been considered a form of criticism.[49] Often criticism acts as a "catalyst for an aggressive response."[50] There are many types of criticism, but in the interpersonal realm, most criticism can be summed up in four categories: intentional, constructive, unintentional, and vengeful, which is often called deconstructive.

---

[47] Young et al. (2005).
[48] Vangelisti & Young (2000); Young et al. (2005).
[49] Leary et al. (1998).
[50] Young (2005) as qutd. by Roloff (1996).

Vengeful/Deconstructive Criticism: can harm self-esteem, confidence, pride, and have lasting effects. This kind of criticism can inspire anger and aggression. Destructive criticism can be unintentionally hurtful if the person doesn't realize what they are saying, but most often destructive criticism is given purposefully and for malicious reasons (vengeful). I hope you are not using this in your relationships.

Constructive Criticism: highlights mistakes and problems, but in a way that shows how improvements could be achieved. Constructive criticism is intended to help others as opposed to hurt or maliciously attack.

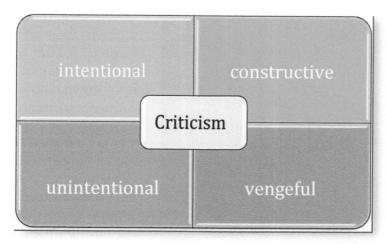

Violent Communication

As discovered by Young et al. (2006), **violent communication** was one of the only hurtful events studied thus far that has a sex or gender difference. Women are more likely to respond to a hurtful event with negative effect. Men are more likely than women to respond with violence. Verbal aggression has been shown to be a more common male characteristic in general (Shuntich & Shapiro, 1991). It may be the difference in physical size that keeps women from engaging in violent reactions to hurtful messages; socialization of gender norms may also be a reason. The manner in which language is posed is important both in how the victim responds and why the perpetrator chooses to display violent communication. Young et al. (2005) found there is "a clear relation between how a hurt-evoking comment is stated and how receivers respond" (p. 135). Regardless, all forms of violent communication are wrong and not appropriate, excusable, or justifiable ways to initiate or deal with conflict. If you find yourself in a violent communication, you should leave that relationship immediately and seek help from others.

Forms of violent communication include physical and verbal aspects, which may include incidents, such as:

Pushing
Punching
Kicking
Physically harming with objects
Bullying
Destructive criticism
Name calling
Threats

It is important to remember that children who are victims of violent communication or who witnessed ongoing violent communication, are more likely to view this behavior as normal, enter into relationships with abusers, and be unable to leave their abuser.

Jealousy

Jealousy is an emotion many people experience which generally refers to feelings of insecurity that may cause a sense of resentment against others. People who are jealous are often resentful

of another's success or advantages. Research suggests that men and women differ in their communication of and feelings toward jealousy in romantic relationships (Webb et al., 2005). It is argued however, that men and women experience the same amount of jealousy but women are more open and honest about their jealousies and thus it appears they are more jealous. Other research has shown that women have higher expectations/standards for loyalty and displays of love and that may in turn explain these differences as well.

In the United States taller men tend to be less jealous than shorter men and women of a medium type are less jealous than short or tall women. Children struggle with jealousy as well. Usually children display jealous tendencies when it comes to getting attention from their caregivers. This is especially evident when children talk of parents "love." These childhood jealousies can last long into adulthood

Figure 10.15 Romantic jealousy is the most common type of jealousy and is considered "normal".

and alter sibling relationships forever. Experts suggests parents spend one-on-one time with their kids in an effort to show love and give saturated attention. Experts also suggest parents try to let children end their arguments instead of constantly solving the problems and stopping the arguments themselves. This is sad to be effective because children won't be able to argue that a parent took the side of the other sibling. Parents must always diminish the opportunities they provide their children to accuse them of unfair treatment and favoritism. Sibling jealousy often continues into adulthood and is highly unhealthy in many circumstances. When one sibling begins accomplishing things or become successful, purchases big items, or obtains praise this can trigger old feelings of jealousy all over again.

Jealousy has been reported to have positive effects on romantic relationships;[51] however, it can also incite other hurtful events to occur (While & Mullen, 1989). Guerrero (1998) mentioned that jealous people may actually appear less attractive because their jealousy may make them appear desperate to their partner. Young (2006), Canary, Spitzberg, and Semic (1996) found that jealously may provoke anger in the accused hurting their partner to the point that the victim may soon become the perpetrator of a different hurtful event. While we we commonly think of jealousy in terms of our romantic relationships there are other types of jealousy: professional (work related) jealousy, sexual jealousy, friend jealousy, and family jealousy. While jealousy in general is normal, acting out on our jealousies consistently is not. We can feel jealous, but we don't have to act on that feeling and we certainly don't have to hurt people. Ways to control jealous behaviors:

1) talk openly with your partner- don't hold back
2) reflect on why you are feeling this way- is it your past that is harming your future?
3) limit the situations that trigger jealous reactions.
4) don't let emotions build to an explosion- communicate continuously and in a healthy manner of speaking.
5) use clear language when discussing things with your partner. Do not expect people to "pick up the hint" tell them plainly.

Disassociation

Individuals with little regard for their partner's feelings (i.e., low relational satisfaction) will often begin active or passive disassociation. At times, **disassociation** occurs as a result of past hurtful events. Breaking up is one of the least forgivable offenses in the hurtful event genre.[52] Disassociation is regarded as one of the most hurtful events in a romantic relationship.

Figure 10.16 Some people increase emotional distance in relationships as a way of dealing with emotions, but it can be very harmful to a relationship.

---

[51] Yoshimura (2004).
[52] Bachman et al. (2006); Bachman et al. (2003).

Now that you understand the relationship between attachment and hurtful events, let's examine some of the fundamental components of conflict and discuss some factors that may influence your darker communication movements. Toward the end I will provide you several tips and tricks to help you have more successful conflicts in the future.

Conflict

Interpersonal **conflict** requires a few components:

1) Two people
2) Perception
3) Incompatible goal

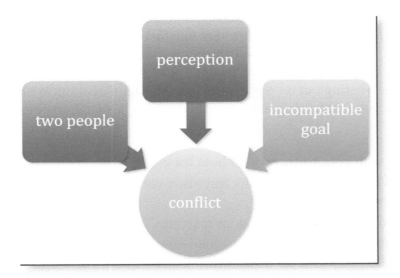

Given that you now know a lot about perception, I'm sure you can discern some of the potential hiccups people encounter in conflict as a result of perceptions. What did we learn in the perception chapter? We learned that perceptions are formed based on a number of factors and our experiences and our cultures can affect our perceptions greatly, which in turn can cause us to act in bias ways. So, if we start with a bias perception, it is likely that our "perceived" conflict might not be a real conflict at all. A lot of times in relationships, what seems like conflict and incompatible goals is really just different people not communicating effectively about their goals.

Part of the reason people don't communicate well during conflict is because our society has given conflict a bad name. Conflict has become synonymous with drama, anger, fighting, and argument. But, conflict is none of those things.
In fact, conflict is great because it:

1) allows people to respond to what others have been arguing in their own minds,
2) allows relationships to heal,
3) can show others our true intentions instead of our perceived intentions,

4) can bring us toward a solution,

5) makes people feel like they mater,

6) faces problems instead of ignores them, and

7) allows people to give voice to their emotions.

Alright, conflict can also be bad. You are right. Conflict can be bad as well, but most of the time when conflict is bad it's because the people involved didn't use communication competence and certainly didn't apply communication skills as well as they could have. Conflict can be bad if:

1) people are not fighting fair (below the belt),

2) the purpose of the conflict is to hurt rather than to help, and

3) conflict escalates and creates a hurtful event and manifests distance.

Research has demonstrated that different people have different ways of approaching conflict and those different approaches have varying outcomes. Sometimes we use different approaches to different situations, but for the most part there is usually a certain conflict mentality that we have adopted over the years. I will outline five of the most prominently discussed types of interpersonal conflict. See which one seems to reflect your style.

Collaborating

I would like to start with a positive conflict style, collaborating. **Collaborating** is a wonderful style because it is just as it seems, a style that considers both people's concerns. This conflict style allows the people involved to feel heard and valued. If you could strive to be any conflict type, strive to be this one.

Compromising

The compromising style of communication is positive in some ways, but not quite as fabulous as the collaborating style. The **compromising** style allows for people's concerns to be voiced and heard, but it doesn't let anyone really be truly happy. Fundamentally both parties compromise, someone loses something. This is the kind of conflict your parents set you up to expect, "you win some, you lose some." Compromising conflict styles do loose a little, but they don't lose completely. Unfortunately, sometimes that slight loss can have devastating side effects, but it really just depends.

Accommodating

Accommodators are basically the opposite of the competing conflict type, but just as bad, because they also only care about one person and are ignoring the other. Avoiders care most and sometimes only about the other person's feelings and concerns and little about their own. This practice can be harmful and certainly doesn't help maintain happiness in a relationship. Accommodators like to call themselves "people pleasers" this is not the case, because constantly sacrificing your own needs for the needs of others does not make you someone who is kind enough to please others, it makes you a doormat. Stop letting people wipe their feet on you. Sure, once in a while we should be accommodating, give in, but as a common conflict style, this is not recommended.

Competing

Competing is not what I would call a positive conflict style. The competitive style of conflict is an ugly little thing, because it fundamentally says that the other person's feelings are unimportant and irrelevant. Competitive conflict style individuals tend to be louder and display signs of anger, aggression, and hostility far more than any other conflict style. In interpersonal relationships this conflict style is the kiss of death, or rather the kiss goodbye. Humans don't want to be in a relationship with someone who is competitive in their conflict style all the time, most of the time, or even commonly.

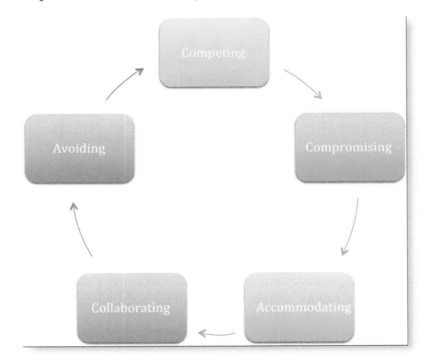

Avoiding

You might think that avoiding is not that bad of a conflict style initially. You would be wrong. **Avoidance** is a very bad thing in communication. We cannot avoid communication in our relationships or bad things tend to happen. The whole premise behind avoiding is problematic. Think about it, if you don't mention something does it make it less real? Really? I don't think so. In fact, some research shows that people who avoid and keep their emotions in, are more likely to obsess and feel internal pain about the situation than others do. Avoiding conflict doesn't make the problems go away. Often times avoiding conflict makes the situations worse.

Tips to Have Successful Conflict

(1) Consider the Surroundings

One of the interesting things I see when I consult people on conflict is where they decide to have these conflicts. It really does matter where you have a conflict, so choose the location wisely. In the chapter on nonverbal communication we discussed proxemics and I told you this story, "When I became a professor I had a great number of students who confided a great many things to me. Among them were usually conflicts with their parents. Student after student wanted to assert their independence, their desire to be their own person, to make their own choices, to be respected as an adult and not treated as a child. And each and every student reported these conversations going poorly for them. My first question to these students is always, "where were you for this conversation?" I usually get a look of bewilderment or irritation. Clearly, I must not be paying attention to the point of their story if all I am asking about is where the conversation happened. But, where this conversation takes place is of great importance, because the surroundings communicate and it changes the way people communicate. Surroundings can alter our perceptions.

Remember back to Chapter 3 and my discussion about conversations between children and parents and the setting of these conversations? Time after time, students reported that these big conversations about not wanting to be seen as children anymore were taking place in their "childhood" homes. This is not good. I explained that if they want to have a chance at this conversation, they needed to have the conversation at a place that is neutral or that gives them (the student) the upper hand. I recommended picking a place their parents did not frequent, but the students did. I recommended picking an environment that is quiet and respectful. A fast-food restaurant, for instance, is not a good choice; it is too informal and noisy. A restaurant they went every Sunday after church as a family is not a good choice either, as this will only serve to remind the parents of their "baby" and moments of "childlessness." These are not memories you want stirred up when you are trying to convince people you are an independent, responsible adult. I often recommended quaint coffee places that have a hint of sophistication, but still a "hip vibe", which let the student, feel comfortable, and places the parents not in a place that constantly reminds them of their "baby."

The same premise is true for conflict. If you intend to engage in conflict, then think about where you are going to have this conflict. Where is an appropriate place to have this conversation? If you are going to discuss your sex life, do you think you should have this conversation in your bedroom? Nope. Absolutely not, you need to have this conversation in a neutral area where there are no reminders of the sexual experience. I'm not, however, suggesting you pick the nearest Mom and Pop restaurant, please no. You also don't want to discuss your sex life in a place that is hyper sexualized either. Instead opt for the kitchen table, the living room, or in your backyard. I guess I am presuming that those places are not places that you commonly have sexual relations. I could be wrong, in which case, perhaps take a stroll in the park or a walk around the block. My point is, when you have conversations that you know are likely to end in conflict then you need to consider the surroundings. Our surroundings affect the way we feel and what we remember. If you can control that a little bit, you might give yourself a little bit, of an advantage or at least even the playing field.

You also want to ensure that the surroundings are private enough for your conversation or loud enough to not be the center of attention in the room. I remember once a boyfriend took me to a night club to discuss our relationship over cocktails. I thought this was odd. We were shouting back and forth about our desires for the future. In truth, I was happy, I wasn't ready for that talk and loved getting out of having to discuss things that I couldn't "hear." It wasn't the best decision on his part. By the end of the night he was disappointed and frustrated. I quickly suggested that we stop trying to talk over the music and enjoy the remaining songs and drinks. He wasn't pleased.

Considering the level of privacy, the noise level, what the location will remind them of, are all important things to consider when selecting an ideal surrounding. Now, you might be thinking that this sounds like a lot of work, and well, it might be.

But, relationships are work, and if you put work into them they run a lot more smoothly. I also understand that sometimes you might feel the conflict couldn't wait until a later time. In this case, I ask you to really consider that. Is it possible that it could have waited? Was it more that your emotions got the best of you? Or was it really appropriate and necessary for you to address the situation at that moment? You will know what the right thing to do is depending on your answer. But, be sure to ask yourself these questions and be honest next time. If we can wait till later when we can think calmly, rationally, and plan a surrounding, it often ends up being to our advantage.

(2) Consider Culture

We all come from different cultures, so before you get into a big conflict really consider the cultural implications of the situation.

I recommend asking yourself a few questions:

1) Are there any rituals in _____ culture that might affect this situation and make _____ react this way?

2) Does _____ 's culture teach _____ that this kind of behavior is idea and expected or normal?

3) Was this kind of communication normal in _____ culture growing up?

4) Are there possibly tings I don't know about a culture that _____ belongs to that might be affecting this part of our relationship?

5) Am I judging based on my conception of what a man/woman/wife/husband/mother/sister/father/brother/parent/etc. should be based on certain things my culture taught me that's culture did not?

These are just a few questions to get you started. Now, please don't misunderstand, I am not suggesting that because you and your person are from different cultures you should always just give in, not at all. I am, however, saying you need to address the possibility that you are missing some bits of information and suggesting that you be prepared to respectfully ask for access to that information. I am also saying that you should be critical of your attitudes and beliefs and really understand how they came to be constructed, this will help you understand why you think the way you think and perhaps make it easier for you to communicate.

(3) Make Sure All Parties Are Ready

Before you start a conflict, please make sure all people involved are actually ready to participate. One of the easiest ways to ensure that a solution to a problem will not be found is to start a conversation with a person who is not ready to have that conversation. Before you have a big talk with anyone important in your life, I recommend giving them a bit of notice so they can emotionally prepare for the conversation or at least give you their full attention. Providing advance notice decreases the chance that they will feel attacked. If people feel like they have been ambushed, they get defensive and once someone becomes defensive their ability to listen diminishes significantly.

Let's get personal...

Looking back at my childhood, I can recall my mother watching TV, or reviewing a script (she was a speech/performance/coach). At any rate, she was clearly into what she was doing, and my dad would begin to have a "big" conversation with her. You could see from her nonverbal body language and facial expressions that she felt caught off guard and ill prepared to participate and respond with such little notice. Not to mention she was in the middle of something else entirely. Her inability to respond quickly frustrated my father. It was my impression that he perceived her slow response as disrespectful and not caring to engage in the conversation. I think it was honestly more of a matter of being completely ill prepared for the conversation and in the middle of doing her work. In the end, those types of conflicts never ended well. My father never really got the solution he was looking for and mother never felt respected enough to be given notice. Nowadays they are much better at communicating. They control their tones and facial expressions so much better today than they did back then, years of practice I suppose.

— *Andrea D. Thorson-Hevle*

---

(4) Define the Fight

This seems kind of silly on the surface, but I can tell you from experience and from a research standpoint that a great deal of conflict occurs between two people talking about two totally different things. When you start to have a conflict, define your terms. If you say Sam is unsupportive, you need to define what "unsupportive" means to you. If you say "rarely" define what rarely means to you. Do you remember our discussion about time in the chapter on nonverbal communication? In that chapter we discussed how being "on time" means different things to different people. That same idea is true

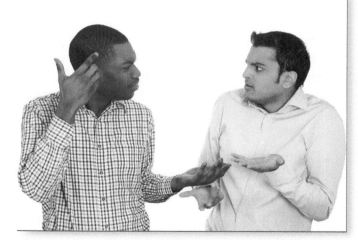

Figure 10.17 Have you ever had a fight and then suddenly after ten minutes of arguing you realize you were arguing over two totally different things because you misunderstood what someone meant by a term they used?

for most things in life. Before you start your big conversation, define your terms, fully explore and give examples of what you mean by certain words. This will serve to clearly define the parameters of the debate. Defining terms also helps keep the conflict on task and from including unnecessary information, examples, and experiences.

(5) Check Your Perceptions

As you learned in an earlier chapter, the perception checking process is always valuable. Because our perceptions are so often a reflection of our own insecurities, biases, or past experiences, it is important that we perform basic perception checks before we take big actions in our relationships. **Perception checks** help us ensure we fully understand.

There are three basic steps to the perception checking process: describing, interpreting, and clarifying.

Perception Check Process

☐ Describe their behavior

☐ Interpret what you think that behavior may mean (two options)

☐ Clarify the behavior and interpretation

This process is vitally important and can even save a relationship. I'm sure you can think of an occasion in which you misinterpreted what someone else said or meant and thus reacted inappropriately because of it. Had you followed this simple process all those nasty side effects might have been avoided.

(6) Check Your Self-Esteem

In Chapter 2 we discussed self-esteem and the many ways that can change your perceptions of the world around you. Before you engage in a big conversation ask yourself if low self-esteem may be affecting the way you perceive the events and behaviors. If you are experiencing low self-esteem, you are more likely to feel hurt when others would not, you are more likely to react emotionally, you are more likely to get depressed, and you are more likely to withdraw (avoid) or hyper attack. As a reminder, I posted the signs of low self-esteem below.

Indicators of Low Self-Esteem

1) Feeling unhappy
2) Feeling less important than others
3) Feeling anxious
4) Feeling generally negative about yourself
5) Self-blame and self-criticism
6) Playing "the victim"
7) Reacting with extreme emotion

8) Lack personally set goals

9) Feel other's goals are most important

10) Fearful and timid

11) Responding to others with neutrality

12) Deep feelings of panic and fear

13) Obsessing with what could have been

14) Assigning the actions of others as reflections of your worth

15) Making excuses for negative behaviors without taking responsibility or saying sorry easily

16) Over analyzing what others said

17) Needing to have people agree with you

18) Inability to remain ethical and calm

19) Feeling impatient with others

20) Takes criticism poorly

I hope this section helped you understand the role of conflict and how it can impact your relationships. Most importantly I hope it helped you see how it can be helpful in your relationships if you choose to approach it with sensitivity and with the right style. Conflict doesn't have to be bad, we can use it to make our relationships better and to bring us closer.

Conclusion

This chapter sought to show you ways to minimize the likelihood that your behaviors and words will cause others pain and to increase the likelihood that solutions will come from our conflicts. In this chapter I discussed conflict, attachment, and hurtful events in relationships. I hope this chapter gave you inspiration to create better communication in your interpersonal relationships and gave you cause to think about the ways you communicate, why you communicate, and where you communicate. I wish you the very best of luck in your relationships. Remember, in the end, you can't be much in a relationship if you don't first know, accept, and love yourself.

References

Ainsworth, M. S., Blehar, M. C., Waters, E., & Wall, S. (1978). *Patterns of Attachment: A Psychological Study of the Strange Situation*. Hillsdale, NJ: Erlbaum.

American Psychiatric Association. (1994). *Diagnostic and Statistical Manual of Mental Disorders* (4th ed.). Washington, DC: Author.

Anders, S. L., & Tucker, J. S. (2000). Adult attachment style, interpersonal communication competence, and social support. *Personal Relationships, 7*, 379–389.

Andersen, P. A., & Eloy, S. V. (1995). Romantic jealousy and relational satisfaction: A look at the impact of jealousy experience and expression. *Communication Reports, 8*, 77–85.

Bachman, G. F., & Guerrero, L. (2006). Forgiveness, apology, and communicative responses to hurtful events. *Communication Reports, 19*, 45–56.

Bachman, G. F., & Guerrero, L. (2003). Relations among apology, forgiveness, and communicative responses to hurtful messages. Paper presented at the annual meeting of the International Communication Association, San Diego, CA.

Bartholemew, K., & Horowitz, L. M. (1991). Attachment styles among young adults: A test of a four-category model. *Journal of Personality and Social Psychology,* 61, 226–244.

Bartholemew, K., & Shaver, P. (1998). Methods of assessing adult attachment: Do they converge? In J. A. Simpson & W. S. Rholes (Eds) *Attachment Theory and Close Relationships* (pp. 25–45). New York, NY: Guilford.

Benjamin, L. S. (1993). *Interpersonal Diagnosis and Treatment of Personality Disorders.* New York, NY: Guilford.

Bevan, J. L. (2004). General partner and relational uncertainty as consequences of another person's jealousy expression. *Western Journal of Communication,* 68, 195–218.

Bifulco, A., Moran, P. M., Ball, C., & Bernazzani, A. (2002). Adult attachment style: Its relationship to clinical depression. *Social Psychiatry and Psychiatric Epidemiology,* 37, 50–59.

Bippus, A. M., & Rollin, E. (2003). Attachment style differences in relational maintenance and conflict behaviors: Friend's perceptions. *Communications Reports,* 16, 113–123.

Bowlby, J. (1973). *Attachment and Loss: Vol. 2. Separation: Anxiety and Anger.* New York, NY: Basic Books.

Bowlby, J. (1979). *The Making and Breaking of Affectual Bonds.* London: Tavistok.

Bradford, S. A., Feeney, J. A., & Campbell, L. (2002). Links between attachment orientations and dispositional and diary-based measure of disclosure in dating couples: A study of actor and partner effects. *Personal Relationships,* 9, 491–506.

Carson, C. L., & Cupach, W. R. (2000). Fueling the flames of the green-eyed monster: The role of ruminative thought in reaction to romantic jealousy. *Western Journal of Communication,* 64, 308–330.

Casidy, J., & Berlin, L. J. (1994). The insecure/ambivalent pattern of attachment: Theory and research. *Child Development,* 65, 971–991.

Cayanus, J. L., & Booth-Butterfield, M. (2004). Relationship orientation, jealousy, and equity: An examination of jealousy and positive communicative responses. *Communication Quarterly,* 52, 237–250.

Collins, N., & Feeney, J. A. (2000). A safe haven: An attachment theory perspective on support seeking and caregiving in intimate relationships. *Journal of Personality and Social Psychology,* 78, 1053–1073.

Collins, N., & Read, S. (1990). Adult attachment, working models, and relationship quality in dating couples. *Journal of Personality and Social Psychology,* 58, 644–663.

Dainton, M., & Aylor, B. (2001). A relational uncertainty analysis of jealousy, trust, and maintenance in long-distance versus geographically close relationships. *Communication Quarterly,* 49, 172–188.

Evans, L., & Wertheim, E. H. (2005). Attachment styles in adult intimate relationships: Comparing women with bulimia nervosa symptoms, women with depression and women with no clinical symptoms. *European Eating Disorder Review,* 13, 285–293.

Feeney, J. A., & Noller, P. (1991). Attachment styles and verbal descriptions of romantic partners. *Journal of Social and Personal Relationships,* 8, 187–215.

Fraley, R. C., Waller, N. G., & Brennan, K. A. (2000). Information on the experiences in close relationship—Revised (ECR-R) adults attachment questionnaire. *Journal of Personality and Social Psychology,* 78, 350–365.

Guerrero, L. K., & Eloy, S. V. (1992). Relational satisfaction and jealousy across marital types. *Communication Reports,* 5, 23–31.

Guerrero, L. K., & Jones, S. M. (2005). Differences in conversational skill as a function of attachment style: A follow-up study. *Communication Quarterly,* 53, 305–321.

Hazan, C., & Shaver, P. R. (1987). Romantic love conceptualized as an attachment process. *Journal of Personality and Social Psychology,* 59, 511–524.

Jones, R. L. (1996). *Handbook of Test and Measurement for Black Populations.* Hampton, VA: Cobb & Henry.

Lieberman, M., Doyle, A. B., & Markiewitz, D. (1999). Developmental patterns in security of attachment to mother and father in late childhood and early adolescence: Associations with peer relations. *Child Development,* 70, 202–213.

Meier, P. S., Donmall, M. C., Barrowclough, C., McElduff, P., & Heller, R. F. (2005). Predicting the early therapeutic alliance in the treatment of drug misuse. *Addiction,* 100, 500–511.

Mikulincer, M. (1998). Adult attachment style and individual differences in functional versus dysfunctional experiences of anger. *Journal of Personality and Social Psychology,* 74, 513–524.

Mikulincer, M., & Florian, V. (2001). Attachment style and affect regulation, implications for coping with mental health. In G. Fletcher & M. Clark (Eds), *Handbook of Social Psychology: Interpersonal Processes* (pp. 537–557). Oxford, UK: Blackwell Publishers.

Mikulincer, M., & Selinger, M. (2001). The interplay between attachment and affiliation systems in adolescents' same-sex friendships: The role of attachment style. *Journal of Social and Personal Relationships,* 5, 439–471.

Mongeau, P. A., & Schulz, B. E. (1997). What he doesn't know won't hurt him (or me): Verbal responses and attributions following sexual infidelity. *Communication Reports, 10,* 143–152.

Pietromonaco, P. R., & Barrett, L. F. (1997). Working models of attachment and daily social interactions. *Journal of Personality and Social Psychology, 73,* 1409–1423.

Ricks, M. (1985). The social transmission of parental behavior: Attachment across generations. In I. Bretherton & E. Waters (Eds), *Growing Points in Attachment Theory and Research, Monographs of the Society for Research in Child Development, 50,* 211–230.

Shechtman, Z., & Rybko, J. (2004). Attachment style and observed initial self-disclosure as explanatory variables of group functioning. *Group Dynamics: Theory, Research, and Practice, 8,* 207–220.

Sibley, C. G., Fischer, R., & Liu, J. H. (2005). Reliability and validity of the revised experiences in close relationships (ECR-R) self-report measure of adult romantic attachment. *Personality and Social Psychology Bulletin, 31,* 1524–1536.

Simon, E. P., & Baxter, L. A. (1993). Attachment-style differences in relationship maintenance strategies. *Western Journal of Communication, 57,* 416–430.

Spitzberg, B., & Chou, H. (2005). I did it on purpose: A model of strategic infidelity. Paper presented at the annual meeting of the International Communication Association, New York, NY.

Spitzberg, B., & Tafoya, M. (2005). Explorations in communicative infidelity: Jealousy, sociosexuality, and vengefulness. Paper presented at the annual meeting of the International Communication Association, New York, NY.

Thompson, R. A. (1999). Early attachment and later development. In J. Casidy & P. R. Shaver (Eds), *Handbook of Attachment* (pp. 265–281). New York, NY: Guilford Press.

Tokar, D. M., Withrow, J. R., Hall, R. J., & Moradi, B. (2003). Psychological separation, attachment security, vocational self-concept crystallization, and career indecision: A structural equation analysis. *Journal of Counseling Psychology, 50,* 3–19.

Vangelisti, A., Young, S., Carpenter-Theune, K., & Alexander, A. (2005). Why does it hurt?: The perceived causes of hurt feelings. *Communication Research, 32,* 443–477.

Vangelisti, A., & Maguire, K. (2002). Hurtful messages in family relationships: When the pain lingers. In *A clinician's guide to maintaining and enhancing close relationships* (pp. 43–62). Lawrence Erlbaum Associates, Publishers.

Vangelisti, A. (2001). Making sense of hurtful interactions in close relationships: When hurt feelings create distance. In *Attribution, communication behavior, and close relationships* (pp. 38–58). Cambridge University Press.

Vangelisti, A., & Young, S. (2000). When words hurt: The effects of perceived intentionality on interpersonal relationships. *Journal of Social and Personal Relationships, 17,* 393–424.

Vangelisti, A., & Crumley, L. (1998). Reactions to messages that hurt: The influence of relational contexts. *Communication Monographs, 65,* 173–196.

Vangelisti, A., & Sprague, R. (1998). Guilt and hurt: Similarities, distinctions, and conversational strategies. In *Handbook of communication and emotion: Research, theory, applications, and contexts* (pp. 123–154). Academic Press, Inc.

Vangelisti, A. (1994). Messages that hurt. In *The dark side of interpersonal communication* (pp. 53–82). Lawrence Erlbaum Associates, Inc.

Wearden, A., Cook, L., & Vaughan-Jones, J. (2003). Adult attachment, alexithymia, symptom reporting, and health related coping. *Journal of Psychosomatic Research, 55,* 341–347.

Webb, L., Warford, E. M., & Amason, P. (2005). Thoughts of, feelings about, and communication responses to jealousy in romantic relationships: The influence of biological sex and relational proximity. Paper presented at the annual meeting of the International Communication Association, New York, NY.

Yoshimura, S. M. (2004). Emotional and behavioral responses to romantic jealousy expressions. *Communication Reports, 17,* 85–101.

Young, A., & Acitelli, L. (1998). The role of attachment style and relationship status of the perceiver in the perceptions of romantic partner. *Journal of Social and Personal Relationships, 15,* 161–173.

Young, S. L. (2004). Factors that influence recipients' appraisals of hurtful communication. *Journal of Social and Personal Relationships, 21,* 291–303.

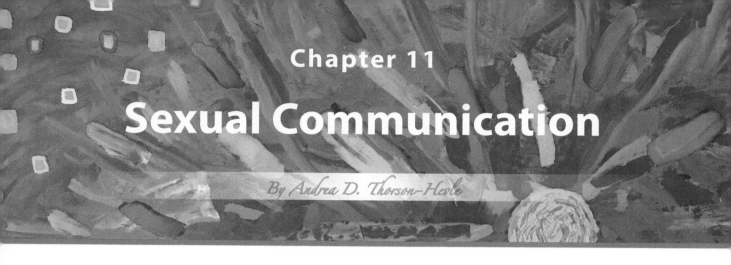

Chapter 11
Sexual Communication

By Andrea D. Thorson-Hevle

Let's get personal. . .

In my house, growing up, talking about sex wasn't really something that was encouraged. I remember if couples kissed on TV my father would be upset. We certainly wouldn't be able to openly talk about sex in the home. I do however, remember my mom having the "talk" with me, but I also remember being so afraid, nervous, and anxious that I didn't actually listen to anything she said. I concentrated on providing her fake nonverbal signals that I was paying attention and understood. Inside I was really just totally freaking out.

— Andrea D. Thorson-Hevle

You need to read this chapter

- To learn how intimacy and relational satisfaction are related.
- To understand the importance of sexual communication in relational satisfaction.
- To improve our intimate relationships.

Intimate Communication with Our Sexual Partners

This section is written to help you communicate with perhaps the most important person in your life. The previous pages have been devoted to overarching ideas and strategies for communicating more effectively. This section is not in most textbooks about interpersonal relationships, in fact, it is left out of all the books I am familiar with.

I have had a few candid concerns tossed my way, "Andrea, you can't really talk about sex ... it's too much don't you think?" "Andrea, this is a book that college students will read and I don't know if we should be talking to our students about sex." To these people I confirm their concerns and I understand their fear, but if we can't talk about it, if communication experts, professors of interpersonal communication, scholars and researchers of sexual and relational communication aren't the appropriate people to have this conversation, then tell me please, who is? I couldn't in good conscience leave this section out. How could I possibly tell my readers or students that I did a good job of helping them have successful relationships with their partners if I never talked about the one aspect of that relationship that makes that relationship different from all the other relationships they have?

Honestly, this is perhaps the most important section of the book, because it will provide you information that you are not getting anywhere else and it will allow you to reflect on your practices and your relationship in a new way. This section will specifically talk about the role of communication in your sex lives and how that affects your relational happiness and success. Ready? Let's go!

Communication in the Bedroom

In our society sex, especially communicating about sex, is not always the easiest task or most accepted behavioral topic. Why is this? Why can't we engage in effective communication about sex?

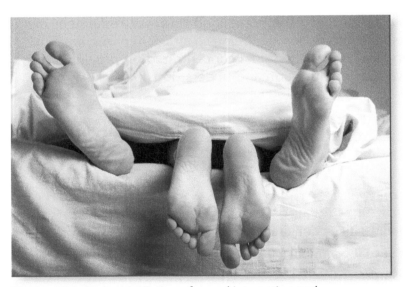

Figure 11.1 Partner initiation of sexual interaction and communication has been shown to be a strong predictor of sexual satisfaction.

Knowing how to get what you want in the bedroom, and how to please your partner in the bedroom, means communicating with them. More importantly, the communication, or lack thereof, in the bedroom can affect your general communication in all aspects of your relationship with your partner. Communication in the bedroom can ultimately affect communication out of it. *Sexual communication* may be responsible, at least in part, for our relational communication and thus relational satisfaction. Relationship communication skills seem to be the most reliable predictors of relationship satisfaction.

Concurrently, partner initiation of sexual interaction and communication has been shown to be the strongest predictors of sexual satisfaction.[1] In studies, sexual interactions have been essential contributors to a lasting successful marriage.[2] As such, relational communication has been accepted as an important part of relational success. Conversely, *sexual communication* has not. Sex therapists agree that a good sexual experience involves good relationship experiences and vice versa.[3]

1 Bridges, Lease, Ellison (2004); Veilleux (1998); Cupach & Comstock (1990); Flowers & Olsen (1989)
2 Henderson-King & Veroff (1994); Hurlbert & Apt (1993).
3 Veilleux (1998); Bridges, Lease, & Ellison (2004).

In about 1930, researchers started to collect sexual data. The research wasn't specific to communication, but it did show that people were having sex, and they were having a lot of it. Alfred Kinsey, a Harvard entomologist, discovered what has been verified year after year since, that most men had sex before marriage (about 85%) and as you might expect that number increased once they were married. We now know that that number is similar for women as well. This was shocking to the conservative 1930s culture, and it still shocks people still today sometimes. But, the fact is most everyone really is having sex and research shows it is an important factor in relationships and sexual satisfaction, so we absolutely need to understand the role of sexual communication in our lives. If you want to know about sex research you might want to check out he HBO show "Master's of Sex," which depicts the research and life of another famous sex researcher.

This section of the chapter will focus on understanding how our communication (language choices) can affect our relationships. This section is heavy in research because I have found research is easier for people to listen to and accept. I will still use my voice, but I want to be sure you see that research does, in fact, support my claims. It is my hope that you read this section and understand how important your communication about the intimacy in your relationship really is. I also hope it allows you to reflect upon your practices, habits, and norms and make communicating about sex and intimacy an easier and more normal part of your relationship.

Examining the role sexual and relational communication play in long-term relationships will improve our understanding of the importance of these relations, while also giving us insight into how we can improve these special relationships. It is important for us to know the role communication plays in our relationships, especially when it concerns (wink, wink) sex. So, hang in there, let's put on our adult hats and have an adult conversation while we investigate the relationship between *sexual communication* and *relationship satisfaction*.

Sexual Communication

Sexual communication can be understood as verbal interaction regarding sexual relations in a long-term committed relationship. Admittedly this definition has ambiguity, but necessarily so because of the broad arrangement of elements to consider unique to each committed couple. Past research has shown that *sexual or intimate communication* is associated with *sexual satisfaction* and relationship satisfaction.[4] Research also demonstrates that communication is associated with changes in relationship and *sexual satisfaction* over time.[5] A few studies have measured specific elements of *sexual satisfaction*.[6] According to Woody, D'Aouza, and Crain (1994) contributing variables to *sexual satisfaction* include attitudes, partner relationships (sexual communication and initiation), and self-relationships (masturbatory practices).

Sexual communication has been lumped in the same category as **sexual initiation**. Sexual initiation is the act of showing or telling someone that sex is desired. This is problematic, yet understandable. Initiation of a sexual act is different from communicating about the act of sex, or feelings that one experiences result from communication or lack thereof during the sexual

---

4 Cupach & Comstock (1990); Flowers & Olsen (1989).
5 Byers (2005).
6 Woody, D'Aouza, & Crain (1994); Bridges, Lease, & Ellison (2004).

experience. Initiation is an important aspect of a sexual encounter and clearly is an act of sexual communication, but there is a multitude of other sexual communication as well. For instance, being able to tell your partner what you want, need, or are not comfortable with, or the degree to which you feel safe and comfortable opening discussing sexual aspects of your relationship.

Numerous studies have been conducted and countless theories of **relationship satisfaction** proposed in hopes of determining which relationship processes ultimately create a harmonious, happy, satisfying relationship. Various variables are examined in these studies. And isn't that what we all want to know? We all want to know how to craft our relationships into the happiest, most harmonious, and satisfying relationship with our partners that we can. Studies have tried to get to this answer from a sexual and relational perspective since about 1974, when Lo Piccolo and Steger examined the role of sexual function in relationship satisfaction. About 10 years later, similar studies continue with Banmen and Vogel (1985) concluding that *sexual communication* and the resulting *sexual intimacy* can determine the entire successor satisfaction of the relationship. The study of marriage and marital counseling has been said to be best "advanced through a better understanding of communication processes."[7] From further back than even Bienvenu's research communication skills have been considered the "key" to any successful relationship.[8]

Beyond the obvious importance of general *relational communication*, *sexual communication* is also important and not studied to the same degree as general *relational communication*. Some researchers argue that general communication is irrelevant. These researchers argue that *sexual communication* is the lone predictor of a successful relationship.[9] So, we know it's important and yet most people feel uncomfortable talking about it. Why? For some people, they lack the words to communicate effectively. For others, it is embarrassing to talk about sex and intimacy. And still for others it hasn't been something we have been taught how to do so we just are not very good at it.

Figure 11.2 "Talking about sex can be difficult, but research tells us to get over ourselves and get communicating!"

7 Notarius, Markman, & Gottman (1983), p. 118.
8 Bienvenu (1968).
9 Banmen & Vogel (1985); McCabe (1999); Bienvenu (1980).

Bienvenu puts responsibility on society, saying that children are not allowed to express themselves sexually in our society. "Parents do not communicate with their children about sex. Consequently, young couples have less than adequate preparation for understanding their own sexuality and for later marital dialogue."[10] Bienvenu makes a good point here, generally it is easily agreed that this is the state of which we currently reside. Sexual communication is a taboo subject, it's arguably more taboo than the act of sex itself, for it is much easier for a person to engage in the act of sex than to actually communicate about sex.

The nationally representative survey commissioned by PPFA and the Center for Latino Adolescent and Family Health (CLAFH) at the Silver School of Social Work at NYU conducted by Knowledge Networks discovered that 57% of parents still find it uncomfortable to talk to their children about sex. So perhaps you can relate, that might be uncomfortable, it's sex after all, but why do so many adults feel uncomfortable talking about sex with their adult sexual committed partners? Well, I had my own ideas about this and went to investigate. This is what I found. Most people avoid talking to their partners about their sex lives, wants, needs, and limits candidly and often because they:

1) Worry their sexual preferences might be judged.
2) Teel they are being selfish.
3) Believe sex should be organic and intuitive.
4) Fear of rejection.
5) Are embarrassed to use sexual words and/or directive language.
6) Fear direct and open communication may be seen as a power play.
7) Are afraid to break gender/sex-based role expectations.

Modern Maturity (1999) magazine and the AARP polled 1,384 adults aged 45 and older and found that 56% of adults were unsatisfied with their sex lives. This is appalling; if anyone should have sexual experiences figured out it's the people who have been doing it the longest. But that is simply not the case. So why are so many people unsatisfied? (Retrieved from http://www.health.harvard.edu/newsweek/Excerpted_from_Sexuality_ at_ Midlife_and_Beyond.htm, 2014).

When *sexual communication* begins to fail so does that of the relationship strength. When negative feelings are created and neither member of the couple can express their needs and desires, resentment, anger, and frustration can result. Such feelings often manifest themselves into extreme negative relational behavior. This negative behavior often begins with something small then escalates quickly as it infects the relationship one section at a time. One such example of this is when a member of the relationship seeks out an individual outside the relationship. Often such behavior occurs in order to fulfill their sexual needs, feel comfortable with *sexual communication* and/or obtain attention their partner is not giving them.[11] A full investigation of the hurtful events involved in the lack of *sexual communication* and *sexual initiation* with language or nonverbal indicators is discussed in the chapter about the darker side of relationships.

10 Bienvenu, (1980).
11 Marano (2005); Rempel, Ross, & Holmes (2001).

Figure 11.3 People often wonder if the things that want sexually are "normal." This wonder often grows into a fear and that fear keeps them from having open conversations with their partner, which is sad because they have just avoided a conversation that may have gone far better than they imagined.

Sexual Communication and Sexual Satisfaction

The psychology community has accepted the topics of sexual communication and sexual satisfaction much earlier and with less resistance than the communication field. The reason for this is due in part to the terminology and the taboo subject matter. Several somewhat limited studies have been conducted regarding sex and sexual engagements, but rarely do we engage in the area of sexual communication. Psychologists and the public at large consider the sex life of a couple unquestionably linked to the overall relationship of the couple.[12] Indeed, we can all agree that

Figure 11.4 "Being willing to communicate about sex means being willing to accept criticism and perhaps being open-minded."

12 Sprecher (1998); Wincze & Carey (2001).

if you are engaging in a sexual experience, you are undoubtedly communicating something to someone. With this in mind, it then becomes an important aspect of sex. Since we can agree that *sexual communication* is important to sex, we can then agree that it has importance concerning the relationship in general, as sex is a part of the relationship.

"Even if you just have a little bit of anxiety about the communication, that affects whether you're communicating or not, but it also directly affected their satisfaction" stated Elisabeth Babin, expert of Health Communication in 2012.

(LiveScience, 2012, Retrieved from http://www.livescience.com/22934-talking-about-sex-satisfaction.html, para. 3).

In order to understand and identify the concepts involved in *sexual communication* we must examine the research concerning **sexual satisfaction**. The idea of *sexual communication* was only and first examined because of the research that was being conducted concerning *sexual satisfaction*. In the past, researchers have demonstrated that there is a measurable positive association between *relationship satisfaction* and *sexual satisfaction*.[13] Researchers were able to identify specific traits that combine to create the variable of *sexual satisfaction* and aid in determining the level of satisfaction. Variables that contribute *sexual satisfaction* include feeling the partner is available and there, feeling they are loved, feeling respected during conversation, having positive conflict that doesn't escalate into abusive language or abusive events, and/or closeness.

Figure 11.5 "Research tells us to communicate openly about sex if we want to have better sex and stronger relationships."

Sandra Byer's article, "Relationship Satisfaction and Sexual Satisfaction: A Longitudinal Study of Individuals in Long-Term Relationships," examined associations between *relationship satisfaction* and *sexual satisfaction*. "Sexual satisfaction and relationship satisfaction were found to change concurrently" (Byers, 2005, p. 318). In order to have any degree of *sexual satisfaction*, one must engage in *sexual communication*. Byers alludes to this idea of *sexual communication* in her study that the quality of "intimate communication accounted for part of the concurrent changes in relationship satisfaction and sexual satisfaction" (2005, p. 318). This conclusion is revolutionary;

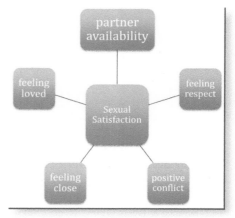

Figure 11.6 Components of Sexual Satisfaction

13 Haavio-Mannila & Kontula (1997); Purnine & Carey (1997).

her article has given both communication and psychology a new avenue from which to arrive at conclusions regarding sex, relationships, and communication. The bottom line is, if we want to have those happy successful relationships, a major component of that is using our words to communicate about our intimacy and that includes talking about our wants, needs, and limits sexually.

Three Schools of Thought

Generally speaking, there have been three main themes woven throughout the research concerning *sexual satisfaction* associated with *relational satisfaction*. The first of which, is that *relational satisfaction* will carry over into *sexual satisfaction*. So, if you are happy in your relationship then you will just end up being happy sexually as well.

The Interpersonal Exchange Model of Sexual Satisfaction (IEMSS) is applicable in this situation proposing that the quality of a given relationship directly affects the level of *sexual satisfaction* experienced in that relationship.[14] The IEMSS examines interpersonal relationships in terms of what each partner gets out of and puts into the relationship; it's a cost and benefit way of thinking. This kind of model asserts that humans engage in a kind of thinking that assesses how much they are putting into something against what they get out of it. Some research has demonstrated this possibility, including a study conducted for the purpose of measuring the effect of nonsexual marital counseling on a couples' sex life.[15]

O'Leary and Arias found that relationship counseling void of sexual counseling did have a significant affect on sexual satisfaction. The study showed that counseling significantly increased the couples overall *sexual satisfaction*.[16] Therefore, there is some evidence leading to this theory.

Second, it is possible, and some research suggests, that sexual satisfaction affects relational satisfaction.[17] In order to measure a relational satisfaction, most research use "intimate communication" as a tool and measuring device. Those studies include ones that employ the use of the didactic scale. Haig (2004) conducted a study seeking to understand the "nature of sexual satisfaction and its relationships with other variables such as personality, trait affectivity, socio-sexuality and adult attachment."[18] Haig found a significant relationship between openness and extroversion

14 Lawrance & Byers (1995); Byers (2005).
15 O'Leary and Arias (1983).
16 O'Leary and Arias (1983)
17 Byers (2005)
18 Haig (2004), p. 6376.

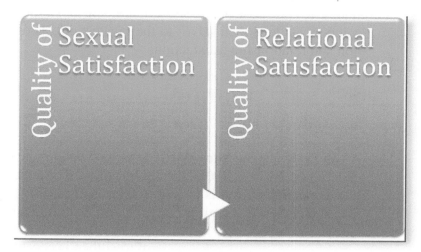

and sexual satisfaction. Haig's study did not find a link between the frequencies of sexual encounters and relational satisfaction, but did find that conscientiousness, openness, and attentiveness served as significant predictors of sexual satisfaction (2004).

"Awareness, openness, and attentiveness serve as strong predictors of sexual satisfaction."

The third option, and the possibility which leads us to our concept of sexual communication, is the association between the two variables (sexual satisfaction and relationship satisfaction). The concept is called the "third variable" according to Byers (2005). This third variable suggests, and evidence supports, the possibility that the quality of "intimate communication" is the catalyst for the changes in relationship and sexual satisfaction. To elaborate, the greater the sexual communication between a couple is, the greater their sexual satisfaction will be, and thus their relationship satisfaction (Byers, 2005, Byers & Demmons, 1999; Cupach & Comstock, 1990; Flowers & Olson, 1989). According to Byers' article, a study of newlyweds was conducted in 1994, which established this connection.

Figure 11.7 "Don't assume women want sex less frequently then men do, much research suggests that is simply not true."

All the previous research suggest in varying degrees the importance of sexual communication. Byers suggests that it may be that for men decreased sexual satisfaction leads to decreased relationship satisfaction, whereas for women, the opposite is true.[19] I disagree with the sex-based assumption. These kinds of assumptions often result as a part of a larger societal belief that women don't need or like sex as much as men do. But a great many studies have found that sexual satisfaction is just as important to women as it is to men, we just communicate about it differently. Stacy Rosenfeld (2005) identified psychological correlates of sexual communication, which included sexual partners, gender, relationship

19 Byers (2005), p. 115.

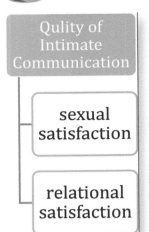

status, sexual self-esteem, self-esteem, and self-efficacy. I think these components lend themselves to the greatest effects on sexual satisfaction and relationship satisfaction.

Sexual Communication and Relational Communication: The Link

A couple that engages in positive relational communication may in turn experience positive sexual communication. Conversely, if a member of this relationship feels unable to trust their partner to not hurt them, then the person will be less likely to trust that individual when engaging in a sexual experience. This lack of trust then is capable of manifesting into fear and a lack of communication regarding the sexual experience. This fear of sexual communication can then alter itself into the regular communication of that relationship.

Another example would be, if a person feels they can trust their partner enough to tell them anything, even if it's embarrassing, or demanding, or experimental, they are more likely to feel that their partner will be more receptive in their relational communication as well and vice versa.

Figure 11.8 "Trust is essential in any relationship", but especially in sexual relationships.

Generally, researchers in communications, psychology, and sexology along with the persons currently in or out of a committed relationship agree that sexual communication is an important aspect of a healthy sexual experience and overall relational satisfaction. Past research has shown relationships between relationship satisfaction, sexual satisfaction, and relational communication. It is not then a very large leap to assert that sexual communication may be directly associated with relational communication and thus relational satisfaction. With this in mind, answer the following questions:

1) What variables do you associate with a satisfying sexual communication experience?
2) What variables do you associate with a satisfying relationship?
3) Do you think your partner would answer these questions similarly? If not, how could this be affecting your relationship and how can you use this information to your advantage now?

Canadian research has shown not only that communication about sex is low in relationships overall, but it's surprisingly low in long-term relationships. What's most interesting about Byers studies perhaps is that it discusses self-disclosure. **Self- disclosure** is the act of telling other people information about yourself that they wouldn't otherwise know. Research tells us that unfortunately, couples don't communicate about what they want and need sexually very much.

What humans tend to do is assume that their partner wants and needs things that are similar to their wants and needs. In actuality, it is theorized that we know less than a fourth of what our partner finds sexually unattractive or distasteful.

Common practices of great sexual communicators and sexually satisfied adults:

1) They put aside judgments -verbal and non-verbal communication displays a desire to listen, consider, be open-minded, honest, and caring.

2) They try any means necessary to communicate. Some couple send each other love notes detailing what they love about their sex life. Those who are too shy to say the explicit sexual words often find writing their partner a letter is easier.

3) They communicate frankly and specifically. Using concrete language instead of vague general statements ensures listeners fully understand what is being said.

So, we have established that talking about intimacy and sex is important and that it can alter the chances for our relationships to last. But, what do we do to start talking? Well, first, it may be helpful to understand why you are currently not talking.

The primary reasons people shy away from open and honest sexual conversations are:

1) We feel embarrassed.
2) We don't want to hurt our partner's feelings.
3) We don't want to make our partners feel inadequate.
4) We worry about what others will think.
5) We don't want to hurt other people's feelings.

Sexually Satisfied People:

☐ Put aside judgements

☐ Communicate in any way needed

☐ Communicate plainly, specifically, and often

6) We don't want to be perceived in a certain way.

7) We don't want to be rejected.

8) We don't want to look foolish.

9) We don't want to be seen as weird or abnormal.

While these concerns are understandable, they are wildly problematic. You can't consume yourself with fear of what others will think about you at the expense of having an honest conversation and a potentially amazing sexual experience. Being open about sex is important and to be honest, in the years I have spent researching, *sexual communication* I haven't found a ton of weird stuff. People usually want to have their partners initiate sex more, initiate sex in more romantic or sexy ways, provide them compliments, talk more during sex, try new positions, or experiment with simple toys. Sure, different people will view different things more favorably than others, but don't assume that your partner will abandon you because of it. And honestly, if you have a need sexually that you can't communicate because you are certain your partner would leave you if they knew—then perhaps that is not the most ideal relationship for you. Again, research tells us that if you are not happy sexually and communicating affectively about sex and intimacy, then you are not likely to have a happy lasting long-term relationship (assuming that is what you want, of course).

Figure 11.9 If you talk about sex from a place of love it can be easier. Make sure your partner feels love when you communicate with them. It is equally important that you love yourself enough to be honest about what you want and what you need in a relationship and that includes your needs in the bedroom.

Part of the problem is that society has bombarded us with images and scripts of what are "normal" sexual behavior, desires, and needs. It's very much something that is not just marketed to humans as a whole, but is cleverly and strategically marketed to specific sexes, genders, and sexual orientations. John Gognon and William Simon coined the idea of "scripts" in the 1970s, they defined it as guidelines that aide and categorize language about sexual interactions. Our sexual scripts are predominantly constructed by the cultures we interact with and the society in which we live. The scripts that society has set for each sex is highly problematic, but we have been making great strides in recent years to rectify this damage.

In 2011 Sarah Vannier and Lucia O'Sullivan found that most people prefer nonverbal communication to signify that someone wants to have sex (Vannier & Sullivan, 2011).

Nonverbal communication is more common than verbal language communication when it comes to signaling to a partner that sex is desired. The problem with this is this often leads to miscommunication which can contribute to misinterpretation of consent to have intercourse (Jozkowski, 2013). It is recommended that verbal language be your primary form of communication about sex.

Communication in the Bedroom: Kimberly's Story

In high school, my boyfriend would constantly degrade me when we would have sex. He would always tell me that I was never beautiful, I was too fat, and he didn't know why he was with me. I was never allowed to talk, specifically never allowed to say "that hurts." He would get angry at me for moaning or trying to express to him that it started to feel good. He would always finish first. I never had one orgasm the entire 3 years we were together. This was what I thought was "normal" when having sex, until a year later, when I met my fiancé.

The first time we tried to have sex, I was so scared of what he would say or do that I kept telling him no and pushed him off. I would eventually force myself to stop saying no and we would finally have sex. I never said anything or made one sound because I was so afraid of what he would say to me. After a few times, he finally told me that he felt like he was raping me because I never told him what I liked or what felt good. He said it was hard for him to enjoy it because I looked scared the entire time. I realized that my past was affecting me and I told him what had happened and reasons why I acted that way. Personally, I felt horrible that he felt like he was RAPING me— that was the hardest thing to cope with.

As I started to become more comfortable with him, he started to ask me how does that feel or do you like it better like this or like this? He also told me that it turned him on if I moaned or told him it felt good like that. I could not believe that this man was not only talking to me during sex, but that he also wanted me to enjoy it! He was never the first one to finish, I was! And to finally experience not only one, but multiple orgasms was a completely new experience!

After those first few times, I finally realized that sex was not what I thought it was and if you're with the right person, who truly cares and loves you, you'll experience amazing things. After being together for 2 years, I realized that it was his communication that helped me to overcome my fear and past; because of that we now have a very confident and open sex life.

How to Start Talking About Sex

I can't claim to know all the answers, but I can say that based on research and experience these are some of the most effective ways to start having those difficult conversations.

1) Recognize there are different components to sex that should be considered. For instance, emotional components, physical situations, and cultural backgrounds. All of these considerations have a bearing on your sexual experiences and thus should be areas you talk about. Different cultural (sex, gender, orientations, religions, nationalities, etc.) **expectations and norms may be impacting your sexual experiences.** Before you assume that a behavior or comment means what you think it means, assess what cultural implications may need to be considered.

2) Recognize that verbal language doesn't have to be your only form of communication. **Coupling nonverbal communication with verbal communication during sex has been shown to be highly effective.**

3) **Recognize that communicating about what you need before and after sex is just as important** as talking about what you want and need during sex.

4) **Recognize that the way you express any dissatisfaction may hurt your partner's feelings**. It is often best to have conversations about sexual dislikes and anything you want to change well in advance of any sexual contact, this way it's not a fresh wound and everyone has time to process. It also won't kill the intimate moment this way.

5) Recognize that communication about sex after sex is also useful, but **it is important to find the right moment to discuss things**. Any negative feedback should be withheld until later, unless you think it is a criticism that your partner is ready for at that moment or if they specifically asked you for the feedback right after. By the way, when I say to not be critical during the act of sex I am of course not talking about any moment in which you feel afraid, pain, or discomfort. The kind of advice I am giving you in this point is meant more for the simple but potentially uncomfortable conversations. Such as, a discussion about how long the sexual experience lasts, which positions you would like to engage in more often, toys you would like to purchase for use in the future, etc.

6) Recognize that the words you use can make your partner feel loved and supported or condemned and blamed. **Don't blame and accuse when you are trying to have a ncie conversation, instead describe and own your feelings and articulate how you would like things to be in the future and why.**

7) Recognize the importance of compliments. So often we obsess over the negative things and tend to gloss over the positive. Positive reinforcement can go a long way in the bedroom. I can't tell you how many people have told me they didn't know if they were any good at certain acts until they finally had a partner that told them when they did things well, even if it was just a quick simple thing. Research shows the lack of affirmation has been indicated as a reason for not engaging in certain acts altogether. Compliments build confidence and they also increase the chance that your partner will repeat that act again. **Try to sandwich a criticism between or after a couple accolades.** "Honey, the other night I loved how you were spontaneous and fun. I love our sex life and having sex with you, but I was hoping I could talk to about something I don't feel 100% comfortable with …"

8) Recognize that sometimes the "big" sexual conversations will need to be had a couple times or revisited in different ways. **These big conversations might be best accomplished in mini-sessions.** Pick one issue to discuss at a time, unless several are linked to one main idea or if you know your partner is open and able to handle a lot all at once. It's great to discuss multiple issues at a time if you and your partner agreed to have that ind of comprehensive conversation. What you don't want to happen is for your partner to have a minor easy topic to discuss with you and then you give a list a mile long. People need to be prepared to have uncomfortable conversations or conversations in which thir sexual performance may be criticized. Please recognize however, that these are general tips and you know your partner well, you may have a very open communication channel with this person so all of these considerations just are not applying to you; that's okay. Take the tips that can apply to you and leave the others for others to use.

9) **Play a sexual communication game.** Using separate sheets of paper and giving space so no peeking can be accomplished, you and your partner have three minutes to write down your favorite sexual moments (with your partner only). You have two minutes to list your sexual preferences (foreplay, toys, speed, etc.). You now have one minute to write down what you think your partner's favorite sexual turn-ons are. Compare your answers. Have a conversation about the answers. Discuss how it is you knew that your partner liked that and vice versa. this conversation will tell you if your and your partner are paying attention to verbal and/or non verbal communication and what you and your partner have been doing well on the communication front. Don't focus on what you got wrong as being a reflection of incompatibility. Instead, use what you didn't get right as a way of having a conversation about how you can implement that into your regular sexual lives more often (as long as everyone involved feel comfortable with it).

10) Recognize that you most likely are doing something less than perfect in the bedroom, but sex and sexual communication aren't about getting a perfect report card from your partner the first time. It's about listening to your partner, talking, and possibly making changes to have a successful and satisfying relationship, which will lead you to straight A's in the end. **Leave your ego outside, allow yourself to truly listen to your partner, and not judge or become defensive.**

11) **Recognize that society has made you feel like you are supposed to intuitively know what you partner wants and needs. This idea is just silly and not supported by significant research.** You aren't a magician or a mind reader; you have to communicate if you want to know what your partner needs. Don't let society's big narratives about love ruin your chance at a successful relationship.

Well you did it; you survived an open honest and sometimes graphic discussion about sex. And you aren't ruined; you aren't dead. I'm not saying this was the easiest section to write. But, I do feel like it was one of the most important.

As I said in the beginning, it is my hope that you take this information and use it to build the courage to have the conversations you aren't having or to make those conversations more fruitful and successful. I want you to have great relationships, especially with your significant other whom you have intimate relations with. As you can see from the research, communication about sex is a huge part of that.

Conclusion

This chapter was all about helping you deconstruct the verbal communication you are using in your relationships and helping you makes positive language choices for the future. You learned about the foundation of language and meaning and the ways in which you can craft more concrete and affirming language that helps you have successful happy relationships. We also discussed how powerful language is and how oppressive and hurtful it can be, and thus why it is important that we choose our words wisely. We ended this chapter with a candid discussion on the role of verbal communication in our long-term committed relationships, especially when it comes to sex. In sum, we learned how important it is to speak; speak clearly, speak kindly, speak with purpose, think before speaking, speak with culture in mind, and speak to get closer to one another.

References

Banmen, J., & Vogel, N. A. (1985). The relationship between marital quality and interpersonal sexual communication. *Family Therapy,* 12(1), 45–58.

Bienvenu, M. J. (1968). *Premarital Communication Inventory*. Natchitoches, LA: Northwest Publications.

Bienvenu, M. J. (1980). *A Guide to Accompany the Sexual Communication Inventory*. Natchitoches, LA: Northwest Publications.

Bridges, S. K., Lease, S. H., & Ellison, C. R. (2004). Predicting sexual satisfaction in women: Implications for counselor education and training. *Journal of Counseling & Development,* 82(2), 158.

Buller, M. K., & Buller, D. B. (1987). Physicians' communication styles and satisfaction. *Journal of Health and Social Behavior,* 28, 375–388.

Byers, E. S. (2005). Relationship satisfaction and sexual satisfaction: A longitudinal study of individuals in long-term relationships. *Journal of Sex Research,* 42(2), 113–118.

Byers, E. S., & Demmons, S. (1999). Sexual satisfaction and sexual self-disclosure within dating relationships. *The Journal of Sex Research,* 36, 1–10.

Cahn, D. D. (1983). Relative importance of perceived understanding in initial interaction and development of interpersonal relationships. *Psychological Reports,* 52, 923–929.

Cahn, D. D., & Shulman, G. M. (1984). The perceived understanding instrument. *Communication Research Reports,* 1, 122–125.

Carstensen, L. L., Gottman, J. M., & Levenson, R. W. (1995). Emotional behavior in long-term marriage. *Psychology and Aging,* 10(1), 140–149.

Communication research methods: A source book. (1994). New York, NY: The Guilford Press.

Davidson, J., & Darling, C. (1988). The sexually experienced woman: Multiple sex partners and sexual satisfaction. *The Journal of Sex Research,* 24, 141–154.

Fletcher, G. J., Simpson, J. A., Thomas, G. (2000). The measurement of perceived relationship quality components: A confirmatory factor analytic approach. *Personality and Social Psychology Bulletin,* 26(3), 340–354.

Floyd, M., Kelly, B., & Stanley. (1995). Prevention intervention and relationship enhancement. In N. S. Jacobson & A. S. Gurman (Eds), *Clinical Handbook of Couple Therapy* (pp. 212–226). New York, NY: Guilford.

Flowers, B. J., & Olson, D. H. (1989). ENRICH Marital Inventory: A discriminant validity and cross-validation assessment. *Journal of Marital and Family Therapy,* 15, 65–79.

Gottman, J. M. (1982). Emotional responsiveness in marital conversations. *Journal of Communication,* 32(3), 108–120.

Gottman, J. M., & Levenson, R. W. (1992). Marital processes predicative of later dissolution: Behavior, physiology, and health. *Journal of Personality and Social Psychology,* 63(2), 221–233.

Gottman, J. M., & Porterfield, A. L. (1981). Communicative competence in the nonverbal behavior of married couples. *Journal of Marriage and the Family,* 43(4), 817–824.

Gottman, J. M., Coan, J., Carrere, S., & Swanson, C. (1998). Predicting marital happiness and stability from newlywed interactions. *Journal of Marriage and the Family,* 60(2), 5–22.

Glauser, M. J., & Tullar, W. L. (1985). Citizen satisfaction with police officer/citizen interaction: Implications for the changing role of police organizations. *Journal of Applied Psychology,* 4, 350–368.

Haavio-Mannila, E., & Kontula, O. (1997). Correlates of increased sexual satisfaction. *Archives of Sexual Behavior,* 26, 399–419.

Hecht, M. L. (1978). Measures of communication satisfaction. *Human communication. Research,* 4, 350–368.

Haig, J. (2004). Sexual satisfaction; its structure, stability, and correlates. *Dissertation Abstracts International: Section B; the Science and Engineering,* 64(12-B), 6376.

Henderson-King, D. H., & Veroff, J. (1994). Sexual satisfaction and marital well-being in the first years of marriage. *Journal of Social and Personal Relationships,* 11, 509–534

Hurlbert, D. F., & Apt, C. (1993). Female sexuality: A comparative study between women in homosexual and heterosexual relationships. *Journal of Sex and Marital Therapy,* 19, 315–327.

Kristen Jozkowski. (2013). Research: Genders communicate consent to sex differently. Published in the University of Arkansas Newswire July, 02, 2013.

Lamude, K. G., Daniels, T. D., & Fraham, E. E. (1988). The paradoxical influence of sex on communication rules co-relationships. *Western Journal of Speech Communication,* 52, 122–134.

Lawrance, K., & Byers, E. S. (1995). Sexual satisfaction in long-term heterosexual relationships: The Interpersonal Exchange Model of Sexual Satisfaction. *Personal Relationships, 2,* 267–285.

Marano, H. E. (2005). Is my wife having an affair? *Psychology Today,* 38 (1).

McCabe, M. P. (1999). The interrelationship between intimacy, relationship functioning, and sexuality among men and women in committed relationships. *The Canadian Journal of Human Sexuality,* 8(1), 31–40.

Notarius, C. I., Markman, H. J., & Gottman, J. M. (1983). Couples interaction scoring system: Clinical implications. In E. E. Filsinger (Ed.), *Marriage and Family Assessment* (pp. 117–136). Beverly Hills, CA: Sage Publications.

Pasupathi, M., Carstensen, L. L., Levenson, R. W., & Gottman, J. M. (1999). Responsive listening in long-married couples: A psycholinguistic perspective. *Journal of Nonverbal Behavior,* 23(2), 173–193.

Purnine, D. M., & Carey, M. P. (1997). Interpersonal communication and sexual adjustment: The roles of understanding and agreement. *Journal of Consulting and Clinical Psychology,* 65(1), 017-1025.

Rempel, J. K., Ross, M., Holmes, J. G. (2001). Trust and communicated attributions in close relationships. *Journal of Personality and Social Psychology,* 81(1).

Schenk, J., Pfrang, H., & Rausche, A. (1983). Personality traits versus the quality of the marital relationship as the determinant of marital sexuality. *Archives of Sexual Behavior,* 12, 31–42.

Schaefer, M. T., & Olson, D. H. (1981). Assessing intimacy: The pair inventory. *Journal of Marital and Family Therapy,* 1, 47–60.

Snavely, W. B. (1981). The impact of social style upon person perception in primary relationships. *Communication Quarterly,* 29, 132–143.

Sprecher, S. (1998). Social exchange theories and sexuality. *The Journal of Sex Research,* 35, 32–43.

Rosenfeld, S. M. (2005). Psychological correlates of sexual communication. *Dissertation Abstracts International: Section B: The Sciences & Engineering,* 65(9 B), 4849.

Vannier & O'Sullivan. (2011). Communicating Interest in Sex: Verbal and Nonverbal Initiation of Sexual Activity in Young Adults' Romantic Dating Relationships. *Archives of Sexual Behavior,* 40.

Veilleux, Z. (1998). You're asking for it. *Men's Health,* 13(6), 106–108.

Warren, C., & Neer, M. (1986). Family sex communication orientation. *Journal of Applied Communication Research,* 14 (2), 86–107.

Wheeles, L. R. (1978). A follow-up of the relationships among trust, disclosure, and interpersonal solidarity. *Human Communication Research,* 4, 143–157.

Wheeles, L. R., & Grotz, J. (1977). The measurement of trust and its relationship to self-disclosure. *Human Communication Research,* 3, 250–257.

Wheeles, L. R., & Andersen, J. F. (1978). An empirical test of social penetration and indices of its critical components. Paper presented at the meeting of the International Communication Association, Chicago.

Wincze, J. P., & Carey, M. F. (2001). *Sexual Dysfunction: A Guide for Assessment and Treatment.* New York, NY: Guilford. Manuscript accepted August 11, 2004.

Woody, D'Aouza, & Crain (1994).